# BEAUTIFUL AL

# BEAUTIFUL ALIENS

## A Steve Abbott Reader

*Edited by Jamie Townsend*

*Afterword by Alysia Abbott*

**Nightboat Books**
New York

ISBN: 978-1-64362-015-2

Graphic Design: Brian Hochberger
Text set in Clarendon and Century Schoolbook
Cover Art and Interior Artwork by Steve Abbott
Author Photo: Robert Giard

Cataloging-in-publication data is available from the Library of Congress

Nightboat Books
New York
nightboat.org

*for* Kevin Killian

# TABLE OF CONTENTS

# INTRODUCTION

Most of the time where we belong exists somewhere beyond the path laid out between where we've come from and where we think we're headed. When we stumble upon that unforeseen place it can be strange, miraculous, unexpected, terrifying. It can feel like falling in love or falling over the edge of the world.

In October of 2013, I was visiting the Berkshires for a friend's wedding. The day before the ceremony, I took a rainy afternoon detour to browse Grey Matter Books in Hadley, MA. Rifling through a dusty labyrinth of floor-level bookshelves comprising the store's poetry section, I pulled out a slim volume with an oddly compelling title: *Stretching the Agape Bra*. The cover photograph displayed a lanky, mustachioed man (Steve Abbott) and a young girl (his daughter Alysia), both dressed like characters from some lost Southern Gothic film. Steve holds a long stemmed flower in the foreground and Alysia, in a ghostly white dress, stands watch behind him. To their left stretch upward the columns of an antediluvian manor or baroque mausoleum. It opens: "This is not a brilliant book nor was it meant to be. Brilliant books have caused far too much harm already." Dramatic pause. This was my first taste of Steve Abbott, and I was hooked.

While the poems in *Stretching the Agape Bra* themselves presented a series of unassuming gems, what excited my imagination the most that day in Hadley was the potential backstory the book itself conjured. Published by the small Bay Area press Androgyne Books in 1980, over three decades it had found its way to the other side of the country, was acquired by this rural bookstore, and, by luck or happenstance, was now in my hands. I thought about the path it might have traced, imagining that it most likely came from the collection of a poet who might have met Steve through the channels of creative writing that connect seemingly isolated literary scenes in the US: San Francisco and NYC, NYC and the writing program at UMASS Amherst, just several miles away from where I stood. I marveled at the small miracle of how these unassuming books find their way, sometimes decades later, to an eager audience, how it's an act of resilience that poetry can collapse time, can make friends of the living and dead.

With Steve, I was immediately struck by the generosity of his poetry, as well as its sense of wonder at the complexities of human relationships.

The act of writing itself, particularly narrative writing, can be expressed as the process of mediating systems of desire: a meeting ground for wants and needs. Reading on and reading closer I would discover that throughout his prolific life as a writer, publisher, editor, organizer and activist, Steve Abbott hovered in the spaces between these roles, directing his attention toward a restless search for points of connection.

With such a generous, forward-thinking practice, who better than Steve to dream up the idea of a "New Narrative", his designation describing the work of intimate colleagues including Bruce Boone, Bob Glück, Dodie Bellamy, Kevin Killian, and a host of others outside this often recognized core group: Kathy Acker, Dennis Cooper, Leslie Scalapino, Aaron Shurin, Judy Grahn. New Narrative, as Steve imagined it, as a mode of writing first and foremost: "language conscious but arising out of specific social and political concerns of specific communities," making use of "the enabling role of content in determining form rather than stressing form as independent or separate from its social origins and goals," as he states in his introduction to *Soup* issue #2. This vision of New Narrative expands from a small group of friends in the San Francisco writing scene to touch upon a broad survey of work by his contemporaries, writing which merged the personal, political, and emotional; a group of writers who were smart, gossipy, and perhaps most importantly, self-aware.

Writing, particularly uncommercial writing, exists out of necessity within a framework of personal relationships. Its existence presupposes an audience before the fact. The efforts that support the creation of any type of art are never singular. Organizing readings, writing reviews, starting small presses and magazines; this boots-on-the-ground labor is often overlooked or undervalued when laid against the seemingly lasting products, the material or intellectual legacy, of a particular time and place. New Narrative not only foregrounds the relational (the use of friends' names, gossip, confession, the quotidian, the erotic) it provides ample room for community critique through linguistic devices that dissect and open up traditional narrative writing (parataxis, metatext, metonymy, narrative intrusion). As such, it seems an ideal mode for addressing ways in which writing necessitates a social body. Though a prolific writer himself (half a dozen books and chaps of poetry and cross genre writing, several novels, and a collection of essays) Steve's dedication in supportive roles – including organizing readings and conferences, his long-term editorial work at Poetry Flash, his columns in Bay Area periodicals (where he published early reviews of important literary works of his contemporaries, including Lyn Hejinian's *My Life* and Bruce Boone's *Century of Clouds*, among others), and his self-publication of *Soup* magazine – gives witness to this essential, though too rarely focused upon, element in the life of writers.

*

Steve Abbott was born on December 21st, 1943 in Lincoln, Nebraska and grew up Catholic in what's now pejoratively called "flyover country". As a young adult he studied first at the University of Nebraska-Lincoln, and later at Emory University in Atlanta. At UNL he wrote for the school's literary magazine and was actively involved in Students for a Democratic Society. While still an undergraduate, he organized a landmark reading for Allen Ginsberg. Steve's invitation prompted Ginsberg to compose his iconic "Wichita Vortex Sutra" en route, which he premiered in Lincoln. After graduating, Steve spent time at a Benedictine monastery as a novitiate. He became disillusioned by spiritual corruption within the order and soon left to travel Europe for several months before moving to Atlanta to begin graduate studies.

In 1968 Steve met Barbara Binder, a psychology major and student activist, while both were students at Emory University. Steve and Barbara seemed a perfect fit: both were fun-loving, active politically, and progressive in their views on sexuality and romantic relationships. The two married and soon after Steve publicly came out as bisexual in the university's student paper. During this time Steve also became "gay lib editor" at Atlanta's popular alternative newspaper *The Great Speckled Bird*. In 1970 Barbara gave birth to the couple's only child, Alysia. The couple maintained a loving, sometimes difficult open relationship, but after an emotionally crippling breakup with his first boyfriend John, Steve, anxious to continue exploring his life beyond the closet, travelled to live with a friend in San Francisco for several months while Alysia was still an infant. This short first visit to SF proved to be a turning point in his life, setting the stage for what was to follow.

In 1973 Barbara was driving with a friend outside of Memphis, when her car was violently rear-ended. She was thrown through the windshield and onto the pavement, dying before medical help could arrive. Almost a decade later Steve would write in his poem "Elegy": "When I learned my wife's skull was crushed by a truck, my head / swam like an hourglass into a tv set. All the channels went crazy." A devastated, now-single parent, Steve quickly took stock of his life, his passion to write and his desire live openly in a place that might better accept him and provide opportunities for him as a gay artist and a social activist. In 1974, with three-year-old Alysia beside him, he drove across the Golden Gate Bridge into what would prove to be his natural environment and permanent home, San Francisco.

Living as a single father in San Francisco during the 1970s and 80s provided Steve many opportunities for connection but also placed his work apart from other young queer writers, artists, and organizers. Steve's responsibilities (often managed on-the-fly, sometimes shirked) as a single parent, as well as his predilection toward poor choices in partners, created a distance between himself and others even while he enthusiastically participated in the vibrant literary communities of North Beach's City Lights Bookstore, the Cloud House collective, and later Small Press Traffic. Steve also began developing in earnest would become a signature of his creative work, the poetry cartoon. Inspired by comic maverick and friend from Nebraska, S. Clay Wilson, as well as the countercultural irreverence of Zap, Steve took full advantage of the zany humor, anti-establishment politics, and soft surrealism of popular underground comics when illustrating versions of his poetry and queer hippy narratives.

During his first decade in San Francisco, Steve developed an impressive, multivalent body of work comprising poetry, cartoons, event posters, fiction, and critical writings. By 1980 he had published three books of poetry and had become a fixture at readings and discussion groups. At the Mission district bookstore Small Press Traffic he joined a developing queer literary scene playing with autobiography, poetry, philosophical text and sex writing, a scene to which he would later give the name "New

Narrative". In 1980 Steve also began publishing *Soup,* his self-funded literary arts magazine, which became the home for seminal writings by friends and contemporaries, and gathered together the first of the New Narrative writings to comprise a bulk of the magazine's second issue. During this time he also took on the responsibility for revamping San Francisco's hugely important literary periodical *Poetry Flash.* During his tenure as the journal's managing editor he more than doubled its readership, tirelessly championing the writings of friends and heroes, while suffering no fools in his search for sincerity, self-awareness, love and resistance to oppression. Steve also spent much of the late 1970s through the early 1990s as a critic, essayist, and regular columnist at a number of Bay Area and beyond publications, including *The Advocate*, the *Bay Area Reporter*, the *SF Weekly*, *The Sentinel*, and *The Bay Guardian*. As an interviewer Steve displayed his wide-reaching interests, interests that would often introduce him to new friends and communities outside his writing circle, new artistic influences including punk rock and post-modern visual art, and, in the case of his Sentinel profile on Issen Dorsey, founder of the Hartford Street Zen Center, the practice of sitting zazen.

As the new decade progressed more books followed; *Lives of the Poet*, a central New Narrative text; an erotic novel titled *Holy Terror*; a collection of essays and writings as a periodical columnist, *View Askew*; a narrative poem presented in the form of a travel diary, *Skinny Trip to a Far Place.* Throughout the 1980s and early 90s also Steve organized many benefits, and panel discussions, including the landmark Marxist conference Left/Write, the gay literary conference Out/Write, readings for Judy Grahn, Allen Ginsberg, Harold Norse, Manroot Press founder Paul Mariah, and other luminaries of LGBT arts. Steve's prolific writing and social life never seemed to lose much momentum, even throughout bouts of drug addiction, failed and abusive relationships, and shifting responsibilities as a father to Alysia.

Though comprising only four issues, the importance of *Soup* (edited and published by Steve between 1980 and 1985) cannot be overstated. It's where New Narrative's nascent form, for better or worse, first found its definition (In Steve's introduction to the second issue). In *Soup*, he published a range of important works from friends and collaborators.

These include early versions of Bob Glück's *Elements of a Coffee Service*, Dennis Cooper's *The Tenderness of the Wolves* and Leslie Scalapino's *Considering how exaggerated music is*. In her 2006 collection of essays *Academonia*, Dodie Bellamy recollects that the first critical response to her writing was authored by Steve and included in *Soup*'s fourth issue.

In addition to the aforementioned works, Soup is also where foundational critical pieces, including Bruce Boone's "The Pluses and Minuses of New Formalism, and Steve's own "Notes On Boundaries"—an essay which provides a cultural and historical framework for New Narrative—first appeared. *Soup* favored a lo-fi, non-hierarchical feel, and predominant focus on local writers, many of whom were Steve's colleagues. It often featured artists too outré for larger publications at the time and was almost completely self-funded through odd jobs and long hours; a true labor of love. Through the wide and motley net it casted, *Soup* also expanded upon the example of earlier queer publishing ventures, such as James Mitchell's *Sebastian Quill* and The Hoddypoll Press, Winston Leyland's *Gay Sunshine*, and Bob Glück and Bruce Boone's *Black Star Series*.

In the essay "Passing Strangers" Steve notes: "Most of my writing is published in obscure magazines. I like to write on unusual topics: the history of rubber stamp art, avant-garde poetry, tv commercials, horror movies. I want to make connections." This desire to connect also directed Steve's attention to where blockages exist. He wrote interrogatively about boundaries, where they dissolve, where sometimes, even in their persistence, they define a social inclusivity. In his critical writings, friends, queer luminaries, academic poets, beats, social activists, and all combinations thereof found in Steve an attentive audience. His acknowledgement of the differences in these communities, rather than creating impassable barriers, celebrated their unique yet shared resistance against hegemony. As an editor of *Poetry Flash* during the exciting and divisive era sometimes dubbed the "Poetry Wars," Steve's slice of life narratives, reviews, as well as fiery political and literary articles (often focusing on the role of gay liberation in the arts) provided a rich overview of SF culture and politics during the 80s. Steve also edited a number of special issues of *Poetry Flash* including, among others, West Coast Black Writing, Gay Writing, and American Indian Poets of California.

Held in 1981, Left/Write was a watershed moment in Steve's life as an organizer. It gathered over 300 hundred people for a two-day conference spanning dozens of workshops, panels, and informal discussions. Its aim was threefold: "active participation from all sectors of the Leftist writing community," "topics and structure would lead from grassroots experience and concerns to wider and deeper historical and theoretical understanding," and that, after the conclusion of the conference "an ongoing organization or alliance might develop." Left/Write represents the artistic culmination of a thread of political discourse and that runs through Steve's life; in 1968 Steve won a civil trial where, as a conscientious objector to the war in Vietnam, he was charged with draft dodging. Later, while at Emory, he became the leader of Atlanta's chapter of the Gay Liberation Front.

In response to the Left/Write's impact Bob Glück comments: "Steve was a tireless community builder, and Left/Write was an expression of New Narrative's desire to bring communities together." He also called Left/Write a "founding moment for New Narrative." Steve, as the head of the conference planning board, helped focus conference topics toward addressing the specific needs of those groups often unrepresented in broader Leftist organizing. This created an arena for complex and often contentious discourse among panelists. Discussions around inclusion and increased focus on gender and gay politics become a central debate, in addition to panels addressing the marginalization of women and POC groups within Marxist political praxis. In his introduction to the Left/Write transcripts Steve responds to the difficulties in building solidarity, even among aligned groups, and reminds readers that we must actively participate in fighting oppression wherever it occurs:

> *Political divisions are not necessarily bad. Lessons may be learned from them and persons involved can later regroup with an even greater understanding and commitment...At the same time, no one can agree to principles of unity that deny the validity of their own struggles or that assign these struggles to categories of minor importance.*

Steve's interest in the places where social action and creative inquiry overlap mirrors his imagining of what community, specifically his fellow travelers in New Narrative, could do to reclaim the importance of legibility and storytelling in the postmodern era. In that regard, the title of Left/Write's opening panel can almost function as a thesis for an examination of Steve's creative project: "How Does Our Writing Arise From and Affect Our Communities?"

In 1987 Black Star Series published *Lives of the Poets*, a book that perfectly illustrates Steve's focus on nurturing community though conversation. *Lives* is not a singular narrative work of historical autobiography but rather a collage of scenes, interesting and amusing asides and quotations from a wide variety of biographies, often without Steve identifying sources or subjects. A sense of the particulars, the "who" and "when", is suspended in favor of a sociological bleed that hints at a vast community of affinity. "I read biographies to cheer me up," Steve writes near the beginning of the book, later providing a statement that serves as an apt summation of the entire project: "layered memories, layered lives." The autobiographical snippets which comprise *Lives* come from sources as varied as Elvis Presley, Ludwig Wittgenstein, Pier Palo Pasolini, and Lady Murasaki. Moments from Steve's own life fill in the gaps between a range of idiosyncratic, fascinating composites of different lives stretched across epochs, cultures, and genders.

Those that do this type of literary reconstructive work often insist on tidying narratives into a discernable progression. Steve's canny form pressurizes and pulls apart this flat historical record; reading it one can imagine Steve's bookshelf spilling into the cafes, baths and bedrooms of an idyllic gay metropolis – a feeling of, as Aaron Shurin writes in his essay "Narrativity," a "simultaneity of times". In this sense *Lives of the Poet* becomes a synecdoche of New Narrative, particularly how it operates as a sort of ongoing group writing project, an overlapping of shifting lives and concerns that reveal the subjectivity of history, the body, and memory. From Steve's poem "Elegy": "what seemed most outlandish in our autobiography is what really happened."

In Steve's final book of poetry, *Skinny Trip to a Far Place*, we see an inverse of this slippery historical frottage, something closer to Bob

Glück's ars poetica, "I wanted to write with a total continuity and total disjunction since I experienced the world (and myself) as continuous and infinity divided." *Skinny Trip to a Far Place* was written during a two week trip to Kyoto Steve took with Alysia in 1987. It's composed as a variation of haibun, and that poetic form's focus on travel, its mixture of compressed verse and diaristic anecdotes dovetails nicely with the signature detailed observations and overarching running commentary of New Narrative writing. It also provided Steve with the opportunity to write intimately. *Skinny Trip* proceeds like a walking meditation, recording moments of ecstasy, rumination, humor, and self-doubt, as well as allowing the voices of Alysia and a newly found friend named Anna Kristina to intercede and redirect the text. As Steve winds his way through an unfamiliar city, he intersperses travelogue vignettes with haiku, passing conversations, and moments of longing, with the practiced eye of an editor and the unabashed romanticism of a young poet. Glück notes: "more than any of us, Steve was the exemplary New Narrative writer, maybe because his Buddhism allowed him to empty without violence both fiction and lived experience." *Skinny Trip...* plays melancholy and melodrama against each, finding a tenuous balance, as he visits famous Buddhist sites, meets Cid Corman at a coffeehouse, and struggles through a long night trying to locate a gay bar in Kyoto.

In a letter to Alysia in March of 1989 Steve mentions in passing that his white blood cell count had recently dropped below a healthy functioning level. Though never outright stating his diagnosis in this correspondence, Steve had, at some point in late 1988 or early 1989, contracted HIV. Between 1998 and his death in 1992 from AIDS-related respiratory complications, Steve continued to work diligently, writing about the lives of others affected by the AIDS epidemic, including an essay titled "We Will Survive the 80s" which functions simultaneously as a love letter to his community and call to action. During these last years Steve also continued to work on fulfilling a personal goal, completing an MFA at San Francisco State.

On December 2nd 1992, after a two-month stay at the Hartford Zen Center's Maitri Hospice, Steve Abbott passed away. At 48 his death was not just a personal tragedy for friends and family, but a huge loss to the communities he nurtured and found himself at home within. His final book, a hybrid-form novel titled *The Lizard Club*, was published posthumously by Autonomedia in 1993. Though declining in health during its composition, *The Lizard Club*'s formal leaps, its mashing of high art and lowbrow comedy, and its Burroughs-indebted, darkly humorous magic provides a glimpse into the wide-open future of Steve's imagination.

Memory, and its application to struggles in the present, is a vehicle for life beyond the inevitable result of being impermanent. Jean Cocteau writes: "in memory our rules no longer apply. Dead and living alike move together on an artificial stage under fatal lighting. The stage is free." Steve's writing and art approaches this internal danse macabre from a multiplicity of interrogative perspectives. Where do we come from? Where are we going? What happens next?

By the early 1990s the AIDS epidemic had drastically shifted the landscape of San Francisco, socially, politically, and sexually. In Steve's friend and literary executor Kevin Killian's collection of poems, *Argento Series* the loss of his friends, fellow writers, and lovers to AIDS is filtered through the films of Italian horror auteur Dario Argento. On the back cover of this book, in place of blurbs or a traditional artist bio, Kevin writes a condensed history of his life as a gay writer, one that quickly becomes overtaken by a list of losses to the epidemic, as well as events that signal the indifference of the culture at large; "election of Clinton, death of Steve Abbott, *Argento Series* born…". Reading these in order I locate a small constellation of events tracing a larger theme in the history of New Narrative, one mediated through Steve's presence. How does culture, which Bob Glück notes "reflected a resoundingly coherent image of myself back to me—an image so unjust that it amounted to a tyranny that I could not turn my back on", fail it's most vulnerable at every turn? How does a fidelity to personal narrative – Kevin's list of losses – draw out a need to examine a larger failure, the failure of memory, of language (Kevin's refrain: "I saw something important I can't remember")? How does this failure make writing a necessary response? In fact, to stretch this thought to its limit, how does the death of Steve birth *Argento Series*?

Near the end of "Will We Survive the 80s", Steve writes eruditely about gay history, challenges those on the margins of society to resist hegemony, but perhaps most poignantly, in the midst of a culture bent on either destroying him or denying his existence, he poses a series of rhetorical questions toward personal improvement: "In work and in play, how can I free myself from the hype of competitive stress? Can I learn to accept and find joy in the present moment even when it's not what I might prefer?..."Can I wake up from sexism, racism, ageism and career-ism...?" As he concludes his list of questions aimed at self-improvement, even burdened with the knowledge of being antibody positive, he turns the questions back toward the reader: "What are yours" he asks, "what do you hope for?" In his work we feel these questions resonant far beyond the seeming silence of his death. I hope that this collection of Steve's work, which reprints *Lives of the Poets* and *Skinny Trip to a Far Place* in full, and provides a broad selection of Steve's other writings and art – ranging from his funny, erudite essays and keen critical observations, to romantic poems, stories and visual narratives – help a new audience discover one of the hardest working, most talented and thoughtful art-ists of his generation. I also encourage readers further interested in his life and writing to read Alysia Abbott's captivating memoir *Fairyland* (W.W. Norton, 2013).

I'll end this introduction with a missive to the future in the form of a few verses from the *Argento Series* poem "Giallo", where a memory of Steve intercedes like a ghost to again blur the lines between lives: "Steve Abbott told me, when we go we / go out into blank space, like an enve-lope, / on our way to who?"

Jamie Townsend, February 2019, Oakland CA

LIVES OF THE POETS

I searched the house for his biography. He was the biggest hero of my youth. A shy high-schooler himself, he bought wild clothes on the Black side of town for his first concert. He was the first rocker to do a radio interview—to prove he wasn't Black. He adored mom. When he got rich he bought her pink Cadillacs and a big house. He got terribly fat when she died and, even in a corset, could hardly squeeze into his white leather jumpsuit for shows in Vegas. He denied he was a drug addict because others shot him up. There's a photo of him with Nixon getting commissioned into the Bureau of Narcotics and Dangerous Drugs looking too loaded to focus.

I read biographies. The woes of geniuses and stars cheer me up. Destiny in a dewdrop, more harmonious than a song. A few pages and X moves from agony to greatness; then death, how neatly it ties things up. But tiny, unexpected details appeal most: Elvis's brief moment of rebellion against Col. Parker when the singer showed just a flicker of interest in the occult.

He lay in bed all day with the curtains drawn. A large boil on his neck had to be lanced regularly, one on his hand made writing and typing difficult. He wrote in French so as to avoid "style" but mostly he couldn't write. He loved attending a great writer whose mentally unstable daughter fell in love with him. He ignored her till a rejection was unavoidable. The writer blamed him for leading the daughter on. Penniless, he returned home to teach but his students couldn't understand his distracted ruminations. His mother hounded him about his work. He had nightmares about missing trains or racing downhill on a bicycle with no breaks. A cousin he once loved died suddenly, then his father. He later became famous for writing about nothing.

A potential new friend doesn't look gay because his jeans hang low and baggy but he kisses a sweater he's just purchased.

*Nein, das tust du nicht* the earliest words she remembers. To this no she says yes: *Ich werde es zerreissen* (I'm going to slash it). She likes the

3

"hissing, ferocious" sound of *zerreissen* and recaptures her childhood by phrases: "liquid as soup," "You're crazy," "If you touch one of those poles, you'll die."

Marking my place in Nathalie Sarraute's autobiography—an undated letter. "It's okay if you write me," Sam said on the phone, "so long as you don't *impinge* your sexual fantasies." I responded by meditating on the forbidden he emphasized, lingered over:

> *To strike, hit or dash against something; to make inroads or encroach. Syllabic connotations: "m," the centering mantra (mamma, murmuring, milk); "p," sexual, generative meanings (sperm, spurt, spark, spank, speak....or penis, penetrate); "inge" as in "syringe," a soft seductive syllabic cluster like sponge.*
>
> *Bakhtin says we give value and context to utterance by intonation. Thus you undercut your syntactic command with an oppositional ambiguity. Flirtation always proceeds in this manner. It's a discourse of carnival and play but also of manipulation and subversion. It incites feelings the responsibility for which it refuses. If exposed, flirtation feigns surprise. "I love you" or "Let's have sex" would be its death.*

Spenserian enchantments, the damsel who melts into a crone. "In the back of your mind it's really there—it's Coke!"

Men at Cafe Flore: one wears new muscles like a mink, or a teenager the latest fashion; another has gold wire rim glasses. Erudition, frosting on the cake.

Most of what we know of him comes from police records. He took his MA from the University of Paris, then killed a priest. Pardoned, he pulled off a big theft. "Get famous, get laid," he sang waggishly (in rough translation) but, after getting busted again in a street fight, he was sentenced to be hanged. When the king rode by he was exiled instead. I liked him for his vengeance, his unappeasable satiric wrath. His poetry steals many discourses but then he belonged to a gang of thieves. He vanishes from history at the age of 32, the same age I was when I discovered him on the bottom shelf of a used bookstore.

In the financial district: a lady in faded green stretch pants and orange hair plays harmonica and beats a tambourine against her thigh.

He studied engineering and designed a prototype of a jet engine. When his father died he became rich. Influenced by reading Tolstoy and the Gospels, he gave his money away, not to the poor whom it might corrupt, but to other family members whom it couldn't harm. After writing a short book he felt solved all philosophical problems, he taught elementary school, then worked as a monastery gardener. Local fisherman marveled at his skill in taming birds. Cajoled into teaching philosophy again, he repudiated all his earlier positions. He hated stupidity and feared colleagues would steal his ideas. He loved Betty Hutton, Carmen Miranda and American detective novels. Three of his brothers committed suicide, the fourth won fame as a one-armed concert pianist. A year before he died, Wittgenstein visited America. He told his hosts it didn't matter to him what he ate so long as it was always the same.

As I walk from the library with an armload of books, someone asks "You actually read all those?" A poet tells of visiting a small town where the Ideal Cafe was closed at noon.

In childhood he wanted to be the beautiful people he saw. He wept with an overwhelming sense of emptiness and, at age 15, ran away to be a sailor. Instead he lived with prostitutes under an assumed name. Amplifying secrets, his conversation sparked like fireworks. He loved fashion and slept with every famous artist he could. "Astound me!" a ballet impresario commanded. So he ate sugar, and later took opium, to induce dreams. Occult characters graphed the deep confusions of his moulting mind. He believed an angel visited him in an elevator. Either he destroyed young men or he attracted those with a genius for self-destruction. He managed a prize fighter. Of his first famous film he said: "I was completely free because I didn't know anything," and of his last: "I do nothing but follow the rhythm of fables which are transformed by the teller." He died after being interviewed on the death of Edith Piaf.

Everyone's jacket was embroidered with hem-stitching and inlaid pearl to an absurd degree but the women pretended not to notice, carrying on with their make-up instead and fussing about where their fans had got to....Lady K. reminds one of a weeping willow in Spring. She is so vulnerable and so easily dismayed that you would think she was on the point of expiring....Two of the women showed a want of taste when it came to the color combination of their sleeves. Lady S. was scandalized. But it wasn't that much of a faux pas, just that the combinations were somewhat uninspired....Well now, I have discussed their looks, but people's characters—that's quite a different matter.

(from Lady Murasaki's diary, 1000—1010 A.D.)

One of the 7 Sages of the Bamboo Grove, a Taoist literary circle, came into town naked. "Scandalous!" exclaimed a townsperson. "What do you mean?" replied the sage. "The sky is my shirt, the earth is my pants, and by the way, what are you doing in my pants?"

"Though dustie wits dare scorne Astrologie," he believed the world was a lyre and sought to manipulate the effluvia of the stars. He was a prodigious letter writer and owner of his country's largest library, but produced few books himself. He completed one, on hermeticism, in 17 days. At 28 he was imprisoned for attempting to enchant the Queen. Released, he inquired of angels how to find a passage to the Orient, convert the natives of Atlantis and reunite Christendom. Enemies charged he was a "Caller of divels." Like his friend, Sir Philip Sidney, he believed poet, painter, architect and philosopher are one. He sought to revive magical chanted verse as practiced by Orpheus and Amphion whose poetry allegedly moved stones to build Thebes. His own poetry was abominable as was that of his later disciple Aleister Crowley. Pope Sixtus V ordered his arrest but he escaped.

Yesterday I talked to my student Chris. He first smiled only with the right side of his mouth, then his whole face lit up and he smiled completely. Later Frank called to say he persuaded his grandmother to dye her hair bright blue. She likes it but can't return to Florida now till the color wears off.

Blue was her favorite color and she hung out with rich lesbians who smoked cigars. She wore a waist-long pigtail to a private party where Mata Hari danced naked. Her first husband was a drunk. He locked her in his study and forced her to write novels. When she divorced him she began a music hall career. After marrying a famous politician/ journalist, she had an affair with his 16-year-old stepson. She loved her cat more than her daughter whose wedding she did not attend. She was 62 when she honeymooned with her third husband who acted as her literary agent. "I hate writing," she confessed. "Mainly I cross out a lot, delete and add." She established a line of beauty products but made-up a famous actress asymmetrically which discouraged further volunteers. She was photographed by *Vogue*, did subtitles for films. Marlene Dietrich told Cocteau the flag "seemed to live and breathe" as it enveloped her coffin.

Michael says he prefers the Picaro to Cafe Flore because it has a more nurturing atmosphere. Since Finnela's Sauna has been leveled, the Flore juts out on the corner of Noe and Market like a severed toe. From the gloom of my room to the glare of a fair – what's lacking, a comfortable space inbetween.

His mother made him memorize 200 verses of Latin each night before he could eat dinner. She slapped him often and forced him to run to lose weight. His mother's ridicule made him violently ill and he cried for two days when she refused to let him wear her dresses. Yet she combed his fair curls and nursed his frequent colds. His mother committed suicide when he was 18 months old. When she died he threw himself on the floor and tore his hair. "Mamma, your son is ill," he wrote in a poem. "Mamma, his heart is on fire. / Tell his sisters he has no place to hide." When he was bad, mother locked him in a closet in "the tower." When he was good, she took him with her to the shrine on top of Mt. Shaoshan, legendary birthplace of the phoenix. He argued all night with her as to whether Valenciennes lace was made in colors or not. His mother laughed when she heard he walked down the street with her panties on his head. When he was fired from his teaching job for molesting boys, he eloped with his mother to Rome. She cautioned him about his outrageous behavior. He was embarrassed to have to take his mother to a mental institution on the bus. When his third wife refused to make him a spice cake at 5 a.m., his mother made one for him. His mother drank, gambled, was a whore, was a virtuous but cold woman who belonged to a separatist religious sect. He never knew his mother. He first met his mother when he was thirty-six. We know nothing about his mother.

> *(Rimbaud, Pushkin, Hart Crane, Stephen Crane,*
> *Lautreamont, Mallarme, Mayakovsky, Pound, Mao,*
> *Apollinaire, John Lennon, Pasolini, Cocteau, Ginsberg,*
> *Kerouac, Apollinaire, Genet, Beckett, Genet, Bruce*
> *Boone, Homer)*

During the filming of *Judgement at Nuremberg*, Marlene Dietrich tells Spencer Tracy: "I'm not fragile, I'm a daughter of the military. I was taught discipline." When she came to Hollywood, several of her back teeth were extracted to improve her looks.

Before he was born, his mother dreamt he ate berries off a laurel tree and turned into a peacock. His father reminded him that Homer died poor. At nine he fell in love with a girl of eight dressed in a decorous crimson. Love later held his burning heart and gave it to her to eat. He wrote a sonnet asking for interpretations. "Remember Homer," his father again warned. Undaunted, he went off to a party in Rome. Sometimes he was bored, sometimes cruel, but his poems on make-up made him popular fast. Did you see him giggle, drunk at dinner last night? The Emperor felt his love poems corrupted his daughter, not to mention other citizens, and he banished him to a miserable village far away. Boccaccio gives this description in a conversation between two women:

> - There's the man who goes to hell and returns with
> tidings from those below.
> - Indeed, his beard is crisped and skin darkened as if
> by fire and smoke.

Wretched scribbler, unhappy fop, meditate on life's mutability. Ovid and Dante hated having to die in the sticks.

Thinking of boredom, I'm reminded of a security guard in my office building who sits by the door all day asking, "How's it goin'?"

I pick him up again on page 126 as he's about to leave mom and Ireland for Paris. But first London: Jung lectures on the illusion of unitary consciousness. He decides to be "completely born" so goes to bed in 1934 waking up in time to buy corn from Joseph in Egypt. This is the result of analysis. After reading Eisenstein he wants to make movies, then fly planes. Instead, he plays chess and reads Samuel Johnson. Upon arriving in Paris he's stabbed by a pimp. War further delays his career. While his wife sews, he turns to writing plays as a diversion from the "awful depression of prose." He equates writing plays to playing chess. "I'm not interested in success," he says, "only failure. The day I became aware of my stupidity is the day I began to write what I felt." In his most famous play Vladimir says "You should have been a poet" to which Estragon replies "I was. Isn't that obvious?"

Keats learned everything he could from his teachers, then surpassed them. He avoided literary feuds. I stop reading Keats' biography on page 290 because I never want my friendship with him to end.

She was born interested and the divided loyalties of her family during civil war gave her a deep sense of ambiguity. At age nine she moved to a land where there was nothing to see—no fences, creeks, trees or hills. On a trip to buy shoes, she surprised townspeople by quoting Shakespeare. Names had a primitive fascination for her and she used aliases freely. She was also fascinated by foreigners, drunks, actors and suicides, the latter being the subject of her first story. Her first ambition was to be a doctor. "Vivisection's my favorite amusement and amputating limbs would be perfect happiness," she wrote at fifteen. Although she admired strength and independence, even to the point of being ruthless, one of her closest lifelong friends was retarded. Usually a tomboy, she always wore long white gloves to the theater. "It's worthwhile to dress for a concert on the same principle as to dress for one's wedding," she wrote. "Music calls for the best in everything." She never married. Toward the end of her life she attempted to visit Keats' grave in Italy but instead found pomegranates in bloom.

On March 20th, Carl Hall rings my doorbell. He's separated from his wife and wants to make a date. We go to see a performance, then to Spec's where I'm to meet Sue Carlson who I haven't seen in some time. Jack Hirschman doesn't remember Carl even though we all worked on the Left/Write Conference together. I show Carl my story "Passing Strangers." He says his tattoo isn't of a tiger but of Sun-Mu-King, the Monkey King. The monkey has special powers. It accompanies a buddhist to get these valuable scrolls but they forget to tip the librarian who gets pissed and invokes a hurricane to blow the scrolls away. Carl's tattoo shows the monkey jumping up 50 feet to see what's happening.

Layered memories, layered lives. As Stephen Crane advised a younger writer: "The artist must be in some things powerless as a dead snake."

Great-grandson of an African slave, he was nicknamed "the monkey" (also a cross between a monkey and a tiger) for his agility in jumping chairs. At age nine he discovered and read his father's secret porn library. He laughed at VD, spent days and nights in drunken orgies. After one serious illness his head was shaved and he had to wear a wig. Many commented on his long clawlike fingernails. A palmist foretold his exile and eventual murder by a tall, fair-haired man. He disrupted theatrical performances and made lists of enemies as well as of all the women he loved. Church and State hounded him mercilessly. Evoking emotion by sound, he invented a new stanza for his most famous poem. His prose portrayed complex characters in the fewest words influencing his country's greatest novelists. At 32 he married a young flirt who plunged into fashion and extravagant court life. Five years later, deeply in debt, Pushkin is shot in a duel by a tall, fair-haired bisexual French hustler. Although his popularity had declined, thousands attended his funeral.

> *Hemingway wrote standing up at parties.*
> *Proust wrote mainly in bed.*
> *Lautreamont wrote only at night at his piano*
>     *declaiming each sentence aloud &*
>     *punctuating it with a loud chord.*
> *Lew Welch is best known for the lines "Raid*
>     *Kills Bugs Dead!"*

She was a bizarre beauty, always attracted to danger. On Halloween she met one of her country's greatest poets. He forced an education on her more intense than any university. Could she control the violence of her emotions? Amorous rejection was madness and she cloaked personal experience in mythical allusion. Flunking out of school, she sought the world beyond through table-tapping, crystal-gazing, tarot, astrology and numerology. She rewrote compulsively cutting her name down to two letters. She lamented her scant poetic output and unfavorable critical attention, was a lone wolf who desperately wanted to belong. Late in life she wore a lovely dress with pearls, a shoulder bouquet, a little hat and white gloves to receive an award from a prestigious institution. Afterwards, she watched tv shamelessly. "Unlike most ghosts," a famous critic wrote of her last book, "she had the guts to keep coming back."

He was a charismatic jokester who found hair raising situations amusing. He had a talent for meeting weird people and boasted that he looked like Nero or Racine. Could he control the violence of his emotions? "Artists are those who want to be inhuman," he wrote, seeking the voice of the light beyond. "I would have done better if I'd become an engineer." Instead he worked as a secretary, tutor, bank clerk, gossip columnist, book reviewer, art critic, pornographer, orange vender and clerk in a Censorship Office. He rewrote compulsively cutting his name down to two words. An arrest for receiving stolen goods and suspected collusion in the theft of the Mona Lisa only made him more shameless. He lamented his scant poetic output and unfavorable critical attention, was a lone wolf who desperately wanted to eat. He named the most influential literary movement of his century but returned from WWI a ghost of his former self.

When I read a draft of this at Intersection, Kevin said it inspired him. This pleased me since no one knows more about the lives and loves of the stars than he.

The biographer tries to delve into the poet's mind. Interviews become a genre. Do you prefer T.S. Eliot or Hart Crane? Barrett Watten or Izaak Walton? Robert Graves or grave robbers? Would you rather run around a building naked or be chased onto a roof by a monster? Lick stamps or spit images? Split an infinitive or hammer a point home? Make a mistake or masticate mugwort? What is your favorite choler? Can you hear 'dose Saud Amerikins singin'? Would you rather lose your mind or find Jesus? Be a Nazi or not see? Go to a Literary party or get murdered? Write with a pencil or be locked in a pen? Pilfer a pedigree or poop on the Pope? Why do vegetables suffer? Do the walls of the city speak? How long is too long? Would you rather watch tv or tether the sea? Depose a dictator or decompose a text? Echo bones or Rod McKuen? Some poets make lists that are endless. Translations may appear in *The American Poetry Review*.

Samuel Johnson, who originated modern biography with his life of Savage, kept a lock and chain by his bed in fear he might go insane. All his discipline, a laborious and painful daily struggle.

For a year I corresponded with X. We discussed various literary tendencies. Because I was drinking, my letters were either arrogant or abject. When I was arrogant, X. responded abjectly; when I was abject, X. was nasty. (This was the erotic component of our relationship.) Finally, we agreed to have dinner and discovered that, in person, we had little to say.

Born on a tobacco farm, he read Kant's *Critique of Pure Reason* at age thirteen. He was disappointed it didn't solve all life's problems. A year later he went to work for the railroad, then as a detective. His grandmother said he looked like a movie star. While working as an ad man, he began writing poems, reviews, and stories. His main influences were 13th century Icelandic sagas and the novels of Henry James. Attaining success, he drank heavily, lived flamboyantly and argued with publishers over book covers. The FBI investigated him, because of his storyline for the comic-strip *Special Agent X-9*. Gertrude Stein met him on April Fool's Day. They talked about autobiography. For 20 years he was a famous writer who didn't write. Instead he tinkered on film scripts, created popular radio shows and supported leftist causes. Prison guards called him "sir" after he was jailed for communist sympathies. He died penniless after making millions; threw books in the fire after reading them. Andre Gide considered him one of America's best writers because he gave "a foretaste of hell."

The first photo published in *Poetry Flash* showed the door of Artful Goodtimes' car on which was stenciled: "Poetry is the heart of liberty." A famous poet offers to be my lover in a future life.

Cervantes, Whitman, Poe, Stein, Creeley and almost every contemporary poet I know had to finance the publication of their first book. Dante and Zukofsky died before their masterworks were published; Dickinson published only one poem during her lifetime. Beckett's *Murphy* was rejected by 42 publishers; Kerouac couldn't get *On the Road* published for ten years. Paul Mariah told me that only one book of poetry in ten gets reviewed. These are not facts. This is a poet's life.

"And the duckweed on the lake...." A flute accompanying these lyrics intensified the coolness of the dawn breeze. The most insignificant thing can have its season.

– Lady Murasaki

Endless rain was the unforgettable presence of his youth. His father had two knife scars on his face. *Over the carpet of the secretive forest.... a butterfly, bright as a lemon.... I have come out of that landscape, that mud, that silence, to go singing....* Shyness, that "damaging thing," opened him into solitude, the foundation of his self. His first poet friend wore a cordova hat, splendid neckties and the muttonchop whiskers of a grandee. Another was nicknamed "The Corpse." A simple man, he envied their brilliant plumage and Satanic poses but believed poetry was more akin to a ceramic bowl or loaf of bread. After his first book, he deliberately toned down his style. Employed as a consul, he traveled through Europe, India and the Far East. "This is the golden age of world poetry," he wrote. "While the new songs are hunted down, millions sleep by the roadside. There is no housing, no bread, no medicine."

Participants in the 1983 One World Poetry Festival in Amsterdam were invited to a cocktail party by the Lebanese Ambassador. The international assemblage was bussed through electrified gates, disembarked and proceeded to get drunk. When the ambassador asked for silence, so we could listen to a rare gramophone recording of Apollinaire, almost no one paid attention. On this same night, 267 U.S. Marines were killed by a terrorist bomb in Beirut.

"One is Purified by Trial and Trial is by what is Contrarie," Milton wrote in the *Aeropagitica*. Could he have had in mind Oliver Cromwell who, laughing hysterically, smeared filth on the fine dresses of ladies at dinner?

He rejected the notion of poet as outcast and found reading sports mags more rewarding than reading poetry. He raided pop song lyrics and the work of earlier writers. This lax attitude toward literary property caused controversy. One new car he got for tossing off an advertising poem, another for writing about an accident he had in it. Besides participating in literary feuds, he wrote for fashion mags and he wanted to do a biography of a fighter who "boxed objectively." Theater audiences, he argued, should behave as if at a circus or the races. More interested in new methods than perfection, he never regarded his work as finished but always "in flux." Three women loved him: his wife, his mistress and his secretary. "My goal is not a good person but a good world," he said. He studied the lives of major capitalists and, in exile, found hard work a tonic. He loved detective novels and cigars but hated Hollywood where the pressure to conform was strong. His mother suffered from the neighbors' talk. "You can make a new start with your last breath," he said shortly before he died.

He recaptures his childhood by tastes: fircone kernels roasted over a fire, orange-rind dragees and aniseed balls for the Epiphany, ice-cold water-melon in summer, tamarind paste to console him when he cried, quince paste and pancakes made of peach paste, macaroni with chicken liver sauce or with sugar and cinnamon – all these he registers before the age of seven. Later, he often goes hungry. Once, with Alfred Jarry, he drank absinthe mixed with red ink.

I awake from a dream with only this phrase: The odd unadorned dodo.

His mother spoiled him though she lived in abject poverty. He started chipping heroin at 15 and was nicknamed for his love of fried chicken. Deep confusions graphed the ornithological character of his mind. He exploited friends and seldom moulted. Donning dark glasses, he ignored his audience. For this, devotees idolized him. Can you hear his voice of light rising from selfish rage? "He could not only translate his ideas into notes at superhuman speed," one poet wrote. "He was simultaneously aware of half a dozen ways of resolving any musical situation and could refer to them all in passing." During a visit to the Manhattan apartment of Baroness Pomnonica de Koenigswarter, he complained of stomach pains. Three days later, at age 35, he was dead. Many poets, including Jack Spicer, eulogized him.

His first three marriages to 16-year-olds ended disastrously and almost ruined his career. "I find unsuccessful people much more interesting," he wrote. "They haven't lost something human, impulsive and warm, especially if they've always been poor and unsuccessful." He became a millionaire and boasted Carl Sandburg, Upton Sinclair, Max Eastman,

H.G. Wells, Einstein, Gertrude Stein and G.B. Shaw amongst his fans (though Shaw he first feared to meet). Many poets, including Lawrence Ferlinghetti, eulogized him.

An underlined phrase in the biography, a shoreline; an asterisk in the margin, dark star. A well-dressed woman and child turn to a table set up by the Humane Society to look at homeless pets.

Over Christmas I see my brother who teaches piano to Solzhenitsyn's son. The boy has such a highly developed sense of smell he can tell everything a town manufactures just by passing it on the highway. He's brilliant but can't speak in front of a class. Amazingly, his family has little appreciation of music. They are extremely protective of pere S. who, according to my brother, presides over the family like a ghost.

Her house burned down five years before she died. Her last outing, with stretchers and ambulance, was to the opening of the opera *The English Eccentrics*. Then she routed the priest who came to hear her last confession. Her last meal consisted of cold beef, tea, jelly and an egg beaten up with brandy. She bought a new car before she died. He insisted on being buried in a zinc coffin as a protection against worms. After kissing the air and her own hands, she died with a radiant, girlish smile on her face. He died of frostbite, tuberculosis, emphysema, heart attack, AIDS, a heroin overdose, alcoholism. Whitman was the only poet to attend his funeral, not because he liked him, but because he thought at least one American poet should be there. For years she longed for death. Having envisioned death as an act of will, she died combing her hair before the fire. He disobeyed his doctors, felt guilty, then dictated to his housekeeper a satirical observation on the imbecility of doctors. He dreamt he supped with the dead. "You were probably the life of the party," his boyfriend replied. He came close to dying in the pulpit, falling into a fever which, with the help of vapors from his spleen, hastened him into so visible a consumption that beholders said "he died daily." He died reading about football in the *Princeton Alumni Magazine* while his friend was reading a biography of Beethoven. He was shot in the groin by fascists.

He was shot by a rival revolutionary faction. He was clubbed in the head, stabbed and run over by a car. He was knifed in a tavern quarrel en route to an espionage trial. He fell or was thrown off a ship. He jumped off a bridge. He was run over by a dune buggy. He shot himself in the head. He returned to court twice to prove he hadn't committed suicide. He died saying:

> *- Words did this to me.*
> *- Does nobody understand?*
> *- I must go in, the fog is rising.*
> *- I should have been, among other things,*
> *a good poet.*

She put her head in an oven. She walked into the sea. He appeared in a dream to his son after he died and showed him where to look in the wall for the final cantos of his famous poem. We know nothing at all of her death and would have none of her poems except for the happy chance that they were written on linen, torn into strips and used to wrap the dead.

I consider writing about all the poets I have met alphabetically (Ashbery, Berrigan, Creeley, Duncan, etc.) but abandon the idea. Yet all is not lost. Returning my matches, someone in the cafe ignores my outstretched hand and tosses the matches on the table instead.

At age ten he published several editions of a dittoed newspaper, *The Daily Dick*. Nine years later, he moved into a gnostic poet's commune where seances were held. Here he had the first of several breakdowns. He also suffered a variety of phobias which prevented regular employment, in particular, agora/claustrophobia. In 1950, the FBI asked him and his second wife to become spies. They refused. Like Kerouac and Sartre, he wrote much of his work on Speed. He liked secret societies, Van Gogh and had a series of mystical experiences. He participated in a seance to contact Bishop Pike's dead son. After someone broke into his house and blew up his files with C3 or C4 plastic military explosives, he moved to Canada. "I took my cow to town," he told *The Rolling Stone*, "and I didn't even get magic beans." Sixty novels, 5 wives, 3 children, 2 attempted suicides, 1 twin sister dead at 6 weeks from malnutrition and neglect. This isn't a life of George Bataille but it could be.

Walter Savage Landor waited savagely in languor. A dog-eared page marks the spot.

The youngest child of a large family, she was the center of attention. Food and books, books and food were her life then, and her older brother. She hated dad and liked mom only for her rich furs which were pleasant to rub against. Her older brother protected her until middle age when she dumped him. As she listened to her dog lap water, she discovered the difference between paragraphs and sentences: the former emotional, the latter not. "It takes a lot of time being a genius," she wrote. "You have to sit around so much doing nothing." Her most famous poem was painted on the circumference of a plate. She loved model T cars, soldiers in uniform and detective novels because they were all the same but different. She paid to have her first books printed and didn't have a best seller until she was sixty. For a while then she couldn't write. Of Pound she said "He's a village explainer, excellent if you're a village." She also remarked that remarks aren't literature. This is literature. She conquered America in tweeds, golf shoes and a wool shooting cap. Although she disliked Christianity, she found saints interesting because they were "like cubists." She dressed unfashionably but was interviewed by *Vogue*.

Rilke hated the city he was born in. Mallarmé hid behind cigarette smoke. Young Goethe was considered a brainless chatterbox by his friends. Aged Rumi's lover/guru was poisoned by his son. Langston Hughes collaborated on a play with Zora Neale Hurston but couldn't produce it because she was jealous of his new girlfriend. Breton, tedious as rain, plotted the coordinates of his life by what he read. Sterne's friends fell asleep as he read them *Tristam Shandy* which so discouraged him he almost pitched it into the fire. Oppen stopped writing for 30 years. He began again when he dreamt his soul would rust if he did not. Miles Davis, who studied at Julliard, befriended Jimi Hendrix, Prince and Sting. Tom Clark and Ed Dorn vented personal hatreds by publishing an "AIDS Awards for Poetic Idiocy."

> *Dear A.,*
> *Let's put the tapes of our interview with D. into the*
> *Bancroft Library where they belong before they get*
> *lost or ruined. Besides, I need the money.*
>
> *Yours, Etc.*

Born into an impoverished family, he joined the military. For five years he was enslaved by Turkish pirates. He was unable to find work afterwards, perhaps because of his stutter and maimed left hand, so he became a tax collector. At this, and in love too, he was unsuccessful. Scornful of theater that valued profit over art, he used the names of real people in his writing along with characters such as Necessity and Opportunity. Other writers were more popular but he refused to give up. With his country in the midst of plague, war, economic hardship and the Inquisition, he was unjustly imprisoned at the age of fifty. Now he begins writing *Don Quixote.*

Born into an impoverished family, she joined the military. She was drummed out as a lesbian, so she worked in a sleazy bar, then as a nurse. At this, and in love too, she was unsuccessful. She fell seriously ill with a brain fever and talked to birds. Finding a new lover, she moved West. They worked for Left political groups and established a home for battered women. Scornful of poetry that valued art over community, she used the names of real people in her writing as well as characters such as the Devil in the form of Love. Other writers were more popular but she refused to give up. With her country in the midst of war, sexism and homophobia, Judy Grahn began writing *The Work of a Common Woman.*

An anthropologist tried to persuade his informant, a medicine man, to get a university education. The shaman replied: "White man's knowledge all in books. Lose books, lose mind."

Laurie Anderson said in a concert: "NYC has five million people, each with a story to tell."

Less than 20 yards away, two male chimpanzees were sitting on the ground staring at me intently. I scarcely breathed, waiting for the sudden panic-stricken flight that normally follows a surprise encounter at close quarters. But nothing happened. The two chimps simply continued to gaze at me. Slowly I sat down and, after a few more moments, the two calmly began to groom one another. Then I saw two more chimpanzee heads peering at me over the grass from the other side of a small glade, a female and a youngster. They bobbed down as I turned my head toward them but soon reappeared, one after the other, in the lower branches of a tree. There they sat, almost motionless, watching me.
– Jane Goodall, *In the Shadow of Man*

FROM "LOST CAUSES"

# A PSYCHIC HEALING: CHAPTER 3

Kristan Zilstrum sat on the worn marble steps of Emory's old library and set her mouth in the frown of grim determination which she'd perfected at age seven when she told her mother that she hated being a girl, *hated* it, and that no, she *wouldn't* wear the pink dress with the four inch flounce at the bottom, she'd wear jeans to school like the boys did. Kristan's surname meant "oak tree" in Swedish and so she sat now, stiff as an oak. Her back was hurting again and Spencer had persuaded her to visit Hannah about it. But Spencer, as usual, was late.

Others would have checked into the student infirmary but Kristan hated doctors. They liked you weak and helpless; they wanted to awe you into submission. No, pain was simply another challenge, another opponent to be met and conquered. If men could stand pain, so could she.

Kristan was the youngest of four girls. Her father, a self-made millionaire in the construction business, wanted a boy and when Kristan was born, he reared her like the son he wanted. By the age of two he was playing catch with her; at age five, he took her hunting.

In another life Kristan might have been a Joan of Arc. In this one, lacking any great cause, her goals were more mundane: compete with men and win—academically, sexually, psychologically. Actual sex she found tiresome since nature, in its mischievousness, had slanted her clitoris so that it was impossible for her to achieve orgasm. But snaring men she found exhilarating. She liked to let them think they might win when actually she always did.

Kristan winced as another pain shot up her spine. Ignoring it had become impossible. Some mornings she could hardly get out of bed.

"Sorry I'm late." Spencer ran up sweating and out of breath. "Peter said we could use his car but he forgot to give me the keys. When I went back to his office he'd left for Morton's…"

"Your brain's so fried I'm surprised you remembered me at all," Kristan grouched. Her own Capri was in the shop. "Well, don't just stand there. Help me up so we can get going."

Like all guilty people, Spencer wanted to be abused. He thought he could lie and hide his little affairs, but Kristan read him like a book. She also knew how far she could push him without letting on what she knew. All men were shits, after all, and all yearned, if only secretly, to find a woman strong enough to dominate them.

Macho jocks were too easy. What could they fall back on, after all, but brute strength. Spencer, in his effeminacy, was more intriguing. First she had to build up his ego. Only then could she deflate that ego and cock which, surprisingly, was actually much larger than those of the jocks.

Kristan's approach had been direct. She simply walked up to Spencer at a party, shoved a football in his stomach, and said "Wanna ball?" Maybe she sensed he was gay from the start. Or maybe she secretly longed for a lesbian relationship and this was as close as she was willing to go. But no, it wasn't a woman she wanted. There was no glory in conquering women. Kristan wanted a man, a cocky animal she could lead around on a leash. When she tired of her other conquests, Kristan always had Spencer to fall back on. Or at least she did before Peter came along.

Spencer's actual confession of his gayness had been a shock. Kristan knew some of his fraternity brothers messed around, but they did it with each other, not with married faculty. Peter was nine years older. Why did Becky put up with it? Peter must be quite a manipulator to have broken through Spencer's defences. No one else had, except her, and many tried. What hold did Peter have over Spencer anyway?

Often Kristan tried to force the issue, not with Spencer, though she teased him about it, but with Peter. When Peter asked Spencer out, she'd tag along. But Peter was so cloyingly gracious that their skirmishes remained oblique. Some she won, some not. Who'd win the war? As she got in the Walden's familiar green station wagon, Kristan re-examined her campaign.

The mountain trip was a tie. She'd stayed too aloof and had let Spencer and Peter flirt. Maybe it was because her back hurt or because Becky's pregnancy had thrown her off. She should have known better than to expect an ally in Becky. Besides, it was humiliating to need one. They'd have been sisters in misery at best.

Then that night at Club Imaginary—Club Nightmare it should be called! Since this was more of a real date, she hoped Peter might blow his cool. Instead, he won under the guise of the drug ethos. He got them stoned, gave Spencer some MDA, and had him on the dance floor all night. Then she had to endure that "after-the-bar" party full of guys in Alice Cooper drag. And to make matters worse, Spencer had insisted on spending the night with Peter. But at least she'd shown her mettle.

Finally, there was the recent aborted dinner at the mansion. Spencer had resisted her coming but after a nasty fight, gave in. For a while Kristan thought this would be her decisive victory.

They arrived late to find Peter downstairs reading. Even with the fireplace roaring, the livingroom exuded a desolation more profound than any ruin. Peter was obviously pissed. When Spencer apologized for missing dinner, he replied in the tone of an irked shopkeeper scolding a pesky child. Kristan savored their mutual discomfort awhile, then asked Spencer if they could go out for pizza. This time, Peter didn't offer his car.

The walk up Ponce de Leon to the Pizza Hut took longer than expected. Dry leaves crackled under their feet and the wind was brisk. "Let's skip," Kristan said impulsively. Maybe she couldn't match Peter's intelligence but tonight, at least, she knew she'd be more fun. This thought so exhilarated her that she actually began looking forward to returning to the mansion and driving her victory home.

But when they returned, Peter was no longer downstairs. The flickering half-light from the fireplace cast ominous shadows on the manikins animating their expressions with just a trace of mockery. Kristan wanted to leave but Spencer insisted on finding Peter first and saying goodbye. So Kristan trudged after Spencer up the curved staircase to the dark upper hall where the echoing footsteps didn't sound like theirs so much as the irrevocable might-have-beens that haunt all houses built to hide from the world's prying. "Who is it?" Peter's muffled voice called out when Spencer knocked on his door.

"It's me, Spencer."

They entered to find Peter sprawled naked on the four-poster bed with a blond who looked so much like Spencer he might have been his twin. And what the kid was doing between Peter's legs was so revolting Kristan could barely make her way to the Queen Anne couch.

"You remember Jimmy, don't you?" Peter pulled a sheet over himself now that the damage was done. "I didn't know you were coming back and he just happened by."

27

Spencer lingered by the door like a dog that had just been kicked. He knew Peter saw other guys—they weren't monogamous, after all—but the sight of him actually in bed with one threw Spencer into confusion.

"Where's Becky," Kristan blurted (was there no way to wound this shameless man?).

"She took Andrea to visit her parents for a few days."

"Sorry we took so long," Spencer said, gamely trying to be cool.

"No problem." Peter sat up and fluffed the pillows.

Jimmy grinned and ran his fingers through Peter's hair. Spencer ambled over and started trying on some of the caps Peter kept on the bedpost. He donned a 30's cap, the kind newsboys used to wear.

"How's this," he asked, cocking it at a rakish angle.

"You must be Kristan," Jimmy said, leaning forward. "I've heard so much about you."

"I'll bet you have," Kristan muttered.

"Don't let us freak you out," Jimmy cooed. "We're just decadent queens, that's all. Crazy, decadent queens!" Jimmy giggled shrilly at the word decadent.

"Well, let's go down and have some tea," Peter said, slipping on a silk dressing gown. "You must be frozen after that walk. I'm so embarrassed. Like I say, I didn't know you were coming back."

Kristan had been in awkward situations before, but never one like this. She felt dizzy, like she was totally losing control. As she followed the men down the back stairs—dark turnings created by ancient delusions of lust and pride—Kristan felt she was descending into hell.

Jimmy, fearful of his own feelings, thrived on fanning up psychodramas around him. "Oh, I *love* your drag," he jabbered. "Where'd you get those boots? And that denim. I just *love* women in denim." Peter, on the other hand, was so polite it infuriated Kristan even more. Then, as Peter heated water for tea, Roses swept into the kitchen.

"Meet Richard," Roses said of the bearded man on his arm (as if anyone cared). "He wants to put me in a play he's directing." Richard glanced around like a viscount visiting the provinces.

"People blanch when they hear the word 'theater,'" Richard yawned. "But it's become so much more adventuresome lately. The play I'm doing is a satire on Soaps."

"You've come to the right place then," Jimmy giggled. "We're dirty as sin here."

On they droned with their faggy talk. Peter asked if they knew "Edge of Night" had recently alluded to homosexuality. Roses replied it was "Queen for a Day" about a housewife who became a star after doing a tap dance in combat boots.

"It's difficult to achieve greatness in minor genres," Richard lectured. "But that only makes the accomplishment all the more fabulous."

"Do you have any hot chocolate," Kristan asked. "When I was a kid I loved hot chocolate in cold weather."

She hoped this wholesome comment might pull Spencer back to her side. Instead, it exposed her as dishwater dull in this den of Sythian glitter.

"'Fraid not," Peter apologized. "Our commune health nuts claim milk is too mucousy."

"Let's go to Club Imaginary," the sylphid Jimmy suggested. No doubt he figured if their interdynamics were amusing here, they'd be hilarious at the bar.

"Kristan and I have to get back to campus," Spencer sighed. "Classes, ya know." Peter knew Spencer seldom attended morning classes, but flushed with Jimmy's giddiness and the discovery he actually could make Spencer jealous, he graciously agreed to drop them off.

Kristan felt sick. Spencer was sticking with her only out of duty now. If he started to do that, she'd lose him for sure. "Go on," she urged. "I mean it, I can see you tomorrow." Spencer said no, he was tired himself, but when they got out of the car, he slapped the fender a couple times. The gesture cut Kristan to the quick.

Just thinking about this now (and how could she forget) made Kristan's back throb even more as they turned up the mansion drive. That vile house! That spawning ground of every iniquity! Why couldn't Hannah have come to her? She was the one in pain, after all. But it was too late to complain about that now. As Spencer helped her out of the car, Kristan felt like Lee surrendering at Appomattox.

"Spencer got fouled up as usual," Kristan explained to Hannah who greeted them at the door wondering why they were late. Unlike Lee, Kristan wasn't ready to concede defeat yet.

"I thought the West sunroom would be best, if that's okay with you," Hannah said, taking Kristan's down jacket. Hannah looked younger than her 38 years—smooth skin, rich full hair. Whatever her healing methods, they certainly seemed to work for her.

Hannah asked Kristan to lie down on the waterbed. She'd already gotten her birth information from Spencer and learning Kristan was a water sign (a Cancer in the first trine to be exact, moon in Leo, Venus in Scorpio), Hannah knew she could be childish and stubborn.

"I must tell you right off I don't cure people," Hannah began. "One *cures* hams; people *heal* themselves. My job is simply to act as your facilitator and help you get in touch with your own healing power. Where does your back hurt most?"

Kristan said her left side did. Hannah asked Kristan to shut her eyes and began massaging her feet. The first task was to get Kristan to relax. For a while Hannah didn't speak. A tape of ocean sounds played from a small cassette on the floor.

"Okay," Hannah said at last. "Let's try some imaginative yoga. First I want you to just concentrate on the pain in your back; then concentrate on feeling the water underneath you. Have you done that?"

"I feel cold," Kristan said, not sure what she was supposed to be doing.

"Do you feel cold or does the water beneath you feel cold?"

"Both."

"Very good," Hannah murmured soothingly. "And how does your back feel now?"

"Hot, I guess. A hot stabbing feeling."

"Okay," Hannah continued. "If Spencer will help us now, we're going to do something I call 'a run.' First we'll massage your head and feet just to stir up a little energy."

Spencer massaged Kristan's feet while Hannah massaged her temples. Then Hannah asked Kristan to imagine her feet growing two inches downward and her head growing two inches upward. When she'd done that, Hannah asked her to return to her original size. They repeated this exercise three times, finally stretching to one foot. Then Hannah asked Kristan to imagine the front door of her house and to describe it. Kristan pictured the front door of Spencer's fraternity.

"Well, there's a ten foot cement porch with five or six steps going up to it on the right side."

"Is the door open or closed?"

"Open."

"Okay," Hannah said. "I want you to walk inside and tell me what you see."

Kristan described a short hallway with a telephone booth on the right. Photos of different fraternity chapters hung along the walls. Hannah asked what color the walls were. Kristan said gray and the carpet was dark green. Then Hannah asked Kristan to imagine she was on the roof and to describe what she saw.

"I can see the whole campus and Morton's in the distance with little cars driving down Emory Road."

Hannah asked Kristan to imagine she was floating up higher now. For a while Kristan didn't see anything. Then she felt a cool mist and, looking down, she saw patchwork snatches of Atlanta through wisps of cloud. Its curved roads, lush foliage and grid streets intermeshed in an embrace at once feminine and hard, fatal and languorous.

"Okay," Hannah said. "Remember you have the power to fly back whenever you want. You're the person in charge of this trip." For the first time Kristan smiled. "Now just relax and fly into a cloud. See where it takes you."

"Someone wants to hurt me," Kristan said suddenly.

"Can you see who it is?"

"No, it's too foggy."

"Okay, Kristan," Hannah said soothingly. "Let yourself land and tell me where you are."

"I'm...I'm at the edge of a forest. And on the other side there's a tall white...maybe it's a building. No, it's a wall."

Spencer shivered. He'd been dreaming of white buildings himself lately. This exercise was getting too strange.

"Look down at your feet and tell me what you're wearing."

"Sandals, the kind that lace up with leather cords."

31

Kristan was amazed. Everytime Hannah asked a question she saw something. It wasn't imagining or hypnosis, it was *seeing* as if she were watching a home movie of herself. She felt this was her even though she was a guy. It didn't make any sense but she felt overwhelmed with love for this person. It was like watching a movie and being in it at the same time.

"What kind of wall or building is it?" Hannah's voice was reassuring. Kristan felt safe laying next to her.

"I don't know. It's very old and it...it surrounds a city. There's a river or moat going around it."

Kristan told Hannah what she saw but not what she felt. She felt so much love for this city that tears began rolling down her cheeks. But everything was in danger.

"What about the forest?"

"It's about 300 yards away. The trees are very tall and close together. Someone's hiding in there watching me."

"How do you feel about that person?"

"They're sort of mischievous. They've put the city in danger and I've got to find them."

"Why do you have to find them?"

"They've run away and I'm supposed to bring them back."

Hannah looked at Spencer who was turning pale. She reached over and put her hand over his. After a few moments she continued.

"Go into the forest, Kristan, and tell me what you see."

"I...I don't think I want to."

"You don't have to if you don't want to. But if you do want to, you can. And remember, you can leave whenever you want."

For a while Kristan didn't speak. Spencer wondered if she'd fallen asleep when she began again. "I'm following a sort of path. The forest is getting darker and..."

Suddenly Kristan screamed.

"Tell me who you see," Hannah commanded. Kristan's body started jerking and a strong smell of blood filled the room. "Fly, Kristan," Hannah said, grabbing her hand. "Fly back into the sky and into the cloud."

Kristan convulsed at Hannah's touch, then felt herself become light as air. The sickly odor that had invaded the room flew into Hannah's body as if she were a lightning rod. Spencer's eyes widened and he started trembling.

"Who did you see," Hannah asked calmly after a few minutes. Spencer's hands perspired.

"I...I don't know."

She didn't want to say the face she saw was Spencer's and she struggled to choke down his name. And that terrible, murderous look in his eyes. She blanked it out.

"Just relax and float," Hannah said. "You're in control of this journey, remember? You can let go of your pain if you want, the choice is yours."

Kristan breathed in and out deeply wrestling with the habit of a lifetime, of many lifetimes maybe, the habit of holding things in. Who would she be if she let go? She'd get lost in the air. Was that death, just slipping away like that? It seemed so peaceful. Why did she fight it then?

"Breathe deeply," Hannah said, slowly letting go of Kristan's hand. "Let yourself slowly float back into the sunroom here. When you feel ready, you can open your eyes."

Kristan opened her eyes and saw Spencer watching her with a look of intense concern. And Hannah, so peaceful. If only her own mother could have been more like that.

"How do you feel," Hannah laughed. Her laugh was warm and wiped away all traces of the previous disturbance.

"Better," Kristan sighed. She felt embarrassed to be the center of their attention. Even more, she felt tired.

"A healing energy flows through us constantly," Hannah said. "The obstacles are in our minds. When you go home I want you to take a hot bath. Be good to yourself."

As Hannah watched Kristan and Spencer walk down to the station wagon afterwards, she felt tired too. Already they were bickering again and Kristan was digging her heels into the earth. Why did people cling to such painful habits? Did civilization drive people crazy? It was the same conflict Edgar Cayce had described in Atlantis: the Children of the Law of One versus the Children of the Law of Belial. What path would people follow this time? Hannah washed her hands and went to her room for a nap.

That night Spencer dreamt he was locked in a tower. Maybe it was a hotel, he wasn't sure, but from his balcony he could see white beaches and a silvery ocean that the sun bounced off of as blindingly as hammered gold.

In Spencer's room was a large bed, a sunken bath and a table laden with fruit and wine. Mirrors covered the walls. Several boys and girls—he couldn't tell how many because of the mirrors—romped in the bath. Spencer knew they were here for his pleasure.

A boy came up and stroked his cock. His coppery skin was smooth as velvet, his black eyes were black as agate. Only they threw off an emerald fire like the sun does when it sinks over the horizon. The boy smiled. Spencer could feel his warmth. To have sex with someone when you're about to be sacrificed is the hottest sex of all.

Death—that's not the great sadness. Spencer's sadness was that he hadn't known until now how much he loved his life, a life he'd largely wasted. But this sadness also made him horny. Only as long as he was eating, drinking and fucking could he feel certain he was alive.

The boy lifted his legs and Spencer entered him. Spencer wanted to fuck him without stopping but every time he thrust his cock into the boy, the walls shook and the mirrors shattered. As each mirror fell—like the breaking of promises—Spencer felt more free. Then the walls began to crumble, exposing Spencer's body to the cruel lash of the sun's rays. Still Spencer couldn't stop. He fucked the boy until he felt his heart might burst.

What would it feel like to rip out your lover's heart? What would it feel like to eat the heart as it throbbed in your hand? Tomorrow Spencer would die. Tonight he wanted to fuck himself into oblivion.

The ocean is a big blue space. It's as wet as the sweat pouring off your body when you're fucking a boy for as long as you can before your heart is ripped out and eaten. In this bed, in this tower falling from the sky, Spencer fucked a beautiful boy while being whipped into a frenzy by the rays of the dying sun. Only this sun wasn't yellow. It wasn't orange, magenta or red. The face of this sun was black as agate as it threw off emerald fires and sank into the sea.

POEMS FROM "WRECKED HEARTS"

# HOW MICHAEL THE ARCHANGEL WAS FOOLED

No one knows the age of Satan
when he fell.
Maybe he was just fourteen.
Milton says he was marvelous to view
& smart as a whip. We know that much.
   Snaky boy!
Maybe he had long brown hair
which fell like a bruise around his neck
in ringlets. Medusa curls.
Maybe he was androgynous, a hustler
wanting to drag *everybody* down.

We don't know about Satan
but we know one fallen angel who lies
before us now.
"Take me to hell," Beaver taunts.
"I been all over this damn town & I ain't
found nothing I like so well
as a rough fuck." His eyes
dance dangerously. He laughs.
He's syphilitic. We know that too.

   The devil.
   The devil smiles.
   The devil draws back
his claws. "Give me all
& I'll give you shit," the devil says.
"Nobody's as stupid as they look
save good angels.

Michael unsheaths his fiery sword
seduced to punish once again.

## WALKING THIS ABANDONED FIELD

Walking this abandoned field I am looking
for something inside myself, an old
shovel perhaps or some evidence of planted seed.
I come upon a tree
much like one I used to climb as a boy
& lying down, my eyes
roam over the frayed hatband of evening sky.

This is how I used to feel loving you.
How sweet the air smelled then, like rain
in Nebraska after a field was plowed.
Now all I can see is this tree
& the memory of how high we once climbed.

# LINES FOR CHAIRMAN MAO

Chairman Mao had a big globe between his ears
he used to turn carefully as a poem.
After the long march
he gave his fellow revolutionaries some pointers.
The map worked just like he said it would.
China transformed.

So far as I know
Chairman Mao never wore a dress
but maybe he does now
in heaven.

# BIG BOYS DON'T CRY
*for Mark Stoll*

Earhorn would be so nice to be sly to;
sly too, to be nice to the reddest jet in the sky.
The corner where I grew up
has changed into alligator teeth
so I have jettisoned to a big, fat city of hunters.
I could go mad talking about these things,
either go mad or cry.

Don't cry says my Daddy
but when you say: "We need to...
                        we need to...
                        we need to..."
I want to run far, far away, find a shy
looney corner of trees that is not alligators or cities.
Goodbye, teachers. Goodbye.
All the stars over my bed grin deadly.
I can't go to sleep anymore
because they never say "thankyou." Not even once.
I could go mad talking about these things.
I could go mad.

Super synapse-snapping hunters, what you hunt anyway?
You keep stealing my dreams
& throwing them into alligator cages.
Why?
Somewhere must be one tree just for silence,
tree corner where big, big boys can cry.
I could go mad talking about these things,
either go mad or die.

# TO A SOVIET ARTIST IN PRISON

*for Sergei Paradzhanov*

They tortured me today
when I created
collage as a degenerate
stance.
I pictured a montebank mathematician,
his two squinty eyes
wandering on totally different planes,
black on blue
(they kicked me in the ribs for this).
"Zoom 1 plus fat 3
equals zero,"
I wrote under his gaping chin
(for this, they broke my thumbs).
The corners of my poster
   I tore
so it would resemble the State
and I stained it with my own blood
(for this, they hung me by my testicles).

But I was lucky!
When I crawled back to my cell
I found this letter from Karl Shapiro.
"America made me silky, rich and famous,"
   he wrote,
"But I am dying
because no one listens to my words."

# MOST STREETS IN VALLARTA

Most streets in Vallarta are straight
   not crooked
but they lean off to the side
   sometimes
like Lorca's songs and one night
   passing
Carlos O'Brian's full of fat queens from Frisco
   chattering
like Romans, I came upon one lone Spaniard
   hard & lean
as cobblestones who reached out hungrily for a boy
   who fought
picking up a head sized stone
   throwing
it at the lone Spaniard
   crushing
his dreams like Lorca's songs & blood
   gushed darkly
through the crooked dimlit street.

# AFTER READING CATULLUS

I have run after those boys
they with flippant heads, posing
as gods or sacred wrynecks aflutter.
I would elevate them on a pedestal
alright, & hoist them up for all to admire
(O down to Faith's last drop I would)
but I have lost confidence in this religion.
Today it is not bodies or even love men worship
but some oblique gamesmanship, some mime
wherein we pretend to court gods none believe.
It's as if the temple were hung with rags
behind which stand no trace of any word
but word of mouth, & that
from the biggest liar in town.

Yet I rejoice! My heart
is blank & aftertime in the countryside
I have learned to love myself.

# THE DISTURBING PAINTING

A MAN AND HIS WIFE view a disturbing painting painted
by their adolescent son. Dark in color, the painting depicts two
monks kneeling before a skinny woman who is pointing to-
ward a door. Behind them, a ghoulish figure, probably a
corpse, lies on a bed. A naked trollop sits behind the bed
holding what is either a very ugly doll or a baby with a muddy
face. One one side of her grows a tree; on the other side stands a
baroque dresser over which hangs an ornate mirror. A ghastly
face looms from the center of the mirror.

"How disturbing," says the man.
"The face in the mirror?" asks the wife.
"No," says the man. "The fact of these trees growing in the
room of the painting and the fact that the time shown on the
clock on the painting is all wrong."
"Yes," says the wife. They stand in silence, wondering
where they have gone wrong. Then the wife speaks again.

"Our son says this painting symbolizes the expulsion of
Romanticism by Classicism." The wife tries to sound
cheerful.
"How disturbing," says the man, "to think that our son
may be a genius."

The dark walls in the room of the painting are overlaid
with diaphanous lines of silver and blue. Fearing that they
might be spider webs, the man and his wife back away.
"How disturbing," says the man again.
"Yes," says the wife, "to think that our son may be a
genius."

# THE DEPARTURE

I suppose it's all over now.
   Brief as a cloudless sky
   Empty as my daughter's mouth
You are flying home for Christmas.

   Back home
   I read this note:
   "Dear Tooth Fairy,
   Tonight's the night!
   Tooth under her pillow."

Your plane drones on.
I don't know where it's taking you.
I replace Alysia's tooth
with a shiny tin quarter.

   (She, so anxious. For days
   It just barely hung in there
   A dead white star)

Under my own pillow
I dream fitfully.
A sad, savage bird
   Drops you
Into an album of fading wings.

Come morning
I'll be the only good fairy
Left in town.

THE MALCONTENT

When Ted talked seriously about his feelings he lowered his head slightly and leaned forward. His fingers fidgeted but his eyes held steady. If I looked in his eyes too long he brushed up his crew cut and laughed. Ted could laugh mockingly too but that only suggests virtues defined by faults.

Ted and I had another cafe friend whom Ted once described as "honestly insincere." Jack had a great talent for meeting people and, unlike Ted, a good career. But Jack was restless, cynical. Ted felt Jack would put down a new friendship with a twenty year old he'd taken in. Jack's smirk would imply Ted was being "ripped off."

Listening to Ted I thought about my own life. Coming out in the 70s I thought being gay would change the world. No more patriarchy or war. I got a lover and when Mark split after five years I plunged into random tricking. If I didn't get laid at least three times a week I felt hopelessly ugly. But this anonymous life—office worker by day, whore by night— grew tiresome, so for two years I tried celibacy. When I did trick, no one was more lustful; otherwise I relied on friends. So life became orderly and, if not entirely happy, not unhappy either.

Then I met Jim. For over a year he eluded me, flitting through street crowds like a ghost. Oddly, this didn't bother me. I like knowing beautiful people exist whom I might never talk to. Just knowing they're out there is enough. But in Jim's case I did finally talk to him at a poetry reading and invited him to a party afterwards. When he showed up I was surprised. He displayed all the qualities that attract me: a sad, withdrawn charm; delicate features ("his thin nose moving like a sail from the harbor of his ocean colored eyes"); an interest in writing. A black derby gave him a rakish air and his eyes could shift from forlorn to sexy in an instant. I liked his smile too — mischievous. Toking on a painted porcelain hash pipe that passed by, his cheeks caved in. Ah, sweeter than death. Jim mentioned needing a place to stay and within a week he'd moved in.

What was on Jim's mind?

I let him know right off I was gay. He replied maybe he was too, he wasn't sure. He'd had a couple girlfriends but the relationships hadn't worked. Then he told me of his best boyhood friend. Growing up in the

South, they shared loneliness with books, music and drugs. Classmates teased them for being queer. Rick later committed suicide.

Did Rick kill himself because he was afraid of becoming queer? Many men would feel a greater horror in becoming seduced by a man than being rejected by one. Mary Shelly tells of a sinful patriarch whose "doom it was to bestow the kiss of death on all the young males of his family just when they reached the age of promise. He bent down and kissed the forehead of the boys who from that hour withered like flowers snapped on the stalk."

I looked across the dining room table to see if I could find a clue in Jim's face. He stared intently into a small octagonal glass ashtray, which he was rapidly filling. His unkempt hair needed pruning. He looked sweet as a flower but so then did the vampire child in *Carmilla*. How deeply he sucked on his cigarettes, how meditatively he held them. Occasionally he flashed a piercing glance, which contrasted oddly with his shy, bashful smile. Mostly he exuded sadness, elegant to the point of despair.

"You and Rick ever make it together?"

Jim blushed.

"Nothing serious," he coughed. "Rick and I were real close but sometimes he played jokes like filling my bed with shaving cream and..." At this Jim paused, then began again.

"You might think me cruel, very selfish; the more ardent, the more selfish. How jealous I am you cannot know. You must come with me, loving me, to death; or else hate me, and still come with me, hating me through death and after. I was all but assassinated in my bed, wounded *here*," he touched his breast, "and never was the same since."

That Jim was ambiguous was a hook, someone undefined whose roads lay open. His health was fragile too, as were his finances. He fit my life like a glove. I nursed him, fed him, played chess with him, took him to movies and bars. For his part Jim was a good listener and leavened my seriousness with his humor. Within a week I felt closer to him than ever I'd felt with a lover. He could hug me, kiss me, say "I love you," walk arm in arm down Haight Street. All this he enjoyed; or did he merely mirror my enjoyment? Jim reminded me of the skin that used to float on my hot chocolate when I was a kid. If I stuck my finger in I might get burned but I couldn't resist its compelling deliciousness. The rubbery membrane was like a veil and my delight in breaking it plunged me into the mythic. Pleasure, a moist dark secret clinging to my own paler flesh. Raising it to my lips I'd slurp it off.

So this is how I kissed him sometimes: pulling him close and thrusting my tongue in his mouth, or laying my cheek to his. Jim seemed to want to extricate himself from these embraces but his energy failed. My murmured words lulled him into a trance he could recover from only when he withdrew from my arms. Then he blushed. In his eyes I could see a love growing into abhorrence and adoration.

Might I have given a more spiritual love? Self-sacrifice affords a pleasing ethic but while I didn't want to push, I couldn't help my desire either. One night I did something shameful. I ground up half a Quaalude and sprinkled it in Jim's food. We went to a punk club and when we returned at 5 a.m. I picked Jim up and carried him to my bed.

"What are ya doin'," he giggled.

"Taking your clothes off," I replied, pulling off his shirt. Jim took this in stride, as inevitable perhaps, and without another word pulled off his jeans as I removed mine. We rolled into each other's arms. Unlike other lovers who lay back waiting for me to arouse them, Jim wasn't passive. His hips began banging against mine in a delicious, mindless frenzy. Then

"Hey, I'm not getting hard."

In answer I reversed my position, moving my head to his groin. His cock awakened but only half-heartedly. Having proclaimed his impotence, Jim now held back. But he didn't object to my holding him as I jerked off.

The next day I feared my lust might provoke a delayed, negative reaction in Jim. I recalled my own first time, head swimming, stomach curdled in self-contempt. I was with a psychologist who worked for the U.N. He got me drunk at an embassy party and seduced me afterwards. But I really wasn't into it. I just liked playing with the edge, the dare. When morning came I felt sick. Even after my second time I felt like an alien creature drifting in space. So when Jim started to leave about noon I caught him at the door.

"Hope you don't feel upset about last night."

"No, but I don't think I want to do it again for awhile." He smiled coyly.

"But you're okay?"

"Sure," he smiled again and hugged me.

To prove my love was deeper than lust I continued cooking for Jim and supporting him emotionally and financially. At night we continued playing chess and indulging in long conversations. We talked about feminism a lot since Jim's last girlfriend was into it. The moon, according to Irene, was really the Mother Goddess and, when full and brilliant, acted on dreams and nervous people, along with the tides. She said her cousin, mate of a merchant ship, napped on deck one such night and woke up, after dreaming of an old woman clawing him on the cheek, with his features horribly distorted. His face never recovered.

"The moon tonight," said Jim, "is full of odylic and magnetic influence. See, when you look behind you at the buildings across the street, the windows flash and twinkle with silvery splendour as if unseen hands had lit the rooms to receive fairy guests."

As he spoke, a silvery splendour in his own eye caught just a spark of hunger in mine and bounced back to spread a sly smile on his lips. This smile Jim quickly enlarged and threw over me like a net. Then he stood up and stretched. His black crewneck lifted a few inches over his jeans revealing a glimpse of flesh. "Guess I'll go to bed now." He yawned. I didn't argue as he headed for the couch in the other room.

"Well, what I've learned," Ted said, finishing his thought at last. "What I've learned is that you can't get too emotionally involved with these guys, at least not at first."

I recalled him talking about Daryl, an ex-boyfriend of someone else I vaguely knew. Ted had taken Daryl in and he'd run up gigantic phone bills taking calls from some ex-lover in Mexico. Then there was Duane. Was it Duane or Daryl who'd rammed their fist through Ted's window?

"I met this guy in the Stud last night," Ted said simply, looking up to see my reaction.

Oh Ted, you with your talk of inside and outside, subject and object! Happily Jim seldom went to bars so I didn't need them. I might be reading or watching tv and he, reading or writing in the other room. Just feeling his presence was enough...unless:

      a) I was tired of emptying his ashtrays

      b) he slouched off on doing dishes

      c) he stopped paying the token rent he got from mom

      d) my sexual frustration grew too overpowering.

After three months of not sleeping with Jim but living as close as lovers, how acute my frustration became. I'd try to overcome Jim with subtle arguments. Like a dissipated Duns Scotus I lay on the bed watching tv while he sat scrunched in a dilapidated chair opposite me, the third point on a triangle. Was his Southern Baptist upbringing the problem? He'd rail against it, even advance a polymorphous hedonism, but when push came to shove the muscles of his jaw hardened. Then I ran my fingernail down his cheek and accused him of being like his father whom he hated but probably resembled more than he realized.

"You're just a hustler," I hissed one night. "You're afraid to let me screw you 'cause you're afraid I'll throw you out afterwards. Or are you scared you'd like it too much. Maybe that's it."

Jim sat like Job. He couldn't deny those bedroom eyes and coy innuendos he used to wean money from me, but I couldn't argue with someone who refused to talk. Silence became the core of his identity. He sucked on his cigarette and stared intently at the floor in a pose that Sartre or Camus might envy. If only we could get rid of this frustration like the Bedouin brothers at the show: Ali took a lighted torch and jumped down the throat of Muli; Muli took a lighted torch and jumped down the throat of Hassan; Hassan taking a third lighted torch, concluded the performance of jumping down his own throat and leaving the spectators in total darkness.

But the darkness Jim and I experienced was different. I trembled and walked quickly. Then I reflected, and the thought made me shiver, that the creature whom I'd left in my apartment might still be there. I dreaded to behold this monster but feared still more that Ted, who was with me, should see him. Entreating him, therefore, to stay downstairs,

I darted up to my room. My hand was already on the lock before I recollected myself. I paused and a cold shivering came over me. I threw the door forcibly open, as children do when they expect a spectre to stand waiting on the other side, but nothing appeared. I stepped fearfully in. The apartment was empty, my bedroom was freed from its hideous guest. I could hardly believe such luck when I went into the bathroom and what should I see—standing in a cloud of steam behind the smoky black shower curtain—Jim's naked body.

Against the shiny black tiles his ruddy skin was a slap, his pinkish brown nipples two needles thrust deep in my breast. My mouth watered, my eyes, I could barely maintain my composure. I dashed back downstairs past Ted and into the street.

The next day I told Jim he'd have to leave. He'd broken every promise he'd made from doing dishes to paying rent. Reluctantly, sullenly he agreed and moved in with someone else for a while. Then he returned, begging to live with me again.

"I have a new policy," I said. Perhaps my lip curled here. I was eating lunch, not standing before a mirror. "Anyone who stays with me from now on has to sleep with me."

To my surprise, Jim agreed. What should bother him about just sleeping together? That he loved me I didn't doubt. How could he keep hugging and kissing me otherwise? His embraces were as heartfelt and gripping as mine.

One morning I awakened to find him next to me naked. I didn't touch him. Yet that same night he pleaded to sleep in the other room because he was breaking into hives. I was unrelenting. If I had to suffer, so would he.

A week later Jim glued himself to a tv tribute to John Lennon. Explaining I was sick and had to work the next day, I asked him to take the tv into the other room so I could sleep. When he didn't budge I turned it off. Jim stormed into the kitchen then returned.

"Stephen, you're fucking *stupid*!"

I flew at his throat like a demon. For three yards, from bed to door, my feet didn't touch ground. I wanted to kill but Jim was wiry and far stronger than I thought. He seized my head in a vice-like grip as I flailed at him with my fists. We rolled over the dining room table, covered with books and dishes, and crashed to the floor.

"Get the fuck out of here!"

"I would if you'd let me up you damn faggot!"

The words stung. I remembered a fight I'd had with an Indian boyfriend. "You little brown bastard," I yelled after Bill lied to me about breaking something. Bill laughed at me for betraying my buried racism. So too I felt pleased to have smoked Jim out.

When I let go of Jim I was still shaking. Jim backed off, grabbed his backpack and left. It was after midnight and cold outside. Where would he go? Phoning Irene I told her what happened, including his calling me a faggot.

A couple days later I saw Jim on Haight Street. We paused for a second then embraced. He'd taken a room in Berkeley. How he'd gotten across the bay that night or come up with the money he didn't say. I didn't ask.

"Maybe it'll sound weird," I said, "but fighting with you felt terrific, more cathartic than fucking."

Jim laughed but admitted he felt much the same. He took out a cigarette. One match went out, he struck another. Then I brought up the touchier subject.

"Still think I'm a faggot?" Jim looked me full in the eyes.

"I never said that. Irene said you thought I did but I didn't. What I called you was a damn *fuck*head. I'd never call you a faggot even if I was angry."

Jim seemed so certain he shook my own certainty. A few days later he came over to gather up his belongings. He still had no job and was returning to his mom in Florida. He seemed sad to be leaving. I didn't expect to ever see or hear from him again.

Ted leaned back in his chair and laughed. "The trouble with you Abbott is you expect these guys to be grateful. You expect to be able to count on them. Maybe they do love you but just trying to survive takes all their energy."

That was one view. I heard others. Sharon, who was straight and wanted me for herself, considered Jim no more than a leech. Like Bryan, she felt he had no redeeming qualities. Bill and Lendon understood my fascination for lost waifs but considered me lucky to be rid of this one. But Meg, a lesbian mother and astrologer, liked Jim and couldn't understand why we weren't sexual.

"He's a Scorpio," she reasoned. "His chart compliments yours perfectly. Since Scorpios love sex, and your Venus is in Scorpio, you two should be having a ball."

Meg laughed, shaking the crystals, medallions, and scarves wrapped around her neck. She'd heard about my Jim problems for so long she considered them something of a joke. Leaning her elbows forward on the marble-top cafe table, she peered at me through thick, red-rimmed glasses.

"Know what I think?" Before I could answer she continued. "I think you choose wimpy guys like Jim because they're the only ones who can't control you. Maybe you really don't want a lover at all."

Jack didn't have an opinion since he'd never met Jim but Dodie's opinion, as always, was pointed. "Straight guys don't like to hang around with gay guys." Dodie was fascinated with my Jim problem enough to comment on it in one of her poems:

> *I said to the one with the poodle tie, "How could he possibly be in love with you but feel no physical attraction?" He took another bite of lemon cake, obviously not seeing the contradiction. So I went on, "The first thing you have to do is figure out which half of him is lying."*

Judy, like Jack, had never met Jim but felt people didn't need to have sex to be lovers. This was a couple months before she left her own lover of ten years.

Most women I knew felt Jim was gay but in the closet whereas the opinions of my male friends varied. A couple gay men sympathized with him while others felt he was on a manipulative power trip that, by extension, affected them too. Brad, for instance, felt Jim should be spanked and fucked.

Is every frame a frame-up? Like meaning trailing into an endless web of signifiers, my problems with friends also trailed into infinity. Ted was in a rut and wanted to limit me to cafe gossip. Sharon wanted to marry me. Bryan was full of complaints about everyone and Bill and Lendon dropped out of my life shortly after Jim.

Jack was sarcastic and had an irritating habit of poking me in the ribs. Dodie got furious if I was ever late. Brad felt superior to me and once insisted on giving me a lecture on why he didn't take drugs anymore when I was on MDA.

Is this fair? Brad says no. My comments about Ted and others aren't fair either, but that's my point. All viewpoints are skewed. Do we gossip less for this? I marvel at Brad's tenderness as well as his brilliance but I don't fully agree with his portraits of me either. Not untrue — exaggerated. For a complete view we'd have to describe the whole universe.

These are just a few problems with a few friends. There was also W. who was lethargic and unreliable, X. who was insulting, Y. who was opportunistic and never repaid favors, Z. who had such a foul temper I finally broke completely. Make a list of your friends. Which is longer: those kept, those lost, or those you'd like to get rid of?

Then I got a rambling, self-pitying letter. Jim was in the hospital for a groin operation. They'd shaved his "beard" as he put it and he was depressed. I wrote back a warm, cheery letter. Two months, no reply. Then Jim phoned. He had a new girlfriend and was hoping to persuade her to drive to California. Three months more, no word. Finally I got a postcard that said he and Jan would be driving to Santa Cruz in October. Would I mail him some acid? Since he already owed me $300 I replied tartly with this observation from Marquise de Merteuil in *Les Liaisons Dangereuses*:

> *Has it not been known since Alcibiades that young men feel friendship only when in trouble? Happiness sometimes provokes them to indiscretions but never to confidences. I might say with Socrates "I like my friends to come to me when they're unhappy" but Socrates, being a philosopher, was quite able to do without his friends. In that respect I'm not as wise as he.*

A month later I looked up from a book in Cafe Chattanooga. Jim was walking toward me. For once he wore a big smile and, before I knew it, was giving me an awkward hug and introducing me to Jan who stood by nervously.

"Get my last letter?"

"And how," Jim laughed. "It burned my fingers."

My friendly letters hadn't phased him but this nasty one made his eyes blaze. I invited them to dinner, taking extra care to be nice to Jan. Dinner was just tuna and noodles, but I had fun fixing it. While I chopped broccoli, Jim played with a musical gadget which, when you moved a lever, made either a ratatat-tat machine-gun sound or whooshed like a rocket launcher. Jan sensed Jim and I were more than just friends and pointedly noted that her closest friends in Florida were gay and how neat that was. So when Jim invited me to Santa Cruz for Thanksgiving I accepted.

Their house was close to the ocean and had a large redwood hot tub in the backyard. When I arrived we had dinner, then strolled along the beach. Afterwards Jan went to bed and Jim and I played chess. He still sucked on his cigarettes, I noticed. Jim showed me a coffee table he made and then we watched the fire die down in the ironwood stove. Every so often an ember that seemed dead would crackle and throw off a few sparks. Finally Jim got up.

"Can I hug you?" I asked.

"Sure!"

He put his arms around me and lay his head against my shoulder. He was never stiff or eager to end hugs like most straight guys. Hug hug hug—why do I obsess on this word? I wish I could write a prose so clear I could reach in and pull Jim out of it just as I always wanted to pull him out of himself. If you can't be touched you can't be changed. And if you can't be changed you're dead. Jim didn't mind if I hugged him, even in front of Jan or his straight roommates, but the next night in the hot tub he squealed when I grabbed his toe.

"Do you know what he just did?" he cried jerking his foot away.

Jan laughed. To hide her embarrassment, she began telling of a flirtation Jim was carrying on with a high school girl next door. Jim shut his eyes and smiled like a pet that enjoys being talked about regardless of what is said. And so the week continued—lolling in the hot tub, playing chess, and strolling along the beach—until the night before I left and Jim and I were alone again.

"Wanna throw the I ching?"

I agreed and silently asked the question that had been nagging me all week: should I persevere in this friendship or not? The coins came up Pi, hexagram 8, meaning water over earth: holding together: "Seeking union without preparation brings misfortune but if one's virtue is sincere and constant, those uncertain will then come." I don't know if I believe in oracles but the answer certainly seemed appropriate. Then Jim tossed the coins. His hexagram was Ku, 18, meaning wind below the mountain: "Work on what has been spoiled." Jim wouldn't tell me his question.

At Christmas I invited Jim and Jan to San Francisco and for Christmas Eve, I fixed Duck L'Orange and Oysters Rockefeller. My vichyssoise was sharpened by a virtuous french Colombard. Candied yams, gooseliver stuffing, multi-layered Jell-O molds, and apple and mince pies rounded out the feast.

Jan wanted to crash early so, after opening presents, Jim and I went to visit old haunts, his favorite being The Headquarters, an afterhours punk dive. A Nina Hagen record shrieked over scratchy speakers as we entered the womblike darkness. A woman I knew from my political days was wearing a black sheath, passing around poppers and claiming to have been saved by Jesus. As the toilets overflowed with a foul smelling slime, I kissed Jim on the forehead.

The next few days I felt a communal warmth I hadn't experienced since the 70s. Jan reminded me of my ex-wife: earthy, vibrant and enthusiastic. But I wasn't sure if I was growing attracted to her for her sake or Jim's. In any event things were going so well we decided to go bar hopping their last night in town. But something was off. My restlessness? Or was it how Jim clung so tightly to Jan? When we returned to the apartment he fished out a William Burroughs record and stretched out on the floor:

61

"'This is very good for fuck Johnny.' He made a tight brown fist and shoved a finger in and out. 'We take yage then fuck.'"

What draws straight guys to Burroughs? Jim seemed tranquil as I massaged Jan's back on the bed. Pulling my thumbs down each side of her spine, I fanned my fingers outward over her lower back, then under her waist and up. She sighed. Jim lay staring at the ceiling, his hands cupped behind his head so that his elbows jutted out like angel wings. "A dim religious light burns all night in the dormitory...Erections are sanctioned with a sharp ruler tap from the night sister."

"I'm going to bed," Jan yawned. "You guys stay and talk." Jim bounded up to follow.

"Can't you chat awhile?"

He slouched into the dilapidated chair next to my bed, site of so many of our previous encounters. A desk lamp behind a screen cast spidery shadows over our faces. This nocturnal existence begins to tell on me. It's destroying my nerve. I said

"I...I'd love it if you'd give me a back massage."

Silence. Outside, a faint drizzle that reminded me of Philip Glass. I would've liked to let my voice become a soothing echo of it—groan, moan, flown, blown—but instead I said:

"How can you dig Burroughs so much but be afraid to even sit next to me?" Jim jumped as if stabbed.

"All you think about is *sex*. I'm *tired* of it!" His face twisted with rage.

"Whadaya mean? I just asked for a back massage."

Jim stomped into the other room leaving an icy anger in his wake. Red and purple stars popped against my eyelids. Planets collided.

"He gets that way with me too," Jan confided the next morning. "I don't know what's wrong with him. Don't take it personally though."

For two months Jim refused to speak. I was inconsolable. Yet when he and Jan left the next day he still embraced me tightly the way Dame Nature gathers round a foreign body an envelope which can protect from evil that which it might otherwise harm by contact.

In February Jan got a job in San Francisco and stayed with me till she got her own place. She and Jim weren't getting on either now but in March he moved up and in with her again. Fortunately, I'd found a new boyfriend.

Jim and Joe were opposites. Jim had dark hair, Joe blond; Jim was melancholy, Joe effusive; Jim was clinging, Joe promiscuous; Jim hated the Stud, Joe loved it. Tall, gangly and a bit crazy, Joe brought presents of food or flowers when he came over. He also did dishes. But best was his unrestrained lust. Joe would phone at odd hours and ask if he could come over and fuck. After two years of celibacy, this was heaven. Since it was, I felt anxious.

Since my desire focused more on Joe now, Jim gradually resumed our friendship. He still had keys (Joe mentioned, somewhat resentfully, that he'd come over to find Jim "making himself at home.") but as Jim grew closer to me again, his relationship to Jan deteriorated. She resented his bookishness, his laziness, his constant dependence. Then I had a blow-up with Joe.

When Joe and I couldn't communicate we took acid. "It's okay if you love me" he said the first time. Until then I'd held back. Like Venus on the half shell, his stilt-tall body stepped from a clump of clothes. We clasped each other tightly as if navigating rapids. Each upward arch, each fall quickened our desire with its gestures of possession and loss until I felt my body fall away. All we had left to spend now were bolts of energy whipping between us.

We didn't take acid often but when we did it was wonderful. We'd walk through Golden Gate Park, meander the succulent gardens, feel a oneness with each other and nature. Before, my life had been linear, a workaholic frenzy. Joe's lackadaisical drifting was refreshing. Only this trip became a nightmare. At 4 a.m. Joe jumped out of bed.

"Don't you see? We're all *stars*. Nothing else matters."

To illustrate this he began hurling books off shelves and onto the floor. When he tore down my Irish lace screen and grabbed a chair as if to smash it through the window I got worried.

"Please stop," I begged. He continued.

"STOP!" I demanded, throwing a Coke can. He continued.

"We're all stars. Don't you see? We're all *stars*!" Was this his dramatic way of breaking up?"

"Okay, split if you want. But you don't have to destroy my apartment."

We all carry natural opiates in our brains to regulate consciousness. The newly found enkephalins, endorphins and substance-P belong to a growing class of upwardly mobile or "yuppie" chemicals called neuro-peptides. These carry out a bewildering array of functions including the control of emotions. When language was acquired, the right temporal lobe was preempted for the issuance of god-like commands across the thin anterior commissure. Subjects heard voices.

I pushed Joe to the door and said he couldn't return until he regained control of his upwardly mobile neuro-peptides. Since he was naked, I hoped this might calm him. Instead he dashed downstairs. Naked myself, I couldn't follow. Had he ever done anything like this before? I phoned his roommate.

"You're closer to him than I am," his roommate drawled.

Next I called Meg who lived nearby. She came over with one of her husky sons and suggested we go look for Joe. Walking up Haight, she asked a wino if he'd seen a naked man running by. "He was feelin' kind of funny," Meg explained.

"He must be," the wino replied, but he'd seen no one.

After looking everyplace we could think of, I returned home and called Jim. It was now about six. He'd also had a roommate who'd gone nuts once so he knew what it was like. We talked for an hour. The main thing I remember is that I kept getting him mixed up with Joe. But talking was easier than just sitting and looking at my wrecked apartment. I felt like I was in Beirut.

At eight I walked to Cafe Flore, ordered a cup of coffee, and tried to read a newspaper. Being able to successfully complete a normal, everyday task meant a great deal. Bad news: "U.S. SOLDIER GOES BERSERK IN BERLIN DISCO, STABS FIVE!" Somehow this comforted me. Astral influences, that's what it was. Craziness everywhere. Meg was right.

Then I went to Ted's. He was one of Joe's few friends I felt comfortable with. Ted called the city jail—that's where Joe had ended up—and drove me to an automatic teller where I withdrew $100 to bail him out. Joe couldn't remember what he'd done but was appropriately repentant. The police report, which he jokingly bragged about later, explained how they'd found him:

*We spotted the suspect at Laguna and Haight run-*
*ning naked towards Market. "Here it is," he called,*
*waving his genitals. "Come and get it." Asked where*
*his clothes were, he said they'd been stolen by the*
*Texans or Mexicans. When asked if he was on drugs,*
*the suspect replied "of course I am. Why else do you*
*think I'm acting this way."*

"I don't know about you guys," Ted laughed, but I could tell he sort of envied our relationship. Most of Joe's friends put down being lovers (AIDS was beginning to be discussed). Maybe monogamy wasn't so bad after all. "At least if your boyfriend doesn't tear up your house," Ted added. Joe got more serious too and slowed down his lifestyle. Then Jim had a psychodrama of his own which involved his old girlfriend Irene.

They met at a West Portal diner where Irene worked as a waitress. Jim had recently dropped out of school and, with his last few dollars, he sat in the diner dawdling over coffee. Irene, who worked for WAVPAM, was intrigued by his mysterious passivity. I can imagine her peering out the window when he leaves like Chrissie Hynde in the Pretenders' "Waitress" video.

When Jim couldn't keep his apartment, Irene took him into her place with B., a wealthy lesbian she'd known since grade school. B. was jealous, which made the project more interesting. Irene sent Jim to her psychologist and lent him books by Mary Daly. After a few months, Jim owed her several hundred dollars. Irene didn't care since B. was paying for it. Money was simply another chip in their three-way power game. Jim's only power, apparently, was his cock. They began sleeping together, then fucking. He introduced her to rock music and acid. Their relationship got intense. Jim's other weapon was sarcasm, which he utilized fulsomely. Irene punished him by making him sleep in the garage.

Maybe my facts are screwed up but it's how I imagine them. Jim was still in love with her when she kicked him out and he moved in with me. So I consoled him, assured him. I was better than mom.

When Jim returned to Florida, Irene started a women's rock band, which got hot on the punk scene. I saw her at a club once. She had a new girlfriend who looked like Jim. Then she met D.

D. worked for a phone sex outfit and was into lesbian s/m as well as shooting heroin. Together they got gigs as dominatrixes, whipping wealthy men for money. "All men are shits and deserve punishment. All women who aren't into s/m are 'dead women'" (Jim played me a radio interview tape wherein Irene says this). Irene quit her band and split from her old friend B.

Now she calls Jim, asks to see him. Since he still loves her, he's elated. She comes over with D. They give him some acid to hold for them while they run errands. Irene knows from past experience he'll probably take it but, for some reason, he doesn't. When they return, Irene asks if he's looked at the luggage they left. He hasn't. They open a black leather bag and begin showing him their "toys": dildos, straps, handcuffs, whips. "Wanna play?" Jim says no, Jan'll be home soon. Then they leave. Jim's fascinated. He can't wait to tell me about Irene's new life. His only concern is that they might come back and beat him up.

Seeing this as a way to get closer to Jim, I suggest we write a story together, alternating chapters. Putting myself in Irene's place, I try to imagine what she, an s/m lesbian punk singer, would see in him. Here's how the story begins:

> *Velvet lays back on her waterbed and imagines fucking Mark for the first time. One finger, then two disappear into her muff as she pictures him above her, pressing down amidst the crumbling plaster of Finnila's grungiest sauna. Her butt burns. Sweat drips from their bodies. Bracing his arms against the ledge behind her, he dives down biting her neck. Her butt jerks up slapping his thighbones. Their bodies sound like suction cups. Then, the screeching buzz of the doorbell.*
> *Velvet ponders whether to answer. But what if it's Mark? What if he's early?*
> *Jumping up, she runs sticky fingers through*

*her hair, not to smooth it so much as to clean her hand and give herself that come-and-get-me aroma. She tucks in her shirt. An oval mirror makes these gestures seem more endearing than they actually are. Puckering her lips, she blows the little girl in the mirror a kiss.*

*"Just a minute, I'm com-ming!"*

*She skips to the door, opening it as wide as the chain latch will allow; a lanky black kid.*

*"Oh Christ, Lenny! What do YOU want?"*

*"Brought ya a surprise. Can I come in?"*

*"No, I'm working. Ya shoulda called first."*

*"Tried but the line was busy."*

*Velvet exhaled deeply as if Lenny had just announced he had the clap, or worse, that he was hopelessly and utterly in love with her which, as a matter of fact, he was.*

*"Look Lenny, you were a nice fuck but we have nothing in common. I'm a dyke, see? Besides I'm married to my music and love's just a stupid irrelevancy. Got the message?"*

*Lenny's jaw fell open and he blinked.*

*"But I boughtcha this, see?*

*From behind his back, Lenny produced a glossy hardback bio of Jimi Hendrix.*

*"Shove it through the mailslot and I'll read it if I get insomnia."*

*Velvet's eyes narrowed showing no pity, no crevice where the boy could hang his fast-waning self-confidence. He looked at the number above the door wondering if he'd rung the right bell.*

*"Now beat it 'fore I call the cops!"*

*She slammed the door and slumped against it waiting for the inevitable "BITCH!" Instead, after a long pause, something plopped on the doormat. She heard slow retreating footsteps and covered her face with her hands. Why'd she keep picking up such twinks? Woulda been better if he'd yelled, slammed his fist against the door, anything but just slink away like that.*

Jim was Mark in the story but, when he first read it, thought he was Lenny. "You think that's how Irene sees me?" I'd touched a nerve but not as I'd expected. Irritated that I hadn't taken his Irene story seriously, Jim confessed he hadn't told everything.

"Actually, Irene did more than just show me her toys," he began.

> *"D., who weighs about 250 lbs., sat on me while Irene slapped my face twenty times. Next she pulled down my pants and squeezed my balls till I screamed. Then she showed me the handle of her leather whip and asked if I'd ever had anything stuck up my ass. When I said ya, that I'd stuck a Coke bottle in there when I was 14, she was so surprised she lost her nerve I guess 'cause she let me up. But I was really scared. They terrorized me and I couldn't tell anyone, not even you."*

Jim's new story was so unexpected I didn't know what to make of it. What struck me most was the Coke bottle episode. I'd never done anything like that and didn't know anyone else who had. Was I just naive or what?

That fall Jim moved in with me again, then out to the Avenues. For the first time since I'd known him, he seemed ready to take hold of his life. He was cheerful, had a job, and wanted to explore his potential in all directions. We discussed Simone de Beauvoir, Michel Foucault, and *The Society of the Spectacle* by Guy Debord. Anti-establishment theories fascinated him. Jim loosened up physically too. He asked me to massage his back and sometimes massaged mine. One night I asked which strokes he liked best. "That feels good," he murmured as I massaged his buttocks deeply in a circular motion.

Jim began going to the I-Beam and, when I saw him there once, asked me if I'd like to dance. Since the disco was mostly straight, this surprised me. As Grandmaster Flash rapped how NYC was enough to "drive a man insane," Jim's feet beat a tattoo into the floor.

"These pushy straight guys from the Avenues," he griped, sweat dripping from his face. "They hog the whole place."

Afterwards he came over to smoke dope. A couple times he spent the night; no sex, just friendship. When I got him a job doing market research where I worked, we became inseparable. After seeing us on Haight Street one evening, Meg asked: "You two having sex yet? He's ripe I can tell." But I remained skeptical.

As winter moved into spring, Jim and I began doing acid. We called the drug "acid" but what it actually was we weren't sure. Snorted like coke, the blue grey powder worked quickly but didn't have the metallic, jangly taste of acid. Maybe it was mixed with MDA or heroin.

Jim's eyes lit up like a bestiary. Hares leapt over delicate peacocks when he blinked. Griffons and hippogriffs parted to reveal a white unicorn, the gold of whose horn was a spark of light in Jim's pupil, which spiraled between us like electricity. It tingled down our spines and bounced back up through our hearts till we were fucking each other with just our eyes. In one deep gaze, an insurmountable barrier between us crumbled. We laughed and walked through the park like warriors stalking prey.

Then I got scared. My personality was dissolving. "Who are you?" a voice inside me pressed. I wanted to say "a socialist" but every aspect of my identity felt arbitrary, a series of constructs overlaying each other like lines on a computer diagram with nothing underneath but wires and lights. I looked around and saw clouds, trees, bushes—all by Watteau only more sexual. Burroughs' erotic landscapes sprang to life: "A tree of smooth red buttocks twisted together, between each a quivering rectum. Opposite the orifices phallic orchids, red, purple, orange sprout from the tree's shaft..."

I wanted to return home but didn't know which way to go. I imagined Brad looming above me disapprovingly. "I'm a socialist," I repeated over and over but I wasn't sure what that meant. Sitting on a park bench in my black leather jacket and gripping my folded umbrella, I felt like a ridiculous old queen. Jim kept giggling but something about him scared me—an undercurrent of violence. Then the landscape collapsed into infrared like in *The Cat People* remake where Natasha Kinsky turns into a panther. So as to survive, I sought to empty myself of desire.

I assumed Jim would later deny our new closeness but during the next week he seemed as pleased by it as I. "That drug was really something," he kept muttering at work. Then, with a sly smirk: "Here's a question-naire from Mr. Hardcock in Deep Bend, Louisiana."

Jim dogged me to lunch everyday too. Leaning over his hamburger and baked potato, he confessed to every near homosexual encounter he ever had: a wealthy doctor who once stopped him on Powell Street, a college friend who was jealous of Rick, and so on. Jim couldn't get enough of me. True, he spent most nights in the Avenue still or with women who picked him up at "the Beam," but he told me about these affairs as if I was his one and only. I knew our time would come and in two weeks it did.

Choosing a sunny weekend, we bussed to Ocean Beach and, snorting a goodly amount of our "love drug," walked up a tree-lined path at Land's End. Jim led like a girl teasing her beau. We walked past the golf course, through a maze of Pacific Heights mansions and over to North Beach where we had an Italian meal. Then we began walking to Fassbinder's *Querelle*, which was playing down at Fisherman's Wharf.

"Can't we do more of that stuff," Jim begged.

We walked to a dark corner of a parking lot on the wharf and I opened the tiny packet. It was hard to hold steady in the wind. First Jim took a snort, then me. We stumbled into the movie and watched as if through sheets of gauze. Afterwards we caught a taxi home.

"I *love* this drug."

Jim flashed a beatific smile. He looked like a naked lab mouse against the burnt-orange sheet on my futon. He giggled nervously as I drew my tongue up his left side to his nipple, then down to his groin, which smelled like honeysuckle strewn over moist earth. I loved the brown warts dotting his body—"flags" he called them—and kissed every one. Jim shivered, then let out a sigh as I sucked and licked at what polite society would call his private parts. The more private, the more delicious. In gratitude, Jim's hands lightly stroked my hair and shoulders. Finally my mouth went over the treasure I'd been chasing all day—for two years in fact—my own sweet peak of Darien. After nursing there awhile, I flipped Jim over and...

"That's enough!"

Jim's voice had a steely edge as he turned to face me. Then, more gently (or perhaps wearily)

"Aren't you exhausted? I am. Whadaya say we get some sleep?"

In the morning we breakfasted at the Other Cafe and strolled in the park again.

"I really enjoyed last night but I don't want to be your lover," Jim began.

"Don't worry," I assured him. "I wasn't planning on giving up Joe anyway."

"Well what I want to know," Ted interrupted again. "Where does Jim go when you're in bed with Joe?"

"Somewhere else," I laughed. "Unless I'm in bed with Jim. Then Joe goes somewhere else."

Oddly, Jim and Joe weren't jealous of each other. I say oddly because jealousy's been a problem of mine. It almost wrecked my relationship with Joe. When he'd walk off with someone in a bar I'd get furious but, in time, I realized he wasn't going to abandon me. Besides, when Joe was elsewhere I had Jim to hang with; Jim who enjoyed discussing philosophy. Joe and I mainly bantered; we didn't talk. For instance, if I complained about having holes in my jeans, Joe'd say: "How else could you get your legs in," or if I worried about housecleaning, he'd reply: "My room's a mess; I must be a genius." Joe's wackiness lightened my self-seriousness and sometimes that's exactly what I needed.

As for Jim, he didn't exactly "understand" my relationship with Joe but he felt it took sexual pressure off him. It did. And as Jim and I grew closer again, Joe said he was beginning to find Jim attractive himself. Not that I sought a three-way. Jim had other girlfriends, Joe other boyfriends, and I felt lucky to have them both.

"Between them you almost have a whole relationship," Meg quipped. But life is never certain. When Joe took a three-week bike trip, things with Jim soured. Lonely, I picked up a guy at the Stud. He'd just arrived from Oregon. Eric was 19 and so full of energy he could hardly converse without turning somersaults. Although my sexual interest waned after one night, I liked his enthusiasm. He had one quality Jim and Joe both lacked—ambition.

Coming to San Francisco from a small fishing town, Eric asked for advice. Could he get a job as a houseboy? What did I think of hustling, of drugs? Was it possible to make money in porn? With my own sheltered background, I marveled at Eric's courage. I wouldn't have dreamed of such things at nineteen. He was just coming out too.

Beneath Eric's bravado, I sensed his need so I rented him a cot in the room Jim was sleeping in again. Jim wasn't thrilled but he'd become so sullen I didn't care. If he didn't appreciate me, Eric did. Cheerful, help-ful, kind, brave, obedient—that was Eric. He cleaned house, did dishes, put flowers on all the tables. Not only did he make me feel younger, he lifted my self-esteem. He had charisma.

One afternoon, Eric brought an older man home. Carl was in his late fifties, had made hordes of money with a lock company, and owned a small yacht. Eric had answered a newspaper ad to help him sail it. Carl's problem was liking very young boys. He'd ruined two previous careers because of this and was trying to develop an interest in older guys. He said Eric talked about me constantly. Later, Eric remarked on how inse-cure Carl was. He wanted to help him.

Unlike my friends' first impressions of Jim and Joe, everyone took to Eric immediately. "I'm glad you finally found someone who dresses well," Bryan observed. Dodie seemed amused at Eric's flirtations and went dancing with him. Ted laughed when Jack spoke sarcastically of "Steve Abbott's School for Boys," but others admired Eric's vibrance. "He's like a puppy," Joe said. Brad offered sensible advice on what Eric should watch out for if he went into porn and my niece, who had come to visit for two weeks, was thrilled to find he'd not only cleaned the room she'd be stay-ing in but had hung kites from the ceiling and taped rockstar photos on the walls. Not Heavy Metal either; New Wave.

A few days after Eric moved out, I couldn't find my automatic teller card. Thinking I'd misplaced it, I heard from Carl. Eric had robbed him and disappeared. Carl had phoned the Oregon State Police and learned Eric was wanted there for jumping parole. Going to the bank I found $200 missing from my account.

Eric's actions now took on new meaning: his cleaning the apartment so carefully, his constant bathing, his asking what I thought of hustlers. "There're some things you don't know about me," he'd once said. I recalled how odd it sounded too when he bragged about how great he got on with his folks. I hardly knew anyone who felt like that.

At first I was angry but mainly I felt sad. I felt sadder still thinking of Eric's options. Working two shifts at McDonald's hardly pays rent and hustling demeans everyone.

"But you were his friend," Judy protested.

I was his friend, yes, but was my friendship disinterested? He'd brightened my life when I was blue, had brought attractive guys around as if pimping for me. Had I done anything to encourage this?

Eric mentioned going to meet some hot guys on Polk Street. "Bring a few home," I joked. It's the kind of thing gay men often say, playing off the stereotype. But he came home with two gorgeous 16 year olds and asked if they could crash with us. The next morning I made it with one. The impulse just hit me and the boy seemed willing.

"Eric's a Virgo," Meg noted. "He probably calculated everything he felt he did for you and, when he needed money, took his due down to the last penny."

"But he didn't have to rob you," Judy emphasized. "A lot of people are poor and they don't do that."

"Remember the 60s," Ted ruminated. "We thought it was okay to rip off big corporations but never friends. Younger kids' morality has changed. Maybe they won't clonk you on the head, but if you have some money and they need it, they won't mind lifting some."

Was Jim's situation better, or Joe's? Walking through Buena Vista Park once, Joe showed me a spot where he slept when he first hit town. He had a job and an apartment now but when younger lived off whoever he could. Early on I recall Ted saying maybe Joe needed to figure out if he really loved me or had just fallen into a convenient dependence. Self-sufficiency was Joe's ideal.

Jim's troubles stemmed from his parents' divorce. When they demanded that he take sides in their quarrels, he withdrew into a fantasy world. He stayed with his mother who alternatively babied and leaned on him emotionally. Maybe we're all damaged. But Jim and Joe never robbed anyone.

I remembered another young hustler I met during Mardi Gras. I was drunk and in drag. He offered to walk me to my station wagon. Spooky was stunningly beautiful but I didn't touch him. We lost contact till a year later when I saw him peddling his ass in Atlanta. He slept with me again and, though he was still beautiful, I still didn't touch him. Next morning I awoke to find him staring at the ceiling.

"Know what? That night in New Orleans I thought you'd make a pass at me. When you didn't I realized you wanted to be friends. I was happy, real happy, but the funny thing is I was horny and kinda hoped we'd do it."

Spooky then asked if I'd drive him somewhere to buy Christmas presents. I did and was surprised when the only one he got was for me and my wife. He was giving a Christmas party and asked if we'd come. Besides a young drag queen he was dating, we were the only ones there. Not even his sugar daddy showed. Had Spooky ever robbed anyone? Did he have a choice?

"Some guys want ya to rob 'em," Spooky said. "You can tell. They feel cheated otherwise." Spooky started hustling when he was twelve. Now seventeen, he felt he was getting too old.

I could tell of other outcasts I've met, those who later phoned from psych wards and those who betrayed me. *I would reconcile him to life but he repulses the idea.* How aptly Mary Shelley's words apply to Jim, Joe and so many I've loved.

During my Eric episode, Jim left to live with an older woman who proved far more sexually rapacious than I. Feeling smothered, he then moved in with Jan again. She was living in a large flat with several others. I was angry at first, feeling he'd slid backwards, but he did have his own room finally, and was paying rent. At work, Jim was as friendly as ever. Now I was cold. If he couldn't admit the sexual nature of our relationship after three years, I wanted no more to do with him.

For once Jim clearly stated his desire: a non-sexual friendship. I replied like a lawyer. Hadn't he always flirted with me? Wasn't I the one he always returned to? Couldn't he see he'd helped create the sexual aspect of things?

"Think it over. Examine your feelings. If you still say you're 'in love' with me but not 'sexually attracted,' then you're betraying me more hurtfully than Eric ever did."

The comparison would chafe but I wasn't in the mood to be nice. Jim never moved unless pushed. I didn't look forward to another separation either but this time I'd initiated it. Asserting my power felt good. To keep from missing Jim I took extra steps. I bought new clothes and got my ears pierced.

"I can't pick your arguments apart" Jim said when we met again. "I'm not as smart as you. All I can do is rely on my gut instincts. I love you, I've missed you a lot, but I'm not physically attracted to you."

"Why don't we go into Golden Gate Park and fight? It worked once."

Jim smiled. Now he was the adult and I the child.

"How about we see each other once a week as friends?"

Once again I let go of my desire. This worked until Christmas when Jim went into another depression. He quit his job, couldn't pay rent, and lost his new girlfriend.

"I don't care what you do but don't plan on living with me again," I warned. "It's ruined our friendship every time."

Jim agreed and found somewhere else to crash but in two weeks he was asking to sleep with me again. Why did his humiliation so captivate me? His pleas seemed to trigger some erotic, pre-hypnotic suggestion that robbed me of all reason and power. So he moved in again and if, by accident, our bodies touched at night he'd scoot over as if burned. I didn't care anymore but why did he suggest we see Buñuel's *That Obscure Object of Desire,* which so paralleled our own obsessiveness?

Two nights later Jim crawled into bed after dancing till 3 a.m. He woke me up and I was horny. *Ah, yee lecherous Animall, my little Ferret, he goes sucking up and down into every hens nest like a Weesell, and to what doost thou addict thy time to now, more than to those painted*

75

*drabs that are still affected of yong Courtiers, Flatery, Pride, and Venery.* When he fell into the heavy breath of sleep I cuddled close, resting my hand on his crotch. His cock was rubbery soft but swelled after a few squeezes. *O Lord, what a topless mount of unveered mischief have these hands cast up.*

My heart pounded. The tension was delicious. How far could I go without waking him? *No man can be honest at all howers. Necessitie often depraves vertue.* His belt buckle wouldn't unfasten but, unzipping his pants slightly, I reached inside. He stirred; I froze. How easy to tie his feet, slip handcuffs on him. I thought of the three-note chant Peruvian cannibals sang as they ate their victim's hearts:

> *Mayaarii-ha, mayaarii-ha!*
> *Roaring jaguar, roaring jaguar*
> *Who wanders over the bank of the river Eyori*
> *There you are saying*
> *This is how I growl, this is how I growl*
> *Here I am, here I am*
> *Roaring jaguar, roaring jaguar*

Shutting my eyes, I remembered a few nights earlier. I'd come home from the Stud drunk. Actually, I'd first left with someone who I thought was a cute guy but turned out to be a lesbian. She fixed coffee in her kitchen and began talking about someone who had AIDS.

"I can't take this," I gasped, burying my face in my hands and leaning my elbows on her kitchen table. Her warm yellow walls and clean floors only accentuated my grief. Recently, I'd heard Ted's Daryl had been diagnosed with AIDS. A year earlier he'd slept with Joe's roommate Ed who Joe had since slept with. "You don't know what it's like till you really see it" Ted said solemnly. He'd seen Daryl, once so energetic, shuffling into Bradley's with a metal walker.

Suddenly I felt an urgent need to be with Jim. I left the lesbian's and took a cab home. When I got into bed I began to tell Jim what had happened but before I knew it I was vomiting. Jim got up and walked me to the bathroom. The last thing I remember was him sponging off my face with a cold washcloth. He was so loving. Even though he had to go to work in the morning he didn't complain.

"Guess you always wanted to vomit on me," he laughed the next day.

That was one half of our friendship—total acceptance. So how could I even think of raping Jim now. On the other hand I thought of Gilles de Rais, boy killer, and of Montezuma who "ate only those young men he preferred in bed." I thought of Jim's erotic excitement when Irene molested him and of Tobias Schneebaum's account of the cannibals after their feast: "He turned Darinimbiak onto his stomach, lifted his hips so that he crouched on all fours, and entered him. *Mayaarii-ha!*"

Back and forth my mind went, as if doing a dance macabre between metaphors. Was it possible to screw Jim psychically? The morning before Joe had fucked me, a memory fresh enough I could imagine what Jim would feel if I was in him. It tingled wonderfully dancing up and down my spine. I began jerking off. *O lisps and court made only to provoke, not satiate. And even then the thaw of her delight flows from lewde heat of anticipation.* When I came, I inhaled the milky substance and licked if off my hand. Then I cuddled close again, resting my hand on Jim's thigh.

"Gotta work in the morning," he growled, pulling away abruptly.
Had I awakened him? When? He said nothing but a few days later referred to my "diddling." I ignored this comment and didn't follow it up. Then, a week later, Jim left one of his notebooks on the table.

His writing was sporadic: a paragraph here, a few blank pages, a poem, a list of some 16 women he'd slept with. The small letters jostled each other, pushing every which way chaotically, while the tall letters (looped h's, l's and p's) leapt up and down gracefully like gazelles or magical floating towers. Jim's hand was awkward yet strong in its erotic intensity. In content his notes were less interesting, mostly blatherings against the cruel world and his hatred of everyone who "fit." I was about to give up when I came to three pages that began "An interesting thing happened last night."

So he'd been awake all along! Why didn't he stop me then? Curious as to how far I'd go or feeling it was okay if he feigned sleep? Certainly he was fascinated for this passage was far more detailed and better written than any other.

Jim's text spoke with irony of my "love" which he felt my "obsessed and unrelenting lust" disproved. He noted that I'd moved with "admirable stealth." Why admirable rather than treacherous? Liking secrecy himself, did he admire it in others? Or was my stealth admirable because I'd caught him unawares, removing his need to resist?

He'd considered grabbing my hand firmly, he wrote, but decided that would accomplish nothing since my actions proved I didn't respect him anyway. He also considered leaving straightaway but realized I'd "helped" him (he also emphasized this word) by letting him store all his belongings in my garage. So many reasons were adduced as to why he hadn't stopped me that he obviously felt some responsibility. He felt paralyzed, overcome by revulsion, yet over a week later he was still sleeping with me nightly.

Then two new thoughts. First, he'd noticed I couldn't undo his belt; this alone may have saved him from being used more completely. But now Jim was sleeping with me wearing no belt at all. Second, in glibly mentioning the incident but not pressing to discuss it, had he hoped to prod me into reading his notebook?

Sometimes I desired Jim, sometimes not, but the idea of such a perfidious and convoluted duplicity held no appeal. True, I'd fantasized raping Jim but the actual ritual of s/m—at least from my own one brief experience—seemed too simple. "Slap, slap, slap," went the belt. Silly and boring, not dangerous and exciting as in the movie *Maitresse* which I went to see with Joe and which made Joe hyperventilate so that we had to leave.

"You're not doing it right at all," the guy I was spanking protested. He acted as if I were just a role, a cipher. "You don't have the right rhythm at all." No, I guess I didn't. For me, love and language had not yet lost their symbolic power. I didn't have to be spanked to cry.

"What I can't understand," Ted said when I told him my latest Jim episode. "What I can't understand is how can a 30 year old guy still be in this fix? When I run out of money I work."

Meg had questions too. "How could any straight guy sleep with a gay guy he knows wants him and not expect something to happen? And this went on for over a month."

I think I can understand but I'm not sure. Last fall, during one of my philosophical walks to the ocean with Brad, I was surprised to hear he'd revised his earlier opinion about Jim, namely that he should be spanked and fucked. On one hand, Brad said, Jim's indecisiveness was tragic. What a terrible failure to live one's whole life and never decide something so basic as one's sexual orientation. Anyone who loved such a person would be doomed.

On the other hand, Jim's refusal to define himself might be a kind of utopian courage. "My misery lies deeper than any issue of straight or gay," Jim wrote elsewhere in his notebook. This must be read more deeply than the cry of an abject personality.

"Wrong life cannot be lived rightly," Theodore Adorno concluded in a 1944 essay on the homeless. This applies equally to the question of sexuality and friendship today. But what can be salvaged when life is wrong? Something surely: a smile on the street, an hour by the ocean, having a cup of coffee with a friend, realizing that we are all interconnected. Even as you've read this you've become someone else for a few minutes...or maybe you have...

*She opened the door and...*

FROM "STRETCHING THE AGAPE BRA"

# THE POLITICS OF TOUCH

## I.

Poking about earth he stumbles across
a skull.

It could have been a city
given to worms

or was the creature dumb, it's only traffic
to escape the sky?

As the campfire dies, he hears one cry:

some terrible need
tearing at the moon in his ears.


## II.

In the lab department
                              white coats
    hover over this bone
                    like angels.

Such display of lacquer & glue.
Such lavish display of care.

Salvaged
or not salvaged—

                    fuel for thought.

**III.**

Now a child presses her face against glass
leaving behind
a curious residue of oil.

Great shapes fill her imagination
& are almost seen

        to move

outside

where everything is coming apart.




      (It could have been a city
       given to worms
       or some terrible need
       coming home to roost.)

# IT'S A STRANGE DAY ALYSIA SAYS, A GREEN

"It's a strange day," Alysia says, "a green
bug in my room & now this mushroom growing in the car."

She's right. Under damp newspapers & cigarette
butts, from the floor, protrudes a slimy brown thing.

Maybe I should get a new car or at least
clean it up, fix the window like the kids say.

But how can I do this & still talk to angels?

Poets get absorbed in strange quests,
question not the creative regimen of poverty.

I wanted to meditate on this but before I could
a hitchhiker we pick up crushes the mushroom getting in.

Now the rain wants me I can tell by how
it licks & scratches at the window.

I get so tired of poems that look like this
but say absolutely nothing. Don't you?

# SOME BOYS

**I.** *(for Jeff)*

I saw him on the street
but liked his friend more: the walk
& talk.
Some boys carry their shoulders
on eggs.

Battling against landlords.
Battling against teachers, parents, friends.
Battling against alien wishes—always
striking out.

The space of vulnerability
precisely
what first egged us on.

In my dream he says:
"Stephen, you bring me *so close*."

**II.** *(for Sid)*

Yesterday I knew why but today
not much is new anymore.

An assassin lurks by the candy store.
Alfalfa never. His spiked hair & poppers
fevered like this.

**III.** (for Mark)

The egg lady becomes the new star
(300 lbs. & is she really 59, 60?)
We go to play at a play

or was it a movie? Does it matter
& do we remember all the drugs we took?
We go to the Deaf Club.

Now the egg lady dances leather
whips & all. O Mama!
Her sweet lips
drove me into his arms.


**IV.** *(for Jackson)*

There were no flowers in this poem,
only dreams and perfumed scarves.
The other side of a wall.

Scarves for effect and dreams
to carry us back to wonder
who loved who
when, as a memory of sour Gramps
crushing ants with his cane.

Why it lurched
as vulnerability between boys
I don't know.

Like flies to Easter eggs

were we to the gods.
Moving in for the kill, he said:
"Be a sport."
Even now
I cannot forget his face.

# AL(MOST) (SUBJECT)IVE LOVE POEM

There was yr beauty
& unexpected silliness.

Didn't know who sat in each
other's lap
but had fantasies

which killed us.

# WILD KNOTS

Who tied me up when I met you
& paddled my wild bottom?
Was it the witch?

Her hair was yellow ambergris
warm to the touch as your tongue.
Her voice was lyric as serpents
fluttering in a child's eye.

Maybe it was the witch I was in love
with after all.

# TRANSFIGURATION

Draw a picture of a pig
& hang it on a string.

This way, you can become
a spider
                    who thinks big.

---

*These 3 poems are made up from words, phrases & anagrams from the nov-
els of Robert D'Anunzio, a verbal triptych to match the famous painted triptych of
Hieronymous Bosch.*

# DAYS

*The following text is extracted from journal entries: July 31 to August 12, 1979. According to Kush of Cloud House, these 13 days leading to the Mayan New Year are especially troublesome. Wise Mayans stay close to home during this time. However, the poet (alternatively referred to as "I" or "he") does not stay at home but wanders about recording the following observations. It's not clear who the "you" in the poem refers to. It seems that here, as elsewhere, a shifting "I" chases a shifting "you", yet in some cases they may be one and the same. Other interpretations may be equally valid.*

Emptying the garbage, he comes upon a small leather case. Who left it here, full of rags? Empty them out. Who? Why? Where was it or he before this? Curiosity: from sun up to sun down, around, behold this daze of days to which is given a tension. A find or fugued place. A torsion as in Loyola, who set his days on edge by emptying them out. No conceptual body but *this* body, which forgets itself.

One month ago, in Boston, I made love to a man on a roof. It was as if some giant hand grabbed us up and emptied us out. Dangerous nights, stars spilling over a city. And below us, a poet whose work I admire dying of drugs on Joy Street.

This is what the poem says:
"Money used to talk. Now it goes without saying."

At night I turn off my mind, go to a bar. Go with my body, this hunk of meat that dances like wild and crazy flowers in the wind.

I live my life by writing it. You will not know me except by what is said on this page. And my life is an open book.

---

Feast of St. Dominic, his emblem: a star and a dog with a torch in its mouth. Tongues of fire.

Foraging around the garbage, a man. How did he get in? He seems to be straightening it up, stacking cardboard by the wall.
  "WHAT ARE YOU DOING?" the landlord hollers from his window.
  "I LIVE HERE," the stranger shouts back defiantly.
  (He still insists on his pride)
  "NO YOU DON'T. GET OUT!" X. yells back. Two other tenants, husky young men, race down the backstairs to confront the man.
  "OKAY, I'M LEAVING, BUT I CAN ONLY MOVE SO FAST."

  A brick flies from the window, missing the man by inches.
  A cold fist squeezes my guts.

Things lost;     a small leather case, a cat, a feeling inside me that I'm
                 good & beautiful & that this world will continue
                 tomorrow.T

93

With increasing frequency, class struggle takes off its gloves.

On the 30th anniversary of the bombing of Hiroshima, General Tibitz, pilot and commander of that mission, is interviewed on Evening Magazine. He has absolutely no regrets. "I had a job to do for my country and I did it," he explains. Fifty seconds of waiting and then he tastes the explosion in the silver fillings in his teeth. It was a most routine flight he says.

This same day, the Bay Area experiences its biggest earthquake in 68 years; 5.9 on the Richter scale. First, a sharp up and down spasm (P-waves); then a slower but more dangerous horizontal swaying (S-waves). At Marine World animals suddenly separate according to species. Dogs and cats go wild.

Could our words be like these frightened animals? Could they be waiting for something big to happen?

What you read in the newspapers tomorrow is not it. This world does not need our praise. It does not need our dramatic delivery or learned interpretations. What you see before you is the earthquake itself, a lover into whose arms we could fall forever.

Imagine if we spoke only once a year.
Imagine if we were silent until we had something to say.

Full moon in Aquarius: stubborn mountains move on the tongue
and at the epicenter. . . perfect calm.

Wizard kite asparagus wings let-me-take-you-dancing Isis skylab hooks mammocking tendril beany shores of magenta Kitchigoomi typewriters into alembic Richard Irwin plutonium ears (pause, paws) reviewing Allahmorph shocktroop slide of leggy nowhere trombones calipered thru a keyhole of ruby zebras unzipping Promethean dictionary nuts into a black kit & kaboodle bowl of Wheaties.

This is what I found yesterday visiting David Moe.

But this is a lie. Wizards, asparagus wings and tendril beany shores never existed. I never existed except in the poem and nobody can say what they'll find visiting David Moe.

This is simply the earthquake of it shuddering away.

---

He dramatizes his emotions terribly, blows them up like a balloon. When he lets go, his emotions fly furiously around the room making a great deal of noise. Finally, they fall to the floor exhausted.

I/ you/ he/ she/ it/ they . . . . Each day is almost an army of us we could imagine into MA & PA KETTLE GO BONKERS or HOW TO STOP THE REVOLUTION WITH INTELLECTUAL/EMOTIONAL BULLSHIT.

---

This is what the trees said: Each of us grows in our own way.

This is the most difficult revolution to be concerned about.

---

151 years ago today William Blake died and 14 years ago this week Jack Spicer died. A lot of other people died and were born too but the poem doesn't care about this, or that today is also the first day of the Mayan New Year. What the poem wants is that we invent a language to move it forward.


I can't distinguish verbs anymore.

What shall I wear?

I went out with just a book and nothing happened.

Then the winos sang, waking me up.

There's always something I forget, even when I go out with nothing.

(where's the keys?)

Like the shadow of a tall building.

Like my lips running down yr spine, taking you in.

Like what in hell are we doing here anyway?


I'll tell you what I'm doing here.
I'm trying to be as simple & clear & honest as I can be without lying to the music of it.

I hope it shakes you up.

# BODY LANGUAGE

Always. He was always the O tattooing
the floor like a silver ball of tiny mirrors
spinning overhead. He glided over them, his parents
wishes on the dance floor,
everything moving the dancers could not avoid
stepping thru.
Why was it so difficult then
to catch what really moved him?

Let us imagine it's Spring. A sunny morning.
"Open this flower or beware," He says
taking quick risks. And giggling you reply:
"Pretend I'm not here. I don't want to scare you."
Yes, you might have been the one
who knew they were eight years old.
And huge bears lurked behind all the trees.

Attempting a music of ideas
we come to look like this, like maniac dancers
waltzing with huge bears and lions.
Whose? To be in such a state
when all we wanted was to find a bar
that was not boring,
                              language hanging awkwardly
between us like severed tongues
or leprous patterns of light.

## DO POTATOES WANT SEX AFTER HIGH SCHOOL?

*for Shirley Garzotto*

You are looking in the mirror
when the music becomes ominous.
Xmas tree ornaments aggravate your rash
which is spreading
like a smile over Moscow, Idaho.
The sky is so full
you hear footsteps on the roof.
A fleet of jets sign off on the tv screen.
On which plane will you explode?
New Years Eve again:
You count your blessings with an abacus.
You get to the number 5.

New Years Eve again:
Nancy Drew would have known
what to do with it.

# MERCURY IN THE 7TH HOUSE

Making a Z with your eyebrows
you sawed thru the pianostrings of my heart.
How could I tell you:
moments like this aren't in the alphabet.

Everything I'd read in *I Claudius*,
Pindar & Seutonius,
all those naked slave boys sitting on the faces
of eunuchs,
undulating on the war-weary hips of Alexander—
their lips were bright weren't they & brief
as shrinking stars?

Fleeting youth,
tears marked your departure
with a capital O
yet your withdrawal
was more terrible than the flight of cranes.

If I'd loved an older guy
maybe I could have written an older poem,
one without consonants & vowels.


(PS)

Wiring my brain to Akhenaten
I have a sudden vision:

Maybe sex *was* hotter in the old days.

# THE SURPRIZE OF VENUS

Perhaps a rumble or synthesizer,
uninvented musics tell us,

closet health hazards but not
those sulphuric clouds of Venus

under those auspecies isotope remnants
of Argon 40 polka. Muzurka

Dali children of first fiat supernova
halfshell held to our ear.

Faint radio murmurings & the mummy
of Jack Spicer unfolding real fairy tales

for us. You are holding at 10,000 ft.
when the city below dissolves.

It is such a tiny machine. Yr. hair
falling into a new sexualization of language:

orange mushrooms of pink altitudes
where Dead Kennedys rise in the cafe

& Idaho grandfathers fail to read
primordial gasses coming out.

# GIVING WITNESS

Sidelong glance toward chance profile.
                                        At odds
with the high altitude of your own self, a dent in your identity
momentarily fit into. Then there was me.

To be precise it was like egg on your face. I loved
you stuck in the middle of       that intrigued me. No swoop
sweeping of gesture. Thumbs up, we swerved to avoid
ballooning upward over the rooftops, over the trees:

        "Look Ma, no hands!"
                                as if everyday—

but how can I say this to you who've already lost
the meaning of lies in our seduction.
                                Ribbons & rice.


To begin again we munch our lunch (coleslaw & sandwich) each longing
for the delicacy of one line turned in on itself, a tapeloop
or perfect love affair, a perpetual wedding of risk & surprise
        ritual
in which, hand over hand, we climbed the curious beanstalk.
And who at the top but giant Michelangelo murmuring: "This drawing
for you, Master Tomasso," or Leonardo shaking his head: "Not again
Giacomo."
No, genius didn't lay her golden eggs for nothing.


Now my own kid draws me a picture. She values it
with utmost concentration; cries out at every defect.
Who knows but an earthquake will not swallow us both.

I fiddle with Newsweek, with my tv dinner, with the damn knob
on the seat itself. I scratch my leg.

                              I tell you this
that you might not feel so scared & stupid out there all alone.

# HIT BY A SPACE STATION

Certain events are not unlike new snow
but fall as children waking up from dream.
Such it was when I met you. A space
station might thus have fallen upon us.
We wore expressions of perpetual surprise
that we could still be moved by love.

O much maligned Uranians in love
this age would fling us aside as dirty snow.
That we produre is a cause for surprise.
It's said we live in a world of twisted dream
and this is not the least complaint against us.
Yet our hearts melt into vast and empty space

somehow creating a new order of space;
a healing place for nature, our falling in love,
which flows, surges, takes meaning beyond us.
Like Maple sap rising above snow
we rise above cold dogmatic dream
into the sunny music of surprise.

We wear expressions of perpetual surprise
that many cannot comprehend this cosmic space.
Might aliens on UFO's dream
preferable variants of love?
Love frolics as children in fresh snow—
an unexpected wonder between any of us.

So too, protons and electrons charge inside us.
That they dance at all is the surprise
that stops us cold as sudden snow.
Scary too, as falling. But to space

into rigid rules all ways of love
would kill the nucleus, the very heart of dream.

The time has come we must defend our dream,
proclaim *this* as what is best in us.
Where would we be without our variant love?
The world would shrivel, would die. Without surprise
boredom would be the sole master of space
and summer joys would perish under constant snow.

Releasing dream we shower the world with surprise
spontaneous as light. We redeem this space
as satellites orbiting dead snow.


### Coda

Love came apart in his hands.
What hit him? Some said
he wore a mask of rubber bands.
Also a mask of perpetual surmise.

# ELEGY

The first timepieces were encased in delicate silver skulls.
*Momento mori.* You may smile to hear this
since much of what we say is gallows humor. We would die laughing
but time encases us both as we are young & healthy.
It was not always so. I recall floating up
from one wrinkled corpse with total delight. It was maybe
the 16th century and I fled into exile to escape the stake.
First goes sight, then hearing, touch, taste & finally smell;
so say the Tibetan monks who wrote their Book of the Dead.
Whether fire, loneliness or love hurts more than death I don't
know but I'm reminded of driving 14 hours to Key West
& lying beside you only to hallucinate your beautiful face
a grinning skull. I lost the poem that told of this.
When I lost my first lover, murdered by an AWOL Marine,
I drove round all night howling helplessly
yet no one could hear me. The windows were up. Before my wife
died, she dreamt of our fishtank breaking & all the fish
flopping into the street. No one would help her save them.
She was a psychologist & fell in love with a psychotic patient,
a kid who wanted to kill everyone in a small town. He was
fantastic in bed. Altho he hated queers he imagined me
coming toward him like Jesus with a garland of roses on my head.
I knew this boded ill fortune.

                    The dead
communicate to us in strange ways, or is it only because it is so
ordinary we think it strange. I don a dark suit & wear a white veil,
pretend I'm a monastery prefect reading the Cloud of Unknowing.
The top of my head floats effortlessly into past or future perfect.
An ancestor of Virginia Woolf, one James Pattle, was put in a cask of spirits
when he died & thus shipped back to his wife. She went crazy. It's difficult
to conceive what the Black Death meant to 14th century Europe. That
   Hebrew

tribes & Roman Legions massacred whole cities is generally forgotten
but then so too Auschwitz. Life is bleak enough
under the best of conditions. I wonder if a book of poems has ever
been written about murderers. If not, I'd like to write one.
Caligula, Justinian — one could do volumes on the late Roman
   Emperors alone
But what is more terrible than the death of one child?
The last poem would be about Dan White, the Twinkie killer,
& his love for green Ireland. It's terrible beauty.


When I learned my wife's skull was crushed by a truck, my head
swam like an hourglass into a tv set. All the channels went crazy.
Crickets sounded like Halloween noisemakers & I remember explaining
   the event
to our 2 year old daughter with the aid of her Babar book.
Babar's mother was shot by a mean hunter & that makes Alysia sad
   even now.
We distance ourselves for protection, wear scarves when it's cold.
What seems most outlandish in our autobiography is what really happened.
It is only circumstances that make death a terrible event.
She dreamt of our fishtank breaking & all the fish . . .
You should not have to burn your hand everyday to feel the mystery of fire.

# (RUNNING) (GRAVES)

*for Bill Knott*

and if words could make a difference

    (Batman, Robin—
    the whole damn bunch:
    Mars,
    Venus
    . . .
    ghost between us)

starfish would swim the sky

UNCOLLECTED POEMS

## AN "EDUCATED QUEER" ON HEARING
## DAVID BOTTOMS READ AT CALLENWOLD

*for British Sterling\**

The spring of my imagination
is wound tight.
So I'm a city rat
& the boy on the motorcycle
      following me
becomes a Nazi thug.
I tremble at the thunder
of his breath.

I cannot celebrate violence
yet neither can I fear it.
It hangs
like Spanish Moss on Cypress Street,
a dry, grey
companion
riding Whitman's face.

(Some butterflies lie broken,
some bleeding in the dust.)

   Queer,
you may consider me
an hysterical personality.
In this century
we all have had much
   too much
to be hysterical about.

---

*British Sterling, Miss Gay Atlanta in 1971, was murdered by an AWOL Marine on Cypress Street, in October 1972

## FOR REZA BARAHENI, TOMMI TRANTINO
## AND GENNADY TRIFONOV

To break a jaw is not to break
a word or line of truth from what
it otherwise would be. Truth flows,
an invisible river that cannot be
damned, made solitary, or changed
from its invincible course. See
how rivers run down mountains
seeking the sea. This is how
poems are made, not as your rules
or laws, not even as the distant
rich oppress the poor, driving them
to terrorism, but simply as rain
falling, as snow melting in the sun.

"There is an atmosphere in the
cerebellum," wrote Tommi Trantino,
"And when I move my right hand
the whole universe moves."
This too, not because the poet
said or willed it, but because birds
sing and lotus petals fall.

So open your prisons
authorities and fearful ones.
Dismiss your torturers.
Let poets see the sky once again.
That you jail, maim and kill people
is nothing. The Ceasars did as much,
all in the name of Order, yet they too
came to sleep with worms.
Nations, Empires and economic systems—
all grow and die like flowers in a field

and gardeners might sooner stop the seasons
than you could stop poetry
from flowing
thru the rugged mesa of the human heart.

# SEBASTIAN

The beautiful aliens in the movie theater have come
to make love with the beautiful image, yes, even of love
kissing long arrows which kissed the thigh, bit the
breast & tongued the muscular curvature, the very bone of Sebastian—
Ah! His elbow, thigh & embarrassed knee! They came
to dream over this power of his kiss & while we remain
unclear as to the exact nature of sanctity, the long
sigh or erotic moan which wears a leopard's head yet clearly
by the end, by blood & perspiration of the end,
moaning, longing, gradually everyone has become exhausted.
Behold! What Roman coin blazing overhead, a dream
vampyre, a tattered holy card hanging by one thread.

---

Nearing heaven, the aliens have a late Renaissance vision.
The arrows, typifying love, do a lot of kissing. This is
small comfort to Sebastian who dies of them.

The leopard's head represents the incontinence of
those who like erotic movies too much. Roman coins
are what is laid on Sebastian's eyes when he dies.
Being dead, he sees thru them.

The dream vampyre is imaginary but drinks real blood.
Beatrice will explain this & other mysteries of Faith
in heaven.

## SONNET TO BLESS A MARRAIGE

It's Sunday and bells toll
or if not, the birds. When blue
enters a poem all sound flees
fear. Fear, a deeper sliver than Time.

Where will it go your tentative eyes
implore. We were born old.
Little fish in the sky of dreams
spawn children, houses, love.

Touch each other gently, say "I do."
Nothing else matters. No matter
how long we live we'll never be
through. This is the vow anointed
in all choices. It's true,
Even the dreams of mutes are full of voices.

## POEM OF AN EPILEPTIC STUDENT
## CAUGHT IN WATTS RIOT, 1965

Death filled his fingernails
on my spine last night.
I felt them tingle towards
one light bulb in my pad,
then it was alright.
Euthrasia, my cat, pawed & mewed
for she sensed it quite irregular
that our one room should flash
in bathed rainbow hues. Miniscule
vines enveloped a papered patch
of wall, broke forth in flowers,
frenzied over dias in the hall
(not at all resembling grandmothers
back in Iowa) and I thought
how strange that mother, who was a painter,
did not capture this before her fall.

# POEM FOR JOE MAUSER

### I.

Out of the half-shadows—you.
Out of the shadows—a lamp, an eye, a lame
excuse and we trick together
sometime later to become lovers?
No word exists to define our union
(bodies merged in italics) but when we couldn't talk
we dropped acid and walked in the park.
You show me a garden of succulents making me wonder
at so many species, one in particular bursting
with splashes, a yellow explosion. I don't know
its name but wish we could fuck.
At home instead, our tongues entwined
swinging on each other like gates till we fall
half out of bed. O marvelous, my head glides so far
away from all this it seems buried
deep in books I tried to escape from you in.
You touched my body, I came alive.

### II.

All the books we read lie. No prince
or princess kisses sleeping lips.
No forest falls from that castle called "the self."
The moon turns its cyclops eye, goes peacefully
through changes. It doesn't care what anyone thinks
or feels. Why can't we accept this? I wanted
to say something dumb like "I love you" but before I could you ran
fingers silently over my face. Then it rained
and words fled. We shut our eyes when we screwed
till our bodies bled.

# POEM IN ST. PAUL

That's where he was born
on Laurel Street, two flower
boxes on the porch, two balconies
above. Then they moved a few
blocks over to Summit. A shiny
black motorcycle stands in front
of the big brownstone where Gatsby &
something else got writ. "I can just
see little Scott climbing out
the window up there, " says Rick.
Peeking inside I see a baby
grand covered in plastic, a tv
on the floor. They're remodeling.
Yesterday I saw First Ave where
Prince did "Purple Rain." It's
a former Greyhound Bus Depot, art
nouveau. But Prince is off
in Sheridan, Wyoming for his latest
premiere. "This is about as many
folks as were here for the Queen,"
says an AP photographer. Prince's
father, hairdresser & bodyguard
steps from the plane & joins
him in the limo. They speed off
into the mountains. Lisa Barber,
a hotel maid & Prince's date,
is impressed. Sometimes I feel
like Prince in the AP photo. He's
dashing towards his fans like me
my heroes. But St. Paul
has a lazy, noble feel like Gatsby's
Daisy or those delphiniums & I'm also

very glad I don't have to be
anywhere today at all.

# THE MODERN RELATIONSHIP

Taking off on a fast angular plane of his face
saw cloudy doubts & worrying cares.
What cheekiness! To call this rambling a love poem.

"I don't know," X replied, indicating somewhere adrift.
"How can they still afford golden rings like this?"
You pondered, marking the metallic spot. I thot

It was but maybe it was a runway. Two soft birds
flipping over each other, like "Why
did he say that and where is he now?"

Anyone remember to feed the cats? No, the cats
rushed up to us as if we were ticket takers & despair,
joy, all the good stuff woozed in retrospect a silly speck.

Tools dive deep, fixing eloquence: Sonny's got good qualities
& bad qualities," his manager once said. "It's only his bad
qualities that aren't so good."

## TRYING TO FIGHT SEXISM WITH SNAPSHOTS
## AS IF OCKHAM'S RAZOR WEREN'T STILL A GUILLOTINE

I only want poetry books with lotsa pictures
of poets
since even carrying out trash all look
beautiful
as this man I kissed today walking
back
from my dreams "but wait a minute"
you say
"what if" but before more said I realize how
wrong
I speak since sometimes like tonight this
anthology
I read, I must read backwards or I'd completely
ignore
all women not Rich, Sexton, Plath or Waldman &
this
not even for their madonna beauty since even ugly
men like
Spicer, Clark, Kuzma, Schuchat, Obenzinger, etc.
I read
supposedly for the excitement of their
language
thinking this as if in some highschool
locker
room or football field pretending my sexist-fighting
experiment
might punt me unexpectedly beyond even giant Mayakovsky
red
banner in hand I think again of pictures how
exciting
if on the back of my next book you'd find a
polaroid

snapshot of me electrocuted in Paris
kissing
the plain smelly shoes of Genet.

WRITING MY FIRST NOVEL

You might suppose this page is the beginning of my novel. Why? Because it's the first page. On this page a writer is supposed to tell you what he's about (or what you're about) so you'll know if you want to read further. Okay? Try this:

I telephoned Bob last night and, among other things, told him I was going to write a novel, sort of a spiritual autobiography. "What are you going to write about," he asked. I replied: "Oh, my friends, my experiences, parties I've been to, famous people I've met, about my darling daughter Alysia-Rebeccah. She is six months old tonight you know."

"Why are you writing it," Bob asked.

"For myself, to understand why I'm so fucked up. Isn't that why anyone writes?" Bob wisely refrained from questioning my intentions. We both knew they'd probably never pan out.

Actually I don't feel fucked up, not all the time anyway. I feel peaceful. For twenty-seven years in the middle of the United States (Midwest and Middle America both) I've been trying to discover the secret to serenity. And now people come to talk to me as if I were an avatar of the age, a Meher Baba or Aleister Crowley. But if I've ever saved anyone I don't know it. Maybe that's as it should be. Whether or not I have, of course, has no bearing on whether or not I'm fucked up.

While I do receive visitors, more often I sit at home and alone. I don't know whether it's the fullness or the emptiness of life that I listen to. I do know that it's the quiet buzz of our fish tank filter. The fish tank filter is more dependable than I am.

The first time I tried to write this novel I was in a monastary in Northwest Missouri. I spent two years there. The name of the monastary was Immaculate Conception Abbey and it was about one hundred years old. Benedictine monks from Switzerland founded the place when they learned that the Swiss state was about to expropriate their invaluable rare books. I learned this when I first came because I worked in Conception's Rare Book room. I also learned that Byron wrote a famous poem about the Swiss monastary but that no one even one tenth that famous ever wrote a poem or anything else about Conception.

Conception sits in the crotch of a few small hills and looks just like you probably think a monastary should look, only without a thick surrounding wall. It has two small lakes, one polluted and one not. Around the monastary is acre after acre of rich Midwestern loam. Brother monks manage the farms and a print shop. During prohibition they also managed a wine press. Priest monks manage the seminary. God manages the rest.

One year some seminarians planned a Miss Conception contest. Monastary authorities squelched the attempt but were unable to prevent the idea from living on in the minds of succeeding seminarians. I myself fantasized a few elaborations to the idea, namely that James Horner, an enormous, foul-mouthed fat boy from New York City who was obsessed with collecting gold and silver rosaries and crucifixes would win the contest. It's amazing the nonsense seminarians talk about. But more of this later.

# "CHAPTER TWO"

Maybe you're wondering whether I was at the monastary to be a seminarian or a monk. Actually, I first went just to get away from the University of Nebraska. I had thought universities were where one went to seek Truth and Beauty (certainly high schools weren't for that) but after two and a half years I was crumbling apart. My last semester, the one where I was taking all the courses I thought I really wanted, was the worst. I put on the lining of my army-issued great coat (in those days ROTC was mandatory) and lurked about the stacks of Love Library. What was I looking for? Anything obscure, the more obscure the better because then I could maybe deal with it: What a broken peacock feather meant in a certain Renaissance painting, what a philosophy professor of mine had to say about the Evil Genius of Descartes, what Fra Angelico had to say about painting (He only said one thing supposedly: "To paint the life of Christ you must live the life of Christ." For days I went about, the phantom of the library, muttering that sentence.)

Something lost and haunted about me attracted two types of people: those who wanted to save me, and those who thought salvation was either impossible or undesirable. Among the latter were these: S. Clay Wilson (lately of *Zap* comics), my cousin Dennis, a black graduate student named Joe, Frederick C. Bowman, and an assorted group of party-goers who would fit Thomas Pynchon's description of the "whole sick crew."

S. Clay Wilson I met in the Art Department. He was into painting cowboys and pirates who stared out from musky green backgrounds with looks of metaphysical despair. He was also into living the fantasies of his paintings, a sort of demonic Jonathan Winters. Wilson had incredible energy. He would comb his hair down over his chinless face like a stage curtain, then, parting it with his fingers, go into hilarious monologues. He also arranged monopoly games wherein the players came in costume (Slum Lord, Nazi industrialist, Mafia chief). Only Ray Hutton's grandmother refused to get in costume, but the deadly seriousness with which she played compensated for her lack of assumed role. She simply played herself. Since Hutton's apartment was quite small, the table we played on sat half in the kitchen and half in the livingroom. Hutton's grandmother always sat on the livingroom side. I'll never forget the bloodcurdling scream that she once shrieked when she thought we had cheated her out of a turn. She was virtually a hysterical pioneer lady beset by Indians.

Since I was one of Wilson's few friends with a car, he frequently called me to take him on "adventures" as he called them. Once we went to visit the surrealist painter Almquist who lived in Ceresco, Nebraska. It was late November. Wilson dressed in grey: grey homberg, grey angora scarf, grey spats, gold-tipped cane and a button-on shirt collar. It was lightly snowing and we had twice gotten lost. When we arrived, I made the mistake of going down the sharp incline of Almquist's drive into his garage. Inside the garage was a huge Mummy case, the monumental achievement of his high school shop class. We went inside the house but the painter was nowhere to be found.

As we tried to leave, the car kept slipping down the drive. Wilson, dressed in twilight zone colours, kept chanting: "Between the snow and the Mummy case...between the snow and the Mummy case." The only thing Wilson had against me, I think is that he feared I had the capacity to be good.

I can tell you about my cousin Dennis in conjunction with Joe since they both were charter members of the Paladian Club, the oldest club then extent at NU. The Paladians would have been more aptly termed a cult than a society since all members save Joe took pride in being anti-social. Each Friday evening they gathered together, glowered at each other, made snide remarks at whoever was choosen to provide entertainment, and snobishly sneered at the rest of the university, particularly the section known as "Fraternity Row." Although he is probably unaware of it, Dennis bore the name of the patron French saint who was beheaded and who consequently was depicted by holy artists holding his head in his hands. Many times, in a game of chess or at a Paladian meeting, cousin Dennis assumed that very pose. And so I imagine him sitting now.

Joe, on the other hand, was an exemplum of benificent gregariousness. His emblem would be two hands folded over the girth of a vest. I remember how once, after I had missed a few Paladian meetings, Joe came up to me and said in his North Carolina drawl: "Stephen, why don't you frequent us more often." I felt like a Southern preacher had just asked me to the Devil's Banquet.

Joe came to the university to be an intellectual and an intellectual he would be. Part of being an intellectual, he assumed, was to mimic the gait of a sixty-year-old. Another part of it was to continually ask people what they thought of Camus' philosophy, and to ask them whether they thought Dostoyevsky or Shakespeare was the greater writer. To decline discussing these questions meant you were not an intellectual. But the question Joe most frequently asked me was this: "Stephen, do you know of any parties?"

Dennis told me that one summer he remarked to Joe about the rising influx of nuns who took summer school. Joe responded with a decidedly nonacademic gleam in his eye, "Yes Denny, Ah've been in several classes with 'em and ya know, Ah've seldom met a slow nun." On another occasion, when Dennis and Joe were walking across campus, Dennis caught Joe eyeing a girl across the street. "Joe," cried Dennis, "she's beneath your dignity." Joe replied with sonorous tranquility: "Ah've been lookin' for somethin' beneath mah dignity."

Joe was the most distressed, of all my nonsalvationally-inclined friends, at my decision to go to the monastary. "You're just not the type," he said. I realized, however, that Joe didn't think anyone could be "the type" unless they were either dead or nearly dead. The only salvation as far as Joe was concerned was Southern Comfort.

Frederick C. Bowman, if it can be said he belonged to anything, belonged to the fringe of a little circle known as the "Bouwsmaniacs". The Bousmaniacs were students who clustered around the linquistic philosopher O.K. Bouwsma. Fred was eighty percent deaf, ninty percent schizophrenic, with a one hundred percent photographic memory. He had the weirdest mind I have ever known. He would invite me on long night walks, walks where he, with his British accent, would do all the talking, telling me about Leonardo's theories of geology, Spengler's theories of history, his own theories on mathematics, philosophy, and human torture. Dennis once taped an interview with Fred on the latter subject.

At one point, when Fred was describing certain tortures practiced by the Sioux, Dennis asked, or rather shouted, "Fred, do you think the Indians were justified in doing that?" Fred paused; whether astonished at the interruption or the question is not clear. Then, slowly building up steam, he said: "Justified? Justified? White men came, raped their women, killed their children...justification enough!" Although Fred had the moral fervor of an Old Testament God, he didn't believe in God, and therefore, he, like the others, never attempted to save me, not at any rate until it was clear I really was going to go to the monastary.

There were some however that wanted to save me from the very beginning. One such person was Jamile Namour. I have saved Namour for last because his story is so strange, so like a detective novel that no one would have given me the suspension of disbelief if I had tried to tell it before now.

Namour was from Lebonon. While in high school he published a volume of poems that were praised by Khalil Gibran, among others. Until the revolution of 1956, Namour had intended to become a poet but when the revolution came he devoted all his energy to it. He became a propagandist and street orator, and was soon jailed. Only the power and influence of his father got him out of the country. Namour's father gave him ten thousand dollars to establish himself in France but Namour established himself instead in wine, women, and song. He was soon broke.

Why do I tell you about my friends at the university rather than about myself? Because at this time I hardly existed. The only difference between me and the mirror that hung on my closet door was that, to some degree, I chose the people I reflected. But even among these outcasts I felt myself an outcast. I could find no one wierd enough, none strong enough to lead me to myself. The closest I came was with two teachers: Richard Tricky, an art teacher, and O.K. Bouwsma the philosopher.

Mr. Tricky would not have been more like a Buddhist monk had he worn yellow chaffon robes. Other art teachers egotistically tried to make me draw a certain way (like them) or were lost in their own thoughts. Tricky was present and inspired me, yet for the most part left me alone. He would walk around the room twice during our two-hour class. If he liked a drawing he chuckled with his whole body in sort of of chipmunk shimmy. If he disliked a drawing his chuckle became more like, but still short of, a convulsive laugh, a laugh that pulled me in too and made me notice the particular deficiency.

More than anyone else at this time, Mr. Tricky gave me encouragement to be myself. He taught me the most important lesson of my life; being myself was more important than anything I might do or draw or achieve. Unfortunately, he was not strong enough to buffer me against the rest of the art department and after a fight with professor Gail Butt over whether or not I had the right to draw angels in all my work, I dropped out. I naïvely thought I had the strength to go it alone in art.

Oets Kolk Bouwsma was legendary. His students called him the square root of God. Ludwig Wittgenstien, W.H. Auden, and others called him the greatest living American philosopher. Bouwsma once gave an address to the American Philosophical Association entitled: "Who Killed Cock Robin."

I'd heard countless stories about Bouwsma before I ever got into his class, and long before I ever met him. I had met students of his, not ordinary students, men impressive in their own right: Kimmel who had worked on a whaler for a year, Lesley, the Scottish minister, and Namour whom I've already introduced. Not everyone liked Bouwsma. I remember a gaunt Swedish grad student who positively hated him. All great men provoke violently divided opinions.

The first day I entered Bouwsma's undergraduate class I felt utterly insignificant. The room was full to overcrowding. Not with blank farm-kid faces either but a Dickensesque diversity of age and lifestyle. I knew some, the Bouwsmaniacs, and I knew they were far more intelligent than I. I was scared.

Bouwsma entered the room late. He was very old, somewhat stocky with unruly tufts of white hair fluttering about his chubby, freckled face. His eyes were mischievous. Later, he would begin class by asking us if anyone had any thoughts. On this first day he simply looked at us a minute as if we were as miraculous to him as he was to us. "Miller," he said, "Those are nice socks you are wearing. Did your wife get them for you?" Miller and Bouwsma both laughed. "Hello Sheppard. Why are you hiding in the back of the room today?"

After briefly recognizing some of those he knew in this way, Bouwsma sat down on the edge of a desk and begin calling the roll. Every name provoked either a brief etymological discussion or a special nod. Calling the roll for Bouwsma was not simply a chore, he went at it with the care of a magician evoking deities. All words, but especially names, had a special significance to him. As he called roll, there was something magnetic about him that pulled at you, pulled at the depths of your being, made you *want* to communicate with him, not just speak, but speak in as precise a way as possible. What you talked about was not important. What was important was *how* you talked.

In the university catelogue, the class was listed as "Descartes and Hume." We spent seven classes on the first sentence in Descartes *Meditations* and never got past the second meditation. Bouwsma didn't seem to mind. He didn't care if we remembered everything Descartes said or even if we understood (in the usual academic sense of the word) everything Descartes said. Rather, he sought to get us into Descartes way of thinking, to get us to discover how Descartes came to say:

> *It is now some years since I detected how many were the false beliefs that I had from my earliest youth admitted as true, and how doubtful was everything I had since constructed on this basis; and from that time I was convinced that I must once for all seriously undertake to rid myself of all the opinions which I had formerly accepted, and commence to build anew from the foundation, if I wanted to establish any firm and permanent structure in the sciences.*

How did Bouwsma attempt to do this? He asked someone in class to remember back to their childhood. What were the little books on their shelf? What were the games they played? We would fantasize the playground and the details of the games. This was our age of belief when the world was full of hope. We would remember believing in Santa Claus and what it was like when we came downstairs on Christmas morning.

"And now," said Bouwsma,

> "What was it like when you first discovered that
> Santa Claus doesn't exist," and so you run home, you
> run home as fast as you can, and you cry 'Mommy,
> Mommy, Johnny says that Santa Clause doesn't exist,'
> and Mommy says: 'Stevie! What are you talking about?
> Of course Santa Claus exists. Didn't he leave presents
> under the tree for you last year and didn't he give you
> the electric train you asked him for? And who else could
> have eaten the milk and cookies we left out for him? Of
> course Santa Claus is real. Johnny doesn't know what
> he's talking about and you can tell him I said so.'
> And so you run back all the way down the street and
> say: 'Johnny, you liar, my Mommy says you don't
> know what you're talking about because Santa left
> me an electric train last year and ate our milk and
> cookies and he's real and I know it!!' (here Bouwsma
> paused) But Johnny says: 'Stevie, you're so stupid.
> Do you believe everything that your Mommy says?
> Your Daddy is the one who left those presents under
> the tree and I bet if you looked in all your closets
> you'd find this year's presents there right now.'
> And so you go back home, and you tiptoe into the hall-
> way and you climb up on the big chair and peek into
> the closet and what do you see? PRESENTS! And
> next to the presents in a paper bag — a red suit with
> white fluffy trim! Now what do you do? Mommy calls:
> 'Stevie, get your tricycle out of the driveway before
> it gets run over.' What do you think? Do you think,
> 'Mommy lied about Santa. Mommy's a liar. My trike's
> not in the driveway at all.'"

Bouwsma pauses and looks around the room like a mischievious elf. "Is
that what you think?"

Usually at this point some campus intellectual would break in to talk about the distinction between belief and knowledge. Bouwsma would stand, amused as they would try to get the class back to Descartes and "proper" philosophical terminology. Usually too, in their enthusiasm to score points, they would drop some word imprecisely, perhaps a word like "*ir*regardless." Bouwsma holds his finger up. "*Ir*regardless?" he questions. Confused or aggravated they talk on, not really knowing that Descartes too got tripped up on seemingly trivial words, phrases like "clear and distinct ideas," phrases which seemed clear until a little child pointed out that the Emperor had no clothes and the philosopher had no sense. If they went on Bouwsma just smiled, as if he knew a little joke that no one else knew.

Often, during class discussions such as these, my mind wandered. I pulled it together within my own private world, making doddles in my notebook (Bouwsma had told us that our only grade would be the notebook). The doddles grew very elaborate, very detailed, and began to take up more room by far than the notes. It was as if they had a life of their own, one that had to be born. At first I was afraid Bouwsma would be angry that I wasn't paying attention. One day I realized otherwise.

Bouwsma was fond of beginning classes by writing quotes on the blackboard. It might be something he saw on a bus advertisement, or something a student said. One day he wrote Blake's motto of Thel:

> *Can the eagle know what is in the pit*
> *Or must he go ask the mole?*
> *Can wisdom be put in a silver rod*
> *Or love in a Golden bowl?*

I had never heard of Blake before, so I went to the library to look up some of his work. Coming accross an early print entitled "Of Cloudy Doubts and Reasoning Cares" I decided to copy it and give the copy to Bouwsma. I worked very hard. When I was finished I noted that, while to a casual observer the drawings were identical, one saw in close observation a remarkable difference. The lines in my drawing were tight, partly because copied, and somewhat sad. The lines in Blake's drawing, however, were free flowing with an elfish Bouwsmanian quality. I pointed out the difference to Bouwsma and he was amused that I should compare him to Blake. He asked to see the drawings in my notebook and said he prefered them to the verbal exposition of the other students notebooks. I thought he was just being polite. Several years later, when I visited Bouwsma on one of my short leaves from the monastary, I was surprized to see my Blake copy framed and hanging in Bouwsma's study.

On another occasion, Bouwsma and several students were leaving Swedes, a coffeeshop frequented by art, music, and philosophy students and faculty. As we were leaving I said to Bouwsma, "I'd like to be a philosopher but I can't seem to write about anything." Bouwsma replied: "You think don't you."

"Yes."

"Well, you can't very well help yourself then. Once you've started thinking you can't stop and that's the dilemma of a philosopher."

I could tell countless stories of Bouwsma. While I later outgrew my enthusiasm for his philosophical prejudices, I never outgrew my enthusiasm for the man himself. He is the greatest person, the greatest saint I've ever met and as you shall later see I met several. Unfortunately I was too shy and spiritually disintegrated at that time to fully learn from him. Perhaps if Bouwsma had been in Lincoln instead of London during that last fateful sophomore semester at NU I would have never gone to the monastary. But such was not the case. Bouwsma was the opposite of S. Clay Wilson. He loved me because of my capacity to be good.

*from* <u>HOLY TERROR</u>

*from* THE MONASTERY: CHAPTER 3

Snow is never white. It mixes with dust and pollution from the very moment of its inception until when it hits ground, even in the most remote countryside, its whiteness is as inevitably mottled as those third grade diagrams of the soul perforated by tiny pinpricks of venial sin. In industrial areas, snow is black yet we persist in imagining it according to its supposedly original state. So it is with everything we see. We become like the vain water nymph at Salmacia who, spying the hapless Hermaphroditus and having nothing better to do, threw all manner of metaphor over the boy. "She was ready to throw her arms around his *snowy* neck," Ovid tells us, and the result was a fusion that enervated both forever. Had I done this with Robbie or he with me?

Waiting in the snow for him, I considered all the ways I'd known Robbie till now. From the pinnacles of Romance he fell to earth. I'd tasted and squeezed his salty skin. It was not ivory. I'd smelled his armpits, his breath, his farts. They were not ambrosia. I'd memorized every downy hair, every vein and freckle on his body. It was not a map of heaven. In time, I'd come to love Robbie's imperfections even more than his perfections because "perfect" means nothing unless there's some goal to be aspired to, some irregularity to give order its shape and definition.

Robbie's teeth, for instance, weren't quite straight and his lips couldn't pout so charmingly had it not been for his slight overbite. Nor would his arms, which perpetually moved in a sibilant of curves, have so moved me had it not been for the random dispersal of freckles spread over them. I pictured him lying in the grass looking up at me, the stem of a cattail in his mouth. Friend, lover, brother – how quickly the terms we used for each other changed. How quickly Robbie himself changed. Even now, after knowing him for almost a year, did I really see him for who he was?

Although Easter was only two weeks away, a light snow had been falling all afternoon. "A deeper peace than sorrow can ever know," Gabriel Marcel had called Faith in his lecture two weeks earlier. Easy for him to say. He was old and preparing to die. Robbie'd squirmed uncomfortably as the famous Existentialist spoke. Lectures bored him. Classes bored him. Only when we talked did ideas come alive for him.

During summer and fall it had been easy for us to slip away into some field after night silence. Who could ever find us in all that darkness. But with the advent of snow our silhouettes stood out and our footprints betrayed us so we began meeting inside. In the attic storeroom of the Theology building we moved some boxes to make a little room in the corner. Inside we spread a grey woollen blanket. Although the dust made us sneeze, we loved this secret cubbyhole with the passion of kids. For a while we'd discuss the day's events, then we'd give in to the conversation of our bodies.

What is more eloquent than the first speech of fingers, the gentle coming together of hands as if the hand represented the whole human spirit? Or what more instructive than to savor the minute yet vast differences between a fingernail drawn delicately down one's side or a fluttering swim of fingertips down one's back? Different pressures of touch told us who we were too, and how our bodies lived in the world. It thrilled me to feel Robbie shudder, to know the ecstasy I was giving him as I moved my tongue lightly around the head of his cock.

Sometimes we also met in the rare book room to which I still had a key. But making love in a rare book room is not without its perils. Any sound over a whisper might be heard in the hall or in the library reading room. One careless kick and a Gutenberg Bible might come crashing down breaking not only its, but *our* precious spines. Still the very danger of our meetings heightened our senses. To go down on each other amidst so many sacred books added a peculiarly religious, even ritualistic dimension to our pleasure. All the prophets, saints and early Church Fathers witnessed our union. How fresh, sweet and alive, too, Robbie's cum tasted amid the musty odor of these old tomes.

At first it bothered me to break night silence. Silence allowed one's spirit to breathe free. It allowed one to listen to nature, to one's deeper self, to God. One of my happiest times at Inviolate had been a two-week Silent Retreat that fall. The simplest acts, going on walks or eating a meal, assumed whole new proportions. I'd gaze into each spoonful before eating, realizing in full my dependence on this slice of peach, this morsel of bread.

Have you ever looked carefully at a piece of bread? Countless fibers thin as spiderwebs span each other, interlacing into a veritable beehive of nourishment. The simplest bread crust has the unique, dazzling complexity of a snowflake or the Milky Way. That's the real miracle of life. Gratitude flooded through me to rediscover it.

I discovered other miracles too – the sound of fresh milk pouring into my glass, the sound of leaves crackling underfoot or of sparrows chirping as they hopped over dry twigs, the music of a friend's smile. Ah, this *was* something! To learn smiles really can make sounds, sounds as euphonious as a symphony. Filled with the babble of our own voices we're deaf to so much, but in silence, a silence freely chosen and extended, the orchestra of nature makes itself heard. What had I come to a monastery for if not silence?

"Love," Robbie replied. I leaned over and kissed Robbie's shoulder. He was staring up at the ceiling. It was the first time we'd made love inside. "What if a depressed person needs a kind word? Do you think our first talk could have been postponed till the next morning?" The answer, of course, was no. Certain talks can only occur at night because at night one feels more intimate and protected. So silence wasn't for itself but to help us advance in the path of love. Only weren't we often stretching rules more for our own gratification than for any long-range spiritual good?

"There's your Presbyterian grandmother again," Robbie giggled. I had to laugh and admit I felt far more fulfilled under his tutelage than I'd felt the year before under Adelheim's rules. But what would happen to us? I couldn't expect Robbie to hold in his irrepressible nature for long.

Thinking this I heard Robbie's footsteps crunching in the snow. He'd gotten permission to care for Mrs. Zurfis who was ill and I feigned sickness myself. Going to the bunkroom I'd taken Robbie's and my pillows and beat them into a shape that looked vaguely human under an army blanket. We left at separate times and walked the long way round to the bluff so our footprints couldn't be seen. Next to the clump of pines our black parkas wouldn't stand out so much either and anyone approaching from the monastery would be visible for at least three hundred yards.

Without a word we fell into each other's arms. Our kiss was long. Then we gazed into each other's eyes as if by doing so we could melt the chill of the outside world. Robbie was just 18, five years younger than I, but looking into his eyes I felt he was older, thousands of years older it seemed when he was serious like this – or was it just that I felt so much younger in his presence? Even when Robbie was sad, his eyes smiled.

"Robbie," I said finally. "I've decided my vocation to you is deeper even than my vocation to be a monk, but I want you to know that if you ever want to separate, I'll love you enough to let you go."

"Love doesn't need promises, but if you're worried I can say I'm yours for as long as I live."

From our perch high on the bluff we could see over the football field to the small lake and even the trees and a few farmhouses beyond. In the shadows the snow looked blue, almost purple in places, but where the moon shone down it glistened. It could have been an ocean and the monastery, rising up out of it, a Leviathan. Lights in the distant farmhouses glimmered like drops of water on a sea creature's back.

"I prayed before coming here," Robbie continued. "I asked blessings for us, and for Adelheim and Theodosius too. Our being together is God's will. I know it is because," and he touched my face as he said this, "because I've prayed for someone like you all my life."

How had I doubted him, even for an instant? So guileless, so innocent. One didn't have to sleep on nails, live in a cave, or shovel snow off baseball fields to be a saint. One had only to risk all for love and trust God for the rest. It was so simple. I took off a glove and wiped my nose, which was starting to run.

"Let's get naked and make angel wings in the snow," Robbie said suddenly. In a flash he was out of his pants and parka, giggling and tossing snow at me. How quickly his somberness had passed. "Betcha can't catch me," Robbie teased, but I did and enfolded his skinny, naked body within my warm coat. Being less impetuous than he, I'd been reluctant to throw off my own clothes. He wrapped his legs around my waist. Then, from behind us, I heard a shriek.

"SODOMITES! BLASPHEMERS! DEFILERS OF HOLY GROUND!"

Theodosius charged at us like a raging demon. He must have followed Robbie and been hiding behind a tree.

"MAKE A MOCKERY OF HOLY VOWS, WILL YOU? I KNEW I'D CATCH YOU DEVILS IN SIN! TAKE THIS, YOU EVIL SODOMITES!"

The force of his cane on my back knocked us down. He was insane with rage and looked like a golem thrashing at us in his black parka and hooded habit.

"STOP," I yelled, rolling over to escape his blows. "HAVE YOU GONE CRAZY?" Then I realized it was Robbie he was after.

"EVIL, EVIL, EVIL ONE," Theodosius was screaming. Robbie raised his arms, whether in prayer or for protection I couldn't tell, but a sickening crack told me one of his bones had broken under the blows raining down on him. I lunged for the old monk's legs, latched onto one and started to bite, my sole concern to get him off Robbie. But he shook me off. What strength possessed him?

"WICKED, WICKED BOY," Theodosius screeched as he advanced on Robbie again. Robbie was scrambling backwards. He tripped. For an instant he was poised in the air as if flying. Then he was over the bluff's edge.

# *from* THE WORLD: CHAPTER 4

Some of the names for heroin are brown sugar, candy, chasing the dragon, horse, H, henry, junk, liquid sky, mama, milk of paradise, scag, shit, smack and snow, though this last usually signifies cocaine for the sound of sleighbells one hears after shooting it. What it's called matters little for whatever name it parades under, it leads to the same narrow basement of oblivion where every human value is numbed, perverted, twisted — obliteration of all need except the need to end need. Entropy! Then one waltzes underwater as in the river Lethe. Few who enter this kingdom ever escape, for from blood-red poppy to white lime of mummification, heroin is the coward's road to suicide.

"Can the Snow Queen come in here?" asked the little girl.

"Just let her come," said the boy, "and I will put her on the stove where she will melt."

There was a real world out there. A revolution was going on. It came and went, but the world of time was not ours. Tomaso and I were like shades in a dream. We felt no pain, but could only get it on when stoned; then it was intense, utterly unreal. I'm not sure we knew or cared who was fucking us at parties sometimes. Often we just held hands and kissed while strangers plowed us from behind.

I remember one party presided over by the filmmaker Fastbender. Although only twenty-seven, four years older than I, he was already dictatorial and obnoxious. His breath stank almost as bad as his unbathed body, which exuded that sour odor peculiar to drug addicts. Tomaso wanted desperately to work with him. Despite Fastbender's foul stench, Tomaso sat as close to him as possible. Fastbender took this courtship as his right and, inbetween chain-smoking Camels and guzzling Heinekens, blathered about upcoming film projects.

"*Siddhartha*! I've always wanted to do that. What tale better exemplifies the bourgeois German dream? A sensitive youth leaves a protected religious environment to find himself in the world." Fastbender turned his puffy, unshaven face toward me and winked. My monastic background was well known and a frequent source of amusement.

"So our kid goes through a city whose walls are smeared with shit, real shit, not this street graffiti which is springing up everywhere, but wanting more he walks on. He comes to a forest of monumental erections, then a desert where intimacy has been abolished.

"On the desert's edge he encounters a tree, a brook, a bird, and a woman of pleasure. All are eager to school him. The tree grows, the brook bubbles, the bird sings and flies. Ah, the wonders of nature! But best of all is the woman who signs him up for special classes: Nipple biting 112, Cocksucking 205..."

"Her educational methods aren't European but American let's hope," Tomaso interjected. "I mean, is education for the student or vice versa?"

Tomaso's wit was at my expense but I couldn't complain since I was now living off him. Fastbender roared with laughter. "Ach! Uppers to sleep on, betrayal to survive. That's the way with us queers, isn't it? Europe spawned Dadaism but how could it compete with America's Doggie Diner heads and McDonald's Golden Arches? Dadaism simply couldn't survive as an oppositional movement in a society whose entire being strained to imitate Duchamp's toilet."

Here the director paused to eat some snot from his nose. The gesture signaled not only his supreme confidence but also his supreme contempt. I thought of the yogi who, after scolding his colleagues, was asked if *he* was free of defilement. "He who tries to get out only sinks deeper," replied the yogi. "I roll in it like a pig. I digest it and transform it into golden dust or a brook of pure water. To fashion stars out of dog dung, that's the Great Work!"

"So what of the tree, brook, bird and woman of pleasure?" Fastbender continued. "Shall we plant them in America? Shall we bequeath them to Wim Wenders to symbolize a floating crap game of the decline and fall? Or shall we make these figures garish images of purity in a corrupt, decaying regime? Oh poor things! In any event their act doesn't get the kid off so everyone prays to Jesus to find out what's wrong. No sooner does Jesus show his face with just a trace of pubescent beard than Siddhartha sprouts an erection right through his pants, the veins of it pulsing like strobe-lights in a suburban rock festival."

"I'd love to play Jesus sometime," Tomaso again interrupted.

147

"You would eh?" Fastbender's eyes narrowed making the smile under his mustache more ominous. "Jesus?" He giggled. Then he let loose a Teutonic roar.

"BUT HOW CAN YOU IF *I* AM HE? NO MATTER HOW MUCH I INVITE YOU TO SHARE IN THE PAIN OF MY CRUCIFIED SOUL, STILL YOU MUST LOVE ME, *ADORE* ME...ADMIT IT, DON'T YOU ALL ADORE ME?"

Everyone's head bobbed as the director stood. His beer gut sagged over his worn leather belt, as he blasted us with his rotting vegetable breath. He was still punching his stubby forefinger at us but was now yelling fiercely at Tomaso.

"YOU ARE FAMOUS. EUROPE REVERES YOUR NAME. HOLLYWOOD WAITS, STILL THE CONFIDENT SEDUCTRESS. BUT INSTEAD OF MAKING FILMS THERE, YOU ARE HERE, TRAPPED IN THIS VORACIOUS LIFE. AND LIKE ALL AWARE PEOPLE OF OUR TIME, YOU TAKE DRUGS SEEING THAT ART CAN NO LONGER BE JUSTIFIED AS A SUPERIOR ACTIVITY, OR EVEN AS AN ACTIVITY OF COMPENSATION TO WHICH ONE CAN HONORABLY DEVOTE ONESELF. THE CAUSE OF THE DETERIORATION IS CLEARLY THE EMERGENCE OF PRODUCTIVE FORCES THAT NECESSITATE OTHER PRODUCTION RELATIONS AND A NEW PRACTICE OF LIFE..."

Here the director paused to wipe a dirty handkerchief over his sweaty face. He delivered his last words in a hoarse whisper, which seemed only to intensify their force.

"So for the love of God, show us some *real* acting. Make your little Siddhartha here come to life."

Tomaso began to undo my pants. For some time now I had taken to wearing his jeans and leather jacket. I luxuriated in the connotations of their smell: brute, biker, barbarian, cop. But more, I felt it was my only way to get inside Tomaso, to get literally inside his skin. So too, in Albania, sick infants were sewn inside the bellies of newly slaughtered cows, then cut out as if receiving a second birth.

When my, or rather Tomaso's jeans fell to my ankles, I felt myself rise to the ceiling so as to better view this tableau in which I was the central prop. Tomaso got on his knees and began sucking me off. I felt nothing. Nothing happened. The crowd registered its disappointment.

"Stick a finger up his ass, maybe that'll help," someone snickered. A well-known French actor ambled into the kitchen with Gunther Hoffman, "my Bavarian Negro," as Fastbender called him.

"I more or less agree with the Situationists," the Frenchman said. "They say it's all finally integrated. It gets integrated in our spectacle. It's *all* spectacle!"

"Then our role as artists is to steal the show," Hoffman replied.

Fastbender's friends delighted in the spectacle of our humiliation because usually it was they who bore the brunt of his "jokes." One hand slapped me hard on the butt as another tore open my shirt and twisted my nipple. Then a new prop entered the fray.

"Here, try this."

A bright silver tube about fifteen inches long and a little less than a half-inch wide was placed in Tomaso's hands. One end was a flashlight switch.

Tomaso looked at me with a "Gee-I-really-hate-to-do-this" grimace and turned me around. Lubricating the device he inserted it gently up my anus. My ass tingled pleasurably at first and I thought I might enjoy cumming. Then a searing fire tore up my spine. I jumped two feet forward and passed out.

In having a bad protector, as I imagined I'd been for Robbie, I sought to become more like Robbie. This dynamic had happened before — maybe Tomaso sensed I wanted it — and it related to why I'd entered the monastery in the first place. I wanted to empty myself of everything, to give myself wholly to the Other. Like Robbie, I wanted to be a saint, but a saint in a world without God.

Regardless of how Tomaso treated me I still loved him, even more now for his cowardice. If he'd ignored or abandoned me, that would have been unbearable; but in ridiculing and abusing me, he showed he still cared. I'd cast my lot.

Parties blurred as did the cities we lived in — Rome, Munich, Barcelona. Each new city, each new movie Tomaso made, each new set of friends were going to be a new beginning, but each new scene turned out to be like the old ones. Then Tomaso began hanging out with a well-known rock singer and his wife whom, for reasons that will soon be obvious, I shall refer to only as K. and A. Tomaso needed a rest after a Visconti film he'd just finished so, along with Miriam Blissful, we accepted an invitation to stay at the mansion K. had just leased at Villefranche, a fishing village on the southern coast of France. A vacation, Tomaso said. Someplace where we could just sail and relax.

Our new friends had just moved from England, mainly for tax reasons but also because of a disturbing incident they'd had with Kenneth Anger. Anger was into Black Magic as well as filmmaking. A., who was rumored to be into Black Magic herself, wore a garlic necklace to protect herself from him.

Before leaving, Tomaso, Miriam and I stopped at one of the summer homes of Tomaso's father, a stiff, formal man who seemed proud of his son's success while at the same time disapproving of it. While his manner was gracious, he betrayed what he thought of me by occasionally raising his eyebrows as if discovering a stain on his dining room lace. But you don't truly know someone until you see how they are with their mother.

Mrs. Bianchi, I could tell, had once been a great beauty. Watching her glide into a room or put everyone at ease simply by raising a glass to her lips made me realize he mostly took after her. But when the three of us were alone together she changed. "Tommy," she'd coo. "Aren't you going to give mamma a kiss?" And he would. Or "Tommy, why do you *insist* on wearing those *horrid* old sneakers without socks? You're doing it just to spite me, aren't you?" Then she'd sigh. "Maybe he'll listen to you, Armand. I can't get him to do anything anymore." Although she spoke with an air of resignation, I knew — and she made sure I knew she knew — that I'd never have the influence over her son that she did. Tomaso might wince, but he always did what she wanted. Indeed, he played the dutiful son so brilliantly that Mr. Bianchi insisted on sailing us to Villefranche in his yacht.

Lush gardens of grapes, nectarines, bananas, palm, and rubber trees spilled down to K. and A.'s private jetty. We disembarked, waved goodbye to Tomaso's father, and climbed the flagstone steps like kids adventuring to an ogre's castle. When we reached the patio, which encircled the

Spanish Mediterranean villa, we even held hands and skipped. Maybe things *would* improve in this idyllic setting.

Miriam pounded on the carved doors. When no one answered, we went in. Large oak and marble panelled rooms were stuffed with thick Persian carpets, Ming vases and other antiques; a decor no more opulent than Tomaso's family's but decidedly more ostentatious. In one room everything was covered in Naugahyde, except a couch covered in white mink. The whole house seemed to say, "Look, my owners are wealthy," yet despite this opulence and a steady stream of visitors, I soon discovered that K. and A. mostly stayed in their bedroom shooting junk.

The evening we arrived, K. and A. presided over an early dinner of turtle soup, salmon mousse and quail. Miriam and Giselle Glèves sat next to Tomaso and Eric, and an ex-racing driver named Tommy and his wife.

"Watch now how K. watches A.," Michele whispered. "I think he suspects she had a fling with Mick but he's afraid to confront her. That's why he looks like he's about to explode." She giggled.

"Wine making you tipsy?" K. challenged. "Must be if you think you can make it with that flaming rentboy." Tommy guffawed, which reddened his big ears and coarse Irish face. Later I learned he'd smuggled a kilo of coke into the country under his kid's clothes.

"What K. means is that Armi's an American who spent several years in a monastery," Tomaso interjected trying to lighten the atmosphere. At the word monastery, A.'s face lit up.

"An artist too, I hear," K. sneered. "Well, let's get some target practice in while there's still some light."

When not involved in games of infidelity or violence, K. spent at least an hour every day shooting vases off the patio balustrade with a .45. K. and A. enjoyed initiating minors into the world of drugs and kinky sex. A. in particular believed one gained in Magic power only to the extent one was willing to break taboos. When the daughter of their French chef became violently ill after A. shot her up, A. decided it might be better to scout further afield for subjects. Tomaso and I were recruited to help.

It was late afternoon when A. and I neared Nice in a carmine red Jaguar E-type convertible. Tomaso followed in K.'s KJ6. Two farmboys about fourteen and sixteen stood by the road, their thumbs extended like newly bloomed sexual organs. It didn't take much to get them to agree to join us for a "party" or, upon returning to the villa, to sniff a little smack. Soon afterwards they passed out.

"Aren't they little gluttons," A. yawned. "And so dirty too. Look at the smudges they made on my nice white couch. Well we can't leave them here can we? Bring them to the cellar and let's clean them up."

"Can't we fix first?" Tomaso pleaded. "Snorting this shit doesn't do anything for me." A. stood up, her straight blond hair falling past her shoulders and framing her strong, Nordic features. If she wore a helmet, she'd look like a Viking.

"Me neither, hon. But first we work, then play. House rules."

Tomaso knew better than to argue. He lifted the older boy up by his armpits, I grabbed the boy's legs, and we stumbled along behind A. down to the wine cellar. After getting both boys downstairs, we stripped them of their clothes and fastened their wrists and ankles into leather straps that had been attached to wooden pillars that buttressed the ceiling.

"What are you planning?" I asked uncertainly.

"Oh, just some fun," A. replied casually, sponging off the boys' dusty bodies. "Umm," she murmured, as their tan lines grew sharper. "These little butts look like double scoops of vanilla ice-cream."

"Just the dainty dish to set before the Queen," Tomaso quipped. I glared at him.

"Okay, that's fine for now," A. said. "You guys can run and do your thing. We'll play our games tomorrow."

When Tomaso and I got back to our room, I shut the door and unloaded my concerns. Some vacation! First, Tomaso's parents and now this. I didn't know who was creepier: K. with his macho bullshit or A. with her sleazy deviousness. They both made me sick.

"You make me sick with your constant complaining too," Tomaso retorted. "If those punks weren't here, where'd they be? Off banging pussy or bashing fags. And why are you here? Because you really love me or because I've got money and can cart you all over Europe to meet and draw famous people?"

"Shit! If you don't believe I love you..."

"Sure I believe it. But I don't *know* it. I can't know anything, especially when all you do is bitch all the time. And talk about sleaze! You weren't so pure with all those anarchists either. So relax. Let's just fix and then we can make love or walk down to the beach or do whatever you fucking want."

With that, Tomaso shot up. Then he shot me up. Whatever had bothered me before didn't matter anymore. To be high and in Tomaso's arms was heaven.

The next morning K. flew to Switzerland to get his blood changed. It was the only way he could abide cleaning up for a concert tour. This left A. the next couple of weeks to do whatever she wanted. Maybe it was because I was loaded, but her games didn't seem as bad as I'd first feared. One was called "Guess Which Hole." A boy would stick his cock through a hole in a blanket behind which was Tomaso's mouth, A.'s cunt or my ass. If the boy guessed the orifice correctly, he'd get to fuck A. If not, Tomaso or I would get to fuck him.

Another game was called "Cover All Bases." The boys would be given acid and shown stag films till they were peaking and horny as hell. Then one boy would be invited to eat out A.'s pussy while I sucked him off and Tomaso fucked him. Every few minutes we'd change positions till all the bases had been covered.

But this wasn't enough for A. One night we unwound from a coke binge by gulping a few Mandrax followed by swigs of Courvoisier. Within an hour we'd passed out, heaped on top of each other on K. and A.'s over-sized Louis XIV bed. I awakened to the sound of bouncing springs. A. was balling Tommy, the race driver, as his wife lay zonked out beside him. When I later told Giselle about this, she warned me not to let K. find out.

"He's scared shitless of his wife," she said. "He'll only take his rage out on you."

Giselle told me of an earlier houseguest who'd died mysteriously after running afoul of A. Was the power of Black Magic real? Did A. put hexes on her enemies? Giselle and Miriam thought so. This especially bothered me because A. told Tomaso she expected us to help her with a Black Mass that weekend. "Thank god Miriam and I will be gone by then," Giselle said when I told her. "Group sex is too powerful for me, even without the Magic."

153

Group sex, I discovered, was itself an addiction, a thrill not unlike shooting drugs. When lying naked in pitch darkness with three to six others, particularly if of mixed gender, it becomes strangely impossible to tell whose body is whose. Sometimes I couldn't even identify my own arms or legs or where the boundaries of my body were unless I pinched myself. Even then I couldn't always tell.

So who *am* I in such a situation?

One becomes group body, group mind. One melts into the whole group's lust, delirium, hunger, energy and exploration. As perceptions of bodily boundaries dissolve, so does the conscious "I." This feels tremendously liberating. Concepts such as male/female, black/white, gay/straight, arm/leg lose meaning as if devoured by a higher power. Smells, tastes, sounds, feelings, bodily fluids — everything rearranges and intensifies in a wild, playful frenzy. I'd grown so accustomed to orgies that making love to anyone alone, even Tomaso, seemed bland by comparison.

"It isn't group sex I'm against," I said to Tomaso the next morning. "It isn't even the games we've been playing with those boys. What bothers me is A.'s demonic power over us. I feel she's draining our souls."

"Souls? Tomaso laughed, splashing his feet in the water under the jetty where we sat. Waves slapped the red fiberglass speedboat, which was tied to the jetty, and I could hear K. and A.'s macaws squawking in their cages behind the palm and banana trees. The morning sun was hot and as dazzling as a ciborium. I felt silly to be fussing in such a paradise.

"The little monk in you is peeping out again, Armi. Rather we go to a church camp?"

"I'm serious," I persisted. "If you don't think A. has evil power over us, let's prove it by leaving tonight with Giselle and Miriam."

"What? And mess up not only my best set of career connections, but all this free coke and scag? Shit! You don't have enough to buy one snort of anything. Look at yourself, Armi. You're a junkie! Leave now and you'll be crawling back by morning just begging for a fix."

All the excuses I'd protected myself with fell like a house of cards: that I mainly "just snorted," or that on bad mornings I "just had a little flu." My escape from society had become the worst prison of all. I wasn't just empty. I was damned. Tomaso's voice softened as he lifted up my chin with his thumb and forefinger.

"I don't mean to be nasty, Armi, but you knew the life I led before you teamed up with me. And I *do* love you. If it wasn't for you..."

At this he pulled me close, hugging me gently and nuzzling my ear with his tongue. Even now I adored him — his baby smooth skin, his strong firm muscles. In his arms I still felt safe, although if I'd thought I could give ballast to his life I'd failed. But he didn't complain. He simply whispered, "I love you", over and over. Those words I'd yearned so long to hear I now detested. Love too was a prison. And I hated myself most of all.

By Saturday the only ones left were A., two servants, Tomaso and I, and the boys. The servants were closing down the house since A. was flying to join K. in Switzerland on Monday. What vampires they were: K., paying $5,000 to change all the blood in his body so he could tour the States and make millions more for debauchery, and A., living off him, us, anyone she could sink her hands into.

All day A. stayed in her room. What she did I don't know. Maybe she watched soaps or maybe she worked spells and invocations. My earlier conversation with Giselle had set me to thinking of the old ornate chest in A.'s room. She guarded it so jealously I assumed it was her drug stash. Once, when she and K. were gone, I saw she'd forgotten the key. It lay on the bed, studded with rubies. Usually she wore it around her neck on a black velvet ribbon. I'd assumed at first it was just an odd piece of antique jewelry.

I glanced up and down the hall. No one was around. I crept in the room, picked up the key and opened the chest. A noxious, rancid odor overwhelmed me. Indeed, the entire room smelled like a garbage pit heaped as it was with dirty clothes and plates of mouldy food. But the odor from the chest was more powerful. Bits of bone with fur and flesh rotting off, mixed with a sickeningly sweet smell that exuded from a box of black candles. I smelled narcissus, patchouli, formaldehyde. Pungent odors I'd never encountered before seeped out from under the caps of strange bottles: dark oils, grey-green unguents, pink and yellow powders. One large bottle looked as if it was filled with blood. I

155

slammed down the lid and returned A.'s key to the bed. I'd forgotten this until now.

At about 3 p.m., Tomaso and I were summoned into A.'s bedchamber. Her disembodied voice wafted toward us from behind a tall black and red lacquered Chinese screen.

"The ceremony will begin at midnight," she said. "Your instructions are in an envelope by the door. Anything else you need I'll give you later. Prepare the boys too. I suggest you take a nap now so you'll be rested."

At A.'s mention of the boys my stomach tightened. Their early rebelliousness had been swiftly and harshly punished. They'd since been given enough drugs to keep them pliable. As their imprisonment continued, they began to participate in A.'s games with such enthusiasm that I was reminded of circus dogs leaping through hoops. "All men should be taught so well," A. laughed after one playful session. I thought of K., barking and sniping at guests during our first dinner together but cringing and looking down every time A. looked at him.

The servants left the house after dinner. At 11:30 p.m., Tomaso and I appeared at A.'s door, naked under our black cassocks and lace surplices, as she'd instructed. We entered the room to find A. standing naked. Considering how she abused her health, she was still stunningly beautiful. Her body was tanned, her muscles well toned. Her long blond hair shimmered in the candlelight, which doubled its reflection off two wall-sized mirrors facing each other. I saw three of her, three of us. It wasn't easy to tell which figures were real.

A set of black leather vestments was spread out on the bed. We helped her into them. As we did so, she sprinkled droplets from a silver aspergillum over everything, mumbling incomprehensible phrases in a rhythmic cadence. She seemed to be in a trance as urine splashed from the shaker. When we finished dressing her, Tomaso and I each picked up a brass candleholder, in which burned a three-foot-tall black candle. Then we led the way downstairs while A. dipped her shaker into a silver bowl and sprinkled it eclesiastically to her right and left.

The ceremony itself followed the usual pattern of inverting Roman Catholic ritual over the body of a whore. Instead of whores, the boys were strapped stomach down on the makeshift wine cellar altar. During

156

the Confiteor, Tomaso and I fucked them as A. sprinkled us all with her silver shaker. Then she confessed to Satan for any act of soft-heartedness she'd ever displayed.

When we got to the Consecration, A. held up a goblet of the boys' sperm she'd been collecting. She spit into it and added a dash of wine. It must have been a considerable amount judging by how deeply she drank.

"SATANUS VOBISCUM!" she cried, wine and sperm drooling down her chin.

"Eat cum spittle too some more," Tomaso and I mumbled in response.

Then, to my astonishment, A. pulled a live chicken from a crate hidden under the altar. She had so much trouble holding the frightened bird down while Tomaso chopped its head off that I almost broke into giggles. The bird clawed wildly till A.'s arms ran red with blood. Then, trying to hold the headless, spastic chicken steady by the wings, she commanded Tomaso to lift up her leather chausable while she inserted its thrashing neck into her vagina. It wasn't easy and she had trouble standing still — a scene so horrid it was funny. I probably would have laughed out loud but when A. finished, she used the bird on the boys. Now I felt like vomiting. I'm sure I would have if it hadn't been for what happened next.

Having lubricated the boys with chicken blood mixed with our sperm, the demented harridan tossed the flapping bird aside and began to shove her greased hand into the anus of the boy nearest her. Even though his mouth was taped and Tomaso'd shot him up with MDA just an hour before, I could tell by how his eyes bulged that he was in agony. It was more than I could bear. While Tomaso stood frozen in shock I screamed "Stop it you witch! This is going too far!"

"Too far?"

A. looked around the wine cellar like she didn't know where she was and I felt a palpable wind fill the room and push against my chest. Then I heard an unnaturally deep voice spill from A.'s lips.

"NO, NO...NEVER TOO FAR!"

A gleam lit up her eyes that I'd seen only once before, a look so terrible I shall never forget it — Theodosius! My blood turned to ice. I cried out the one word that linked these two experiences.

"ROBBIE!"

The entire room seemed to heave a sigh of relief as I heard a great flapping of wings like a flock of seagulls taking off. A.'s arms fell listlessly to her side. Then a smell of honeysuckle hit my nostrils, the smell of a summer evening's pollen-laden air, and finally, rising over and above it, a sharp, sweet smell of boyish sweat which was unmistakable. From somewhere, from the slaughtered chicken perhaps, a long white feather fell at my feet. But I knew better. Robbie had answered my cry.

"Take A. upstairs," I commanded Tomaso. "Then let's free these kids and split."

For once Tomaso followed my orders instead of I his. He took A. by the arm and led her upstairs as if she were a zombie. I cut the kids loose then phoned the police. When Tomaso came back downstairs he panicked.

"The cops? We're foreign junkie accomplices to kidnapping and you call the cops? Christ!"

I held up a key. "But we won't be here when they come. The speedboat's docked at the jetty, right? I packed our stuff earlier. So let's get our bags and split."

I wasn't as stupid as Tomaso thought. I knew it would take drastic action to get him to leave. By the time A. would be coherent enough to put the cops on our tail, we'd hopefully be out of the country. I had no money myself, of course, but Tomaso did and I also knew he'd be unstinting when it came to saving his own skin.

I'll spare you the details of how we got to Rome. Our drug withdrawal was more difficult. We tried to cut back. Tomaso resumed working and I started drawing again. Although we were often irritable, we never mentioned Villefranche. There were rumors, but Tomaso's agent concocted a story that we'd been in the Bahamas. (People will say anything if you pay them enough.) K. and A. had too much trouble of their own to go after us. Rome had its own dangers.

The strain of work and our relationship gradually pulled us back to our excesses. Tomaso could do anything, even commit atrocities, but only on heroin could he call himself my lover. How unbearably painful too our last night together, those last images which begat one another like the endless list of Moses' forefathers.

Images.

Images falling from the sky like shards of the demon's mirror. And like parting shots of a slow motion film sequence, the final frames played through my dreams for weeks:

Staggering...neck and face a flaming bruise...rasping through clenched teeth "I think it was c-cut with —" ...collapsing into a ratty couch, his head rolling back, his eyes bulging, his body convulsed...drag queens passed out on quaaludes, their '40s furs serving as doormats... someone bursting in "Where is he? We gotta call an ambulance quick." Another voice "No. Just get him outta here"...my own voice eerily distant from me as I touched his face...

I could take no more. As I waited in the hospital (long corridors, a medicinal smell, pale yellow walls, high ceilings) I decided that whatever happened I had to leave. So when the doctor came out and said Tomaso was out of danger, I went back to our hotel and phoned Eva.

"Armi!"

Her voice registered surprise, concern. (Armies of what?) Or was it her pause afterwards that suggested this? I couldn't blame her. We hadn't written or phoned, not even when she and Bill sent a wedding announcement. I hoped we'd at least sent a present but what, a fondue set?

"I know I've been a shit," I began. "My life's such a mess I don't know what to do. I feel like killing myself. If you slam the phone down on my ear I can't say I'd blame you."

Manipulative, yes, but I was too desperate to care. In the back of my mind — ha! Such chaos churned there I felt weirdly detached, yet connected, like a surfer riding waves of some unspeakable...

"Where are you, Armand? What's wrong?"

Eva sounded more awake now. How much could I tell her? Should I talk about the siren, the men in white coats who gently but hurriedly had lifted Tomaso onto a stretcher and into the ambulance, the cold plastic seats of the taxi? I could hardly keep my pain back now — rain, night breaking into daylight, streetlights glowing leprously, the hiss of tires on wet pavement. Suddenly I remembered skipping home in the rain

159

when I was seven. I hated the feel of my feet in those squishy, wet shoes but since I couldn't do anything about it, why not throw up my arms and jump around. While I mumbled incoherently to Eva I massaged my arm, neck and shoulder squeezing the muscles deeply as if trying to convince myself this wasn't just another dream.

"What's your phone number," Eva pressed. "You have money don't you? Okay, I want you to call the airport and book the next available flight to Paris. Will you do that, Armand?"

The way she said this reminded me of my grandmother who covered everything in the house: walls, floors, windows, every table and chair. I shut my eyes and envisioned Early American scenes in sepia on the wallpaper, thick '40s drapes with rose-colored flowers and dark green leaves. These associative blips I remember better than what Eva and I were saying.

When I got off the phone to Eva I called the airport. Then I wrote Tomaso a note: "Dear Tomaso, It's not your fault but..."

I didn't know what else to say. Maybe that was enough. In the suit-case my clothes and notebooks looked like a pyramid of past lives — until I closed the lid that is, and sat on it so I could fasten the snaps. Too bad I couldn't stuff my feelings as easily. Then I made another stab at the note.

"Dear Tomaso, You probably won't believe this but I still..." Still what —loved him, believed love was possible? Still waters done reap, as the saying goes, or something like that.

160

<u>ESSAYS</u>

# NOTES ON BOUNDARIES: NEW NARRATIVE

What typified New York City for me, visiting from Nebraska for the first time, was a feeling of danger. Its primal site was the subways. Against the alienation of these dismal tunnels, yet very much part of this world, was the subway graffiti: sprayed names, attempts of the powerless to assert individual or gang identity. Graffitists can be run down by trains, mauled by guard dogs, killed by police. They stray at the edges, talking to death.

Aboveground, in tranquil, white-walled galleries, art hangs safe. After the high period of Abstract Expressionism, Pop Art and Conceptualism, there's an art of the marginal: Julien Schnabel's figures emerging from a South Bronx of broken plates, Sue Coe's tortured women playing out their dramas on nightmare black, and the raw communal energy of subway graffiti. In this history, the self has been erased only to return with the sacred vengeance of a cry. This mode of reappearance—wherein the central is supplanted by the marginal, toppled by the outcast—is defiant. It complains, yells. It's not quiet but not sure of itself either.

What constitutes the marginal? What constitutes community? "The ceremony of the *pharmakos*/scapegoat," writes Derrida in *Disseminations*, "played out on the boundary line between inside and outside, which it has as its function ceaselessly to trace and retrace. *Intra muros/extra muros*. Origin of difference and division, the *pharmakos* represents evil both introjected and projected...Alarming and calming. Sacred and accursed. The conjunction, the *conincidentia oppositorum*, ceaselessly undoes itself in the passage to decision or crisis."

In other words, what's cast out as "marginal" has to be first within. This is what returns to haunt, a Tell-Tale Heart. "It's an affront to our community," Mayor Koch gripes about subway graffiti. Yes, but it represents community more deeply than the mayor. Everything gets confused. Who's really who when anyone says us?

"How can there be stories?" asks Kathy Acker in *Great Expectations*. "Consciousness just is: not time. But any emotion presupposed differentiation. Differentiation presumes time, at least BEFORE and NOW. A narrative is an emotional moving."

Or Julia Kristeva, in *Powers of Horror*:

> *A narrative is the most elaborate attempt, next to syntactic competence, to situate a speaking being between his desires and their prohibitions...But not until the advent of twentieth century "abject" literature (the sort that takes up where apocalypse and carnival left off) did one realize that the narrative web is a thin film constantly threatened with bursting. For, when narrated identity is unbearable, when the boundary between subject and object is shaken, and when even the limit between inside and outside become uncertain, the narrative is what is challenged first. If it continues nevertheless, its make-up changes: its linearity is shattered, it proceeds by flashes, enigmas, short cuts, incompletion, tangles and cuts. At a later stage, the unbearable identity of the narrator and of the surroundings that are supposed to sustain him can no longer be narrated but cries out or is decried with maximal stylistic intensity (language of violence, of obscenity, or of a rhetoric that relates the text to poetry). The narrative yields to a crying-out theme that, when it tends to coincide with the incandescent states of a boundary-subjectivity that I have called abjection, is the crying-out theme of suffering horror.*

First time I ride a subway, a heavy-set black woman starts yelling: "This subway run over my babies." She talks to no one in particular yet at everyone. The train's crowded, passengers snicker. She screams louder: "I gotta big knife in my bag an' I gonna stab some of you white sons-a-bitches. I like t'see you laugh then!" I didn't know whether to feel sorry for her or scared for myself. On my second subway ride, someone hurls a bag of jellybeans at me when I get off. It feels like a rock when it hits my head.

166

"I'm just a maid around here. No one appreciates me." Mom elaborated her wants, and the anger of those wants, talking me and herself to death. "Don't get all wound up," Dad would say.

That's the first sense I get from the title of Judy Grahn's *A Women Is Talking to Death*. In this case, the woman is even less listened to since she's lesbian. Like a subway graffitist, she's talking to death. Not only is she talking to death (of a male motorcyclist on the Bay Bridge), she's also talking to DEATH (the myth of machismo, power hierarchy, the Dying Young God/Warrior). Bridging the first sense of her title to the second and third, Grahn moves from an individualizing abject in literature to a communal revision of the myth. "Testimony in trials that never get heard," she begins. What's on trial is logocentrism.

New Narrative marks an emotional moving forward. What Grahn and her feminist precursors Pat Parker, Alta and Sharon Isabell do in writing, graffitists do in painting: traditional subject/object boundaries blur. New Narrative shatters linearity, proceeds by flashes, enigmas, and yields to a florid crying-out theme of suffering/horror - in short, to a future. Formalisms implode, stagnate. New Narrative explodes, speaking to and creating community. Where New Narrative parts with the older literature of the abject (Celine, Kafka, etc) is in its communal and political grounding.

When woman, gays, and ethnic writers bring back narrative, why is it different? In an introductory note to *A Woman Is Talking To Death*, Grahn writes: "This poem is as factual as I could possibly make it." Gay writers Bruce Boone and Robert Glück (like Acker, Dennis Cooper, or the subway graffitists again) up the ante on this factuality by weaving their own names and those of friends and lovers into their work. The writer/artist becomes exposed and vulnerable: you risk being foolish, mean-spirited, wrong. But if the writer's life is more open to judgement and speculation, so is the reader's. Boone and Glück, for instance, riddle their texts with direct addresses: "What would you do?" Lured into the writer's real life story (actually, a tangle of stories within stories), readers have to compare to and create their own narrative. Humor too reveals a double social edge. Grahn further notes that she wants "to discuss the crisscross oppressions which people use against each other" and to "define a lesbian life within the context of other people in the world." These devices bare the technique of how our lives and communities are constructed, or may be reconstructed.

"Experience which is passed on from mouth to mouth is the source from which all storytellers have drawn," Walter Benjamin observes in "The Storyteller." If this art is becoming more remote, he argues, isn't it because experience has declined in value? Bruce Boone's "My Walk With Bob" suggests New Narrative's ambivalence. We might "believe in" community, but not in the same way people did a century ago. What's changed since the days of Balzac, Flaubert?

Boone's story begins as he and Bob Glück go shopping and stop off at the Mission Dolores. The plainness of the narrative, a "walk," operates like white: all colors can be found in it if you're willing to look. Seeing the monstrances in the Mission museum, the narrator is flooded with memories from his novitiate days. A church museum, religious faith—what could be more remote from contemporary secular life?

Terror! This is what bursts from the underside of the narrator's highly socialized, intellectual consciousness. "I kept my eyes down," Bruce writes, "because I knew if I looked up—for only one instant!—the host would see I didn't believe in it at all. I would have then been instantly annihilated by the rays from the golden sunburst of the monstrance." (Are there other nuances of catastrophe here? Think of the blinding flash millions of Americans viewed in the TV drama *The Day After*).

The meaning of experience isn't always obvious. Borders shift. As they come upon a Lourdes Grotto in the Mission cemetary, Bruce tells Bob about the miracle of Lourdes since Bob, being Jewish, didn't know the story. Bruce can't recall the saintly peasant girl's name so he scrambles in names from similar tales: Jacinta, Guadalupe, Jose. As they talk, the account develops archaic language peculiarities. When Bruce says "Our Lady," Bob adds "as was her wont" and so on. "This made the story a lot more fun for both of us," Bruce comments, "though the sense of disorientation it introduced encouraged a definite and growing note of hysteria."

As Bruce and Bob trip out in search for pure verbal beauty, "removed from the problems of a real social existence," Bruce emphasizes, he suddenly finds himself thinking about the very thing he has avoided in the story's first nine pages. "For instance, how would I learn to live without Jonathan."

This last sentence drops like a bomb. Its last word—his ex-lover's name—explodes the desultory ruminations, the verbal covering of all that went before. You know the feeling. Try to protect yourself, think of other things. Suddenly, when you least expect it, that sense of loss hits you and you're in terror's grip again. What was safely remote returns defiantly, like a vampire's hand from the grave. So where's the safety zone? Do we really want community again, in the same way, with all its nostalgia and repressiveness.

Ecstasy, death, love, terror—these are the *pharmakos*/scapegoat of New Narrative. In Kathy Acker's *Great Expectations*, primal eros powers her roller-coaster run-on sentences. "I feel I feel I feel I have no language, any emotion for me is a prison." And yet writing attempts to break out of this prison. The narrator changes gender, lover and beloved exchange roles, nightmares of war and squalor juxtapose with lush descriptions from Proust or a gloss of *The Princess of Cleves*. Philosophical meditation vs. the scream; plagiarism in the service of authenticity. Through everything eros drives forward, refusing to be cast out.

Acker's first audience—those she seems to be speaking to and for— were the most marginal of marginals: artists who didn't make it, punks, anarchist intellectuals, a browbeaten husband, s/m folks and women who wouldn't be silenced by the white-gloved sector of feminism. Yet Acker herself grew up rich, was cast out. Now she returns with the defiance of primal eros. Likewise with Dennis Cooper.

Cooper's early poetry celebrated highschool crushes, not only with classmates but also with commodified heartthrob images, boy celebrities such as Shaun Cassidy. The dark side of this impossible Romanticism surfaces in serial poems such as "The Tenderness Of The Wolves." Cooper takes on the viewpoint of the boy-killer (akin to Spicer's fool-killer in his *Holy Grail* book) who rips off youth's mask of innocence as promulgated by the uncomprehending complicity of smug parents, hypercritical coaches and society-at-large. But isn't everyone in Cooper's world empty with only a smudge of codified identity? The killer alone acts, has mobility.

On the cover of Cooper's recent chapbook, *My Mark*, is a large photo of the author's head. He's on his back, his throat exposed as to a guillotine, staring up into darkness. Faces in this short prose piece aren't "human"; they're empty vehicles for an author/movie director to fill with meaning. Like a Romantic symbol, the face has become an elusive signified chased by an endless chain of signifiers. Any metaphor slips from the Real. Cooper compares this unattainability to an odor inside the body

> *which writers leave in obscurity, stumped as to how to describe it, not having smelled it.*
> *Without it Mark's not complete, but lies slightly outside of my grasp like the big ring of keys to the door of the jail cell where somebody somewhere is probably locked up for strangling some kid he couldn't get love from. He'll reach as far as he can through the bars and never get near it. I mean the truth about anyone.*

Yet traces of the Real abound, such as insignificant notes left by ex-lovers. "It's strange how something as tossed off could have been so impressive." Cooper writes, "like the graffiti that piles up on neighborhood walls, which I stopped looking at after a few months, but which I've heard has been raised to the level of Art by the experts, simply because it's expressive of one human being." Art experts are like ghoulish boy-murderers: lacking a real life of their own, they prowl the streets seeking new life to devour.

In *Greystoke, The Legend of Tarzan*, a popular movie in 1983, a young man raised by apes learns English and returns to his family in mid-Victorian England. When he later attends the opening of the Greystoke Room at the British Natural History Museum, he sees dismembered claws, stuffed animals. Nauseous, Greystoke escapes through a side door and stumbles into a zoological lab. He passes dissected monkey and ape cadavers, comes at last to a cage containing his "real" father—the ape who raised him. Freeing this "father," they escape to a park where the ape is shot. Greystoke—half-man, half-ape—rejects his inheritance and returns to his "natural family" in Africa.

Why do people flock to this sentimentalized, distanced film? To see someone romp naked in a jungle? But a participation in the primitive can only be vicarious, voyeuristic (when the old earl tries to slide downstairs on a tray as he did as a child, he cracks his skull and dies).

In this context I think of "Invaders from Mars," an early poem by Robert Glück. Here too, pop and high art merge, and the libido seeks release from the barbarisms of culture. The pink and black of glazed donuts in the '50s becomes the pink and black of "the beauty of regularity in / balanced environments like the salmon & wolf & the beauty of extravagance / we share with animals that live in / extremity..." The poem's final lines meld into a kind of breathless prose:

> *He's on a knoll & looks up, there's a pink cloud relating by contrast to the steel gray sky. He says to himself, "Just look at that pink cloud, just look at that pink cloud, just look at that pink cloud," to summon more & more of himself but it's no use—he & the pink aren't equals & everything, even the pleasure, especially the pleasure, is against him & in spite of him.*

Proust, Kundera, Glück—all emphasize memory, art, music, food, politics, history, scandal and hot sex. And the prose of all three is framed by death. Proust writes of a dying social class; Kundera of a nation crushed by a bureaucratic police state. And Glück? In a story in *Elements Of A Coffee Service* the narrator compares the sordid loneliness of a modern death to an Aztec sacrifice that integrated community—and sexuality. Does the freedom to be anything lead to the fate of being nothing?

In his novel *Jack the Modernist*, Gluck laments the death of intimacy.

Jack can give himself piecemeal to "an empire" of friends but not to one lover. No future, no story. "Desire equals meaning in a cruder, simpler way than we might be comfortable believing (Cupid, draw back your bow)." So what's a narrator to do? Glück triangulates. There's a whole history of love (Romance, porn, personal experience) to play off of (in quote marks). More immediately, there's the death of an older friend's son. When the narrator can't cry over Jack, he cries over Philip's death. Was Phyllis' son gay? Questions about Philip and his death develop sub-textually until, toward the novel's end, the narrator and Phyllis have a talk. Phyllis has been in Glück's writing workshop for two years but thinks Bob doesn't like her. Bob tells her he felt she deflected his attention. Their conversation keeps returning to Philip.

> *I felt that by desiring him I was beginning to understand his death. Phyllis said, "I found caches of his cigarette butts around the house, I hunted for them, and even though I don't smoke I smoked them all." I had a shock of recognition. So, I thought, a parent's love for a child is not different from the love between lovers, not merely as intense but cut from the same cloth.*

Then, an unexpected denouement. Bob walks Phyllis to the bus stop.

> *A pending rain gave everyone in the street a conspiratorial feeling that registered as a tremulous sexuality. We opened our eyes wider, quickened our awareness...(The bus) came faster than we thought. I embraced Phyllis and kissed her on the mouth. The kiss surprised us. I think she held out a cheek. Drawing back, I looked at Phyllis' lips where my lips had been and then at her eyes. They were lowered bashful or embarrassed, but later I realized she was just looking at my mouth where her lips had been and if she glanced at my face I also would have appeared bashful, eyes lowered. My kiss was for*

*Philip as much as Phyllis. It struck me as important*
*that we looked at each other's lips although I can't*
*say why. Maybe it was that our surprise showed in*
*precisely the same gesture and for an instant we*
*spilled into each other.*

Earlier in the novel, Glück talks about a peculiarly modern emotion he calls "excited neutrality." It's the space we occupy between boundaries. On one side there's sensation, ecstasy, pre-language; on the other, identity, future, narrativity. The self hovers precariously in-between. Glück seeks to get as close to the body as words can. "When we see that orgasms are produced by society," he's said, "they can suddenly be talked about." Not docudrama, not stream-of consciousness, but an eye for how our interiority is formed. Yet too much talk and meaning suffocates, collapses or explodes.

Truth, love, friendship, lust, community—everything gets mixed up. So too the narrative, which often breaks into cut-up, poetry, essay, catalogues, highly intellectual or pop codings of experience. Not even the first Mickey Mouse film, which Glück uses to explore erotic discourse, can be read simply. Why does Mickey, a steamboat captain, sing a song full of farmyard images? The war of ideologies, of diverse experience, or past and present, of desire and obsession not only complicates everything; it IS everything.

"History is just a resume of one's job experience," Michael Amnasan writes in an earlier version of a new prose piece. Amnasan grounds himself in his working-class background. His prose is flat, less dramatic and florid than that of Acker, Cooper or Glück. It seeks control. "I want to write such simplicity that you could feel Anna lift a cup from the table," the narrator says in *I Can't Distinguish Opposites*. But it doesn't work. "Somehow I became distracted from that. I once elaborated my feelings into theories so they couldn't hurt me. I can't anymore. I've begun to express them."

What distinguishes Amnasan from the New Wave European novelists, such as Peter Handke and Robbe-Grillet, whom he admires, is his explosive irony. It has a defiant edge, like the humor of Mark Twain. Amnasan's character Tom says, "I'm going to become so specialized in normalcy." He then remembers an uncle who wouldn't watch more than one TV show a night because he was afraid the set would run out of pictures. The next day Tom writes this: "I want to feel like a dog who has had his food and water put out in the same place and same time for ten years. I want to feel that for ten minutes." Still later Tom says:

> *People keep calling me on the phone telling me that*
> *they've got the wrong number. Next time somebody*
> *calls me like that I'm going to say, "Look, my number*
> *is not wrong. You're wrong for having called it."*

Amnasan's characters constantly struggle against those who would fit them into a category. In another episode, the narrator quarrels with a bus driver. The driver refuses to open the doors, then opens them saying, "Bang on my doors like that and you're going to stay out. If you were drunk or something I could see it." The narrator replies, "Next time I'll get drunk...then it will be all right." When a bus passenger next asks to try on his sunglasses he pushes the sharpened frame ends into the passenger's eyes. This is the most fantastic, violent episode to appear in any of Amnasan's writing to date. The intruding bus passenger is blind now, "but at the same time he can't admit to himself that I did it." Repressed violence strains from both sides, grinding rock plates along an earthquake fault.

Dodie Bellamy, like Amnasan, grounds herself in a working-class background and excels in irony, but in her work scenes repeat and shift like the thematic image clusters in George Bataille's *Story Of The Eye*. In "Dear Diary Today," humorous recipes appear throughout the text. In between, Bellamy describes friendships whose borders shift:

> *Could Kurt imagine himself sleeping with a woman?*
> *His answer: Could you imagine yourself fucking your*
> *cat? Lying in his bed, watching the news, he keeps*

*leaning against me. He's fluish, so I figure it's delirium*
*or he wants a mother. Shall I purr or play offended?...*
*Antonio lies in Kurt's bed too, sometimes in the middle,*
*and we both lean against him. More often, I am in the*
*middle with Antonio on the outside and Kurt by the*
*stereo. We eat cookies and popcorn, crumbs getting in*
*the sheets. These moments are as good as a hot bath.*

Feeling guilty about gossip, Bellamy later repeats the scene with
altered names:

*Cachetes lies in Ludwig's bed too. Sometimes he's*
*in the middle and you both lean against him. But,*
*more often, you are in the middle with Cachetes on*
*the outside and Ludwig by the stereo. You eat pizza*
*and get the sheets greasy. These moments are as good*
*as a jacuzzi.*

Still later the scene is worked through an astrological nomenclature.
The script remains constant (who sits where) but its meaning shifts by
how it's described:

*A Leo and two Aquarians sat in the Leo's bed. All*
*three were from the Midwest. This was the position of*
*their moons; Virgo was on the outside. Aquarius was*
*next to the stereo, with Gemini in the middle.*

This shifting is amplified by the other elements in the story, which
also change meaning as they interweave with each other. Nothing
remains fixed.

In "Complicity," Bellamy takes on the theme of shoplifting. A list of
things the narrator's friend Lizzie has stolen for her is interspersed with
accounts of Lizzie's shoplifting techniques, and reflections on how all
modern life is based on theft. Is stealing a substitute for love, as the
radio psychologist says?

175

Gradually, in little ways, the narrator finds herself stealing:

> *Lizzie, breaking her diet with a huge slice of German*
> *chocolate cake, "Doesn't the word 'complicity' sound*
> *like a woman's name?" I smile and steal a bit.*

The question of theft expands. Doesn't the narrator "steal" her story from her friend's life? Isn't the technique of pastiche—as practiced by Acker, Boone, Glück, Bellamy and others—a kind of theft? Isn't all intellectuality, even culture itself, theft?

> *Writing about his job as a sheet metal worker, Dan*
> *uses "synchronicity," "semiotic," "metaphorical level of*
> *exchange." I say, "Why the big words? You trying to*
> *sound smart or something?" He looks down the sub-*
> *way stairs then back at me. "I want to use a vocabu-*
> *lary I'm not even supposed to own."*

From a working-class or marginal perspective, shoplifting—food, sweaters, "art spaces" on a subway, ideas—is no more than taking back what's previously been ripped off from you. If all property is theft, steal. But how much anarchy do we want? How much do I want?

A couple of summers ago, I was having problems with my boyfriend. I wanted a monogamous "couple" relationship. Joe was fond of me but felt my desire for categories was stifling. To bridge our communication gap we took acid. We'd done this before and felt a happy, peaceful oneness with nature, each other. This time was different.

Earlier, Joe had expressed irritation over the title of Michael McClure's *Scratching The Beat Surface*. It wasn't exactly my bookishness that bothered him, he enjoyed reading too, but he felt I reified books, especially poetry and criticism. He was doubtful about professional writers generally.

"What's this 'scratching the surface,'" he exclaimed at 5 a.m. holding up McClure's book in exasperation. "Don't you see, we're all stars!"

To demonstrate this insight, he leapt up from bed and started pulling all my books off their shelves and hurling them onto the floor. "We're all stars, don't you see? We're stars!" No book, no set of civilized cultural categories could encompass the tremendous, undefinable energy that was "us." Furniture was too limiting. He tore down a screen, tried to overturn the dining room table, threw chairs. I pleaded with him to stop, pushed him to the door to calm him down. Instead, he ran into the night naked.

Three hours earlier we'd made love, the kind where you totally lose yourself. Now I faced the other side of ecstasy. My apartment was a shambles. I feared if I went after Joe myself he might even kill me. Next morning I bailed him out of jail. The police had picked him up about a mile from the apartment. I realized what I loved about Joe from the start was his willingness to live on the edge, to cry, to play, to admit confusions, to argue, to cross boundaries. We challenged each other. When Joe returned the next day he cleaned up my place. Instead of breaking up we became closer. Closer?

Subway violence, graffiti art, Derrida and Kristeva, Judy Grahn's feminism, the return of Benjamin's disappearing storyteller, rap singing and breakdancing, Boy George, pastiche in film and New Narrative writing, explosive humor, shoplifting, a nostalgia for love and community but a refusal of its repressive, categorizing elements, the ambiguity of the *pharmakos*—prisoner and healer. It all adds up to an anguish over boundaries. We can't go on; we refuse to give up. And at the edges, between inside and outside, an open-ended free play of possibility.

# DIAMANDA GALÁS: IF THE DEAD COULD SING

If the dead could sing, how would they sound? Coming from neither time nor place, mind nor body, their discourse would truly liquid-ate language. Critics would babble, dogs howl, mothers hurry their children into bomb shelters at the first note. Poets have sought this realm and a few (Dante, Rilke) have at times touched it but no one has so drastically ripped away the veil separating life from death as Diamanda Galás. She doesn't sing to or of the dead; rather she allows them to sing to us through her. Maybe that's why the London gay art mag, *Square Peg*, has called her the world's most intimidating performer.

The first time I heard Diamanda Galás was in 1983. Already a cult figure for her *Litanies of Satan* (Y Records), she was appearing at the New Performance Gallery with a new work, "Wild Women With Steak Knives." No amount of hype could have prepared me for that moment. My skin recoiled into a mass of goosebumps like a retreating army. This wasn't art. This wasn't "an act." This was honest-to-god sorcery. For the next hour I feared to look right or left or even to shut my eyes. I stared straight ahead at Diamanda's face, disembodied by a white pinspot, and at the tiny flame of light dancing below on her red sequined dress. Never had I had such an experience, not even on drugs—not until last night, that is, when I listened to the first two albums of Diamanda's magnificent mass trilogy *The Masque of the Red Death* (Mute Records).

Let's not mince words. This is a mass for people with AIDS. Like all of her work it's highly charged, highly controversial. "Many people warned me to stay away from this subject or to tone it down," she confided to me at Cafe Picaro.

"I realize I may be misunderstood but there is so much cowardice around this subject," she continued. "I had to be honest. I sat with friends dying of AIDS in St. Luke's Hospital in New York City and I stayed a month with my brother when he was in the hospital in San Diego. He was such a hero. He kept working on his art to the end. But our family was actually told by the hospital staff to stay away from him lest we be contaminated."

Her face contorts with pain and anger as she spits out the word. Diamanda tells other horror stories her sick friends experienced. She tells of walking out on a London record producer who made a homophobic joke about AIDS. But nothing she says is, or could be, as powerful as her plague mass itself. It draws upon the whole history of archetypal responses to plague from Leviticus to Defoe to Camus.

The first segment, *The Divine Punishment,* refers to Old Testament texts. Galás, who has performed with the New York Philharmonic at the Lincoln Center and at countless other prestigious New Music festivals around the world, premiered *Masque* at the Osweg shipyards in Lenz, Austria, in June of 1986. Amidst smoke and fire, she sang tottering from a 150 foot-high scaffolding. She believes in art as sacrifice, that a performance is nothing if it doesn't take risks.

To put it bluntly, *The Divine Punishment* is neither pretty nor safe. Leviticus chillingly evokes the first community response to plague—to condemn and scapegoat the victims:

> *And the priest shall look upon the plague*
> *for a rising, and for a scab, and for a bright spot.*
> *And the priest shall shut up he that hath the plague.*
> *He shall carry them forth to a place unclean.*
> *He shall separate them in their uncleaness.*
> *This is the law of the plague:*
> *To teach when it is clean and when it is unclean.*

Next, the victim cries out with Psalms 59, 22 and 88: "Why hast Thou forsaken me?" (the cry echoed by Christ later), "Deliver me from my enemies, oh my God," and finally, the harrowing refrain: "Shalt Thou show wonders to the dead?"

But the real shocker is the conclusion, "Son L'Antichristo," a text written by Galás herself. One after another, terms of approbation are embraced by the sufferer and hurled back into the faces of the judges:

> *I am the scourge*
> *I am the Holy Fool.*

*I am the shit of God.*

*I am the sign.*
*I am the plague.*
*I am the Antichrist.*

In Italian, the language Galás sings this litany in, the word for plague (pestilenza) is even more charged. As the organ crescendos amid a cacophony of rattlesnake sounds, how Galás rasps out these lines is nothing short of hair-raising. Language itself drops away and what you experience, on a raw nerve level, is the gut-wrenching spirits that live beneath language—pure, primordial affliction, and defiance. Difficult listening if you are alone at night!

*Saint of the Pit*, the second album, moves from the external community's viewpoint to the sufferer's inner state of mind. As we're raised to this second archetypal octave, that of purging grief, a spiritual transformation takes place. In pain this intense, even anger boils away.

"La Treizieme Revient," a fluttering organ solo, is followed by "Deliver Me," a vibrato solo of Middle Eastern wailing, so anguished that I was moved to tears. Diamanda's cries are like arrows tipped in fire. Side one's final section, sung in French, is Baudelaire's poem "Self-Tormentor" that begins:

> *No rage, no rancor: I shall beat you*
> *as butchers fell on ax.*
> *As Moses smote the rock in*
> *Horeb—*
> *I shall make you weep.*

And ends:

> *I am the vampire at my own veins,*
> *one of the great lost horde*
> *doomed for the rest of time, and*
> *beyond,*
> *"to laugh—but smile no more"*

Side two, dedicated to Diamanda's brother Philip-Dimitri Galás, hints of a still higher archetypal response—the nobility of accepting one's destiny even in the pit of suffering. Beginning with a more traditional operatic rendering of Nerval's poem "Artemis," it concludes with the stunning Corbière poem "Cris D'Aveugle" ("Blind Man's Cry"). Cris begins with a sustained bat-like shrieking. Gradually, an overlapping heteroglossia of voices overwhelms the *Deus misericors* of the chorus: first, the cackling rasp of a crone; next, a breathy childlike voice of innocence; the mumbled murmurings, screechings, arias (both near and far), squeaks and blatherings, growls and moans, unearthly whispers like air squeezed out of a balloon. If the monsters populating the hell of Heironymus Bosch could speak, this is how they'd sound. Finally, when you think you can take no more, a pause, and then the final text:

> *Pardon for praying hard*
> *Lord, if it is fate*
> *My eyes two burning holy-water fonts*
> *The devil has put his fingers inside*
> *Pardon for crying loud*
> *Lord against fate*
>
> *I hear the northwind*
> *Which bugles like a horn*
> *It is the hunting call for the kill of*
> *the dead*
> *I bay enough on my own*
> *I hear the northwind*
> *I hear the horn's knell*

When I played this album for a friend, neither of us could speak for ten minutes after it ended.

I ask Galás how *Masque of the Red Death* will end.

"I work intuitively, not intellectually, so I'm really not sure yet," she says modestly. "I'm influenced by Artaud's Theater of Cruelty, but by cruelty I don't mean sadism. I mean rigor, honesty, forcing yourself to see what you really don't want to see. I don't think I've arrived at Bataille's 'joy in despair' yet, though it may be there in glimmers. I'll just have to wait till I get to Berlin. Then I'll just let what happens happen."

Galás used this same technique when she did a concert tour of mental institutions in the mid-70s. "The Minimalist performance art scene couldn't understand what I was doing," she says, "so when a friend in the Living Theater suggested the mental institutions tour I thought, why not? In those days I'd stand with my back to the audience, sometimes silently for up to 10 minutes, until whatever was in me would start to come out."

Galás has since worked with such leading European avant-garde composers such as Pierre Boulez, Vinko Globokas and Iannis Xenakis, as well as performed in punk clubs like Club Lingerie in LA or other clubs like the I-Beam, Club Nine and Danceteria, in NYC. Perhaps no other singer has appeared at such a wide range of venues.

I asked if she's studied or consciously uses magic incantations in her work. "It's not conscious...It's not witchcraft or anything like that though for some reason people often think it is. I was approached by someone from the Pan African Congress after a concert in Germany and asked to tour Africa. This man related what I do to a form of witchcraft practiced in Africa."

Is Galás ever afraid of being taken over by spirits, energies or whatever it is that channels through her?

"No, not at all. I'd only be scared if my voice needed to do something it couldn't do. That's why I started studying *bel canto* with Frank Kelly in San Diego seven years ago." (The risk Galás alludes to is that she sometimes pushes her voice so far that one mistake, one momentary loss of discipline and control, might hemmorhage her vocal chords and end her career.) "When I sing Norma, which I can't yet, I can probably handle anything," she concludes with a laugh.

Then Galás has a question for me. She's staying with a friend, Jello Biafra, and wonders what San Franciscans feel about the expensive court battle he and the Dead Kennedys are fighting regarding the alleged obscenity of their last album cover. "Everyone I know totally backs them," I reply. Diamanda says Moral Majority types forced the cancellation of several of her own concerts because of her "Litanies of Satan," soon to be re-released.

*Masque of the Red Death* is the first major musical work on the growing AIDS epidemic. It explodes the usual neat categories separating opera and rock, high art and low, far more radically than Nina Hagen or Philip Glass in *Liquid Days*. How any music critic could fail to list it as one of the top albums of 1986 I fail to understand. Indeed, it may be one of the most extraordinary musical works of the decade.

# EVIL LITERATURE AND A FORGOTTEN CLASSIC

Fyodor Sologub, <u>The Petty Demon</u> (Ardis, 2901 Heatherway, Ann Arbor, Michigan 48104) 1983, 355 pages, paper, $6.95

Imagine trying to evaluate any nation's literature with no knowledge of history. French literature would have little meaning if we didn't understand the dialectic between Descartes and Pascal, Rabelais and Racine. American literature likewise has its dialectic — between Dickinson and Whitman, Melville and Poe. Mailer, for instance, can be seen to follow from Melville, Burroughs or Dennis Cooper from Poe. Gay writing also has its traditions despite heterosexual attempts to erase them. In poetry, our dialectic has been between the mithric and shamanistic impulse but in prose it's more difficult to say. Few know the work of Charles Warren Stoddard, Mark Twain's secretary, and James Purdy's only descendant might be Kevin Killian. New York gay writers might be seen to flow from Truman Capote but there're too many gaps in our historical understanding to tell.

In poetry our familiarity is also apt to be international. Many have read some Sappho, Catullus, Byron, Cavafy or Lorca, but I'd wager far fewer have read any Baron Corvo, Rene Crevel, Mishima, Pasolini or Tournier. Mainstream publishers have allowed us Forester and Wilde because their fiction was "proper" (e.g., vaguely romantic, not sexy. Wilde, of course, was known for stereotypic outrageousness but, like Dorian Grey, was acceptable only as an object lesson and punished for unmentioned "excesses"). Mostly, our sexuality has had to be masked. Our only pre-Stonewall novelists who actually wrote about sex—Genet, Burroughs and Rechy—were admitted because they fit an approved stereotype, namely that gays are evil, sick and self-loathing.

If good equates with the values of Christianity and the capitalist, patriarchal state, perhaps we should embrace this "evil" label and proclaim it as what's best in us. To a rationalist, a puritanical imperialist, eros itself is evil. It's play. It explodes boundaries. It's also ecstasy, a celebration of the body. William Blake knew this long before Nietzsche and Bataille, which is why he made hell more appealing than heaven in *The*

*Marriage of Heaven and Hell.* So evil in this sense—moving from ancient paganism down through gnosticism and its off-shoots—is a tradition of which we can be proud.

I note this by way of introduction of Fyodor Sologub's *The Petty Demon*, which I discovered by accident in a used bookstore. First published in 1907, it's surely the funniest, kinkiest and sexiest of Russian classics. Replete with naked boys, s/m spankings and alcoholic hallucinations, the anti-hero Peredonov is at once victim and monster, silly hypocrite and sadistic dullard.

Not content with spanking boys in school, the pompous schoolmaster goes from house to house trying to convince parents that their sons would benefit greatly from a taste of his rod. As Peredonov's alcoholic delusions get worse, he imagines his wife's cookbook is a text of black magic, that his hairdresser has conspired with his enemies to prevent him from getting a Spanish hairdo (never mind that he's near bald), and that his friends turn into animals to spy on him. Constantly he ponders how to get a certain princess to help him with a promotion:

> *Peredonov began to suspect that what the princess wanted was for him to love her. She was repulsive to him, a decrepit woman. "After all, she's a hundred and fifty," he thought spitefully. "She may be old," he thought, "but what a powerful woman she is for all that." And revulsion became intermingled with fascination. Peredonov imagined that she would be barely lukewarm and would smell like a corpse, and he almost fainted from a savage lust. (229)*

Pushing Gogol's fantastic realism to its breaking point, Sologub moves the plot from Perdonov's promotion quest to arson and murder via one of the most uproarious scandal scenes in world literature: the masquerade ball that the young boy Sasha attends as a beautiful geisha:

> *Sasha, intoxicated with his new situation, became the complete coquette....The geisha would curtsey, raise*

*her delicate little fingers, titter in a suppressed voice,*
*wave her fan, tap one man or the other on the shoulder*
*and then hide behind her fan. Every minute she was*
*opening and closing her pink umbrella. They might*
*not have been clever devices but were sufficient for*
*seducing all. (255-256)*

All but the women, that is. As the party goes on, it degenerates into a
drunken orgy. When Sasha wins first place in the women's costume con-
text, he's attacked by a horde of jealous women.

The electrifying relationship between the androgynous Sasha and
the middle-aged nymphomaniac Lyudmila was so shocking for its time
that 15% of the text was censored (these sections are restored in the
1983 Ardis edition). Even so, Sologub lost his teaching job because of it.
Here, for instance, Sasha's older lover undresses him:

*"Think you'll melt, silly boy, if you sit a while with*
*bare shoulders?" Lyudmila said in a plaintive voice.*
*"You're afraid you'll get sunburnt or your beauty and*
*innocence tarnished?"*
*"But why are you doing it?" Sasha asked with a*
*shameful grimace.*
*"Why?" Lyudmila said passionately. "I love beauty.*
*I'm a pagan, a sinner. I ought to have been born in*
*ancient Greece....They say there's a soul. I don't know,*
*I've never seen it. And what do I need it for? Let me*
*die completely. I'll melt like a cloud beneath the sun. I*
*love the body, strong, dexterous, naked, which is able*
*to take its own pleasure."*

• • • •

*Sasha sighed, lowered his eyes, blushed and awk-*
*wardly removed his blouse. Lyudmila seized him with*
*burning hands and showered kisses over his shoul-*
*ders that were convulsed with shame.*

*"See how submissive I am!" Sasha said, smiling with an effort so that he could banish his embarrassment with a jest.*

• • • •

*Meanwhile Darya and Valeriya were standing behind the door, pushing each other, and taking turns looking through the key-hole and almost fainting from passionate and searing excitement.*

I especially like the voyeuristic porn touch at the end.

Despite, or perhaps because of, its scandalous content, *The Petty Demon* became a Russian best seller. Sologub's next effort, *The Created Legend*, provoked critics even more. Here, the hero Trirodov communes with spirits from beyond, raises dead children from freshly dug graves, reduces enemies to glass prisms and, besides aiding various revolutionary organizations, runs an avant garde school wherein both teachers and students run naked.

Gorky went into a frenzy. In his 1934 address to the Russian Writer's Congress, he singled out Sologub for the deviation of foregrounding "eros in politics." Earlier he tried to destroy the magazine that serialized the novel. He wrote Lunacharsky:

*You know that rotten, bald-headed bastard Sologub? In (his) novel you find his hero, an indubitable sadist, and a certain woman who is a social democrat and a propagandist. She comes to him, strips naked, and after suggesting first that he photograph her, she gives herself to the beast like a chunk of cold meat.*

One might wonder why the Russian Communist Party, noted for its puritainism after Stalin's coup in 1929, let Sologub's work stay in print at all (the Symbolist author himself died in 1927). The supposed mark of Sologub's satire was, of course, the Czarist regime but the same bureaucratic pettiness flourished under Stalin. Gorky was right to be alarmed.

Sologub may not have been openly homosexual but if heterosexuals can claim Whitman and O'Hara for their tradition I see no reason why we can't claim Sologub for ours. *The Petty Demon* was pioneering in many respects. It's one of the first novels I know of to focus on the connection of sex and power, sadomasocism and eroticism, androgyny and revolutionary change. In its Rabelaisian exaggerations, its gender reversals, its gothic supernaturalisms and its frank, kinky depiction of sex, it remains modern in a way Tolstoy, Turgenev and Wilde are not. Finally, it's one of the weirdest, funniest novels I've ever read, not to be matched until we come to the work of Witold Gombrowicz and Jean Genet some forty years later.

Dennis Cooper, outrageous from the start. "We're young punks just like you," he proclaimed beneath a police-type mug shot in his first *Little Ceasar* mag, published in 1976. "We want to be big as *Time,* and type towards that," he wrote in the second. Rimbaud, Keith Richards, and a frontal nude shot of Iggy Pop graced later covers. Inside, poems by Robert Bly, Lou Reed, and Allen Ginsberg rubbed crotches with essays on porn and rock. Dennis Cooper was hot but would he last?

Some thought Cooper would burn out on schoolboy crush poetry. John Kennedy Jr., David Cassidy—how much idol worship could we take? But I saw something deeper in Cooper's obsessive romanticism. When he took the leap to romanticism's flip side, daring to enter the mind of a John Gacy-type boy-killer in "The Tenderness of Wolves," I knew Dennis Cooper was just getting started. But where would he go?

The mark of an author's greatness, as Michel Foucault observed, has to do with the scope and depth of his influence. Not only did Cooper galvanize an exciting scene of younger poets in LA (David Trinidad, Bob Flanagan, Amy Gerstler, Peter Cashorali, Jack Skelley, etc.), he also touched base with some of the best new poets in Chicago (Elaine Equi), Washington DC (Diane Ward, Bernard Welt), NYC (Eileen Myles, Brad Gooch, Tim Dlugos), and San Francisco (Steve Benson, Bob Gluck, Bruce Boone, Kevin Killian, etc.). A whole New Narrative movement was taking shape and Dennis Cooper, among others, was in the forefront.

Then rumors started. Was Cooper as messed up on drugs as some of the characters in his writing? "People actually come up after readings and ask me questions like that," Dennis told me on his last visit here two years ago. He seemed perplexed that people would still confuse the author with his creation. Did Shakespeare live like Lear or Macbeth?

But Cooper's life did take some interesting twists. Before he left LA to work on the St. Mark's Poetry Project in NYC, an LA punk paper played up his spectacular public marraige to a guy in LA. Then he dropped his writing career in NYC to live with a guy in Amsterdam (where he's still living). Despite emotional ups and downs, Cooper kept writing. And his writing kept getting better. The noted art critic/poet Peter Schjeldahl wrote, in a rave *Village Voice* review, that Cooper's nouvella *Safe* spoke for the youth of the 80s as Ginsberg's *Howl* did for the 50s. This is all the more remarkable considering that Schjeldahl is heterosexual.

Not all straights have been so sympathetic. Tom Clark and Ed Dorn have waged a homophobic slur campaign against Cooper far uglier than anything Truman Capote, Tennessee Williams, or David Leavitt had to endure. Why? Cooper's gay characters are not polite, apologetic, or guilt-ridden. Leavitt distances his fiction with a haze of sentimentality, Cooper dishes out gay life brash and raw. If Leavitt's like a page torn out of *Dynasty*, Cooper's more a mixture of *Miami Vice*, the old *Saturday Night Live*, and *Printer's Devils*. Here, for instance, is a snatch of Leavitt's romanticism from *The Lost Language of Cranes*:

> *Sometimes, at night, Eliot really was the boy of his dreams. Together they rode a train through lush Alpine hills, past villages as tiny and perfect as those in Advent calendars. There was a smell of ginger in the cold air, a tinkling of chimes. Philip could feel the chugging of the train as it rolled along toward Zurich, toward Venice. (198)*

And when Leavitt gets really steamy:

> *"Oh baby," he said. Soon his hand was kneading Philip's groin. "Yeah," he said, extracting a tube of K-Y jelly from his jacket, and unzipped Philip's fly. He began to jerk Philip off with one hand and himself with the other, using the K-Y jelly as lubricant. Philip came all over his sweater; the man, more wisely, on the floor; on the screen, the young army private came while being strip-searched by his corporal. (199)*

Philip probably gets his sweaters at Bucks and hangs them neatly in a closet with an Advent calendar on the door (he probably belongs to Dignity as well). Here, by contrast, is Cooper's *Safe:*

> *The man has his face in Mark's ass. It smells like a typical one, but belongs to a boy who's a knock-out, so it's symbolic. It's sort of like planting a flag where no human has been. Well, maybe a few old explorers. It's sort of like putting on make-up in front of a small, fogged up mirror. It's an expression of caring. (54)*

Notice how Cooper cynically comments on the triteness of romanticism while, by the deft addition of a wholly unexpected metaphor, he renews it to still greater force. Now that's 80s. And here's how Cooper trumps Leavitt's Alpine imagery, revealing the ideological underpinnings (and the resultant clash) of both High Art and Low:

> *The man screws his eyes up. Mark's anus is wrinkled, pink and simplistically rendered, but nice. All that licking has plastered its hairs to their homeland, smooth as a snow-covered countryside seen from a distance, at sunset. Closer the ass has pores much like anywhere else, only more refined.*
> *On TV some cowboy is shouting, "Arriba!" It sounds like "I need you" to Mark and he smirks for a second. It sounds like "amoebas" to the man rimming. He's risking them, so he can find out what makes this boy happy. (55)*

Frankly, I can't understand all the hoopla about David Leavitt. It's said he's "empathetic," but only if your coordinates are those of the narrowest yuppie. And the contrast in dialogue! I don't know anyone who talks like a Leavitt character but I've met a whole range of people who talk like Cooper's. Indeed, Cooper can squeeze more social commentary, more levels of meaning into one sentence than Leavitt can muster in a paragraph, as a comparrison of the openings of their two novels shows. Here's Leavitt:

> *Early on a rainy Sunday afternoon in November a man was hurrying down Third Avenue, past closed and barred florist shops and newsstands, his hands stuffed in his pockets and his head bent against the wind. The avenue was deserted except for an occasional cab, which parted the gray water puddled in potholes and sent it streaming. Behind the lighted windows of the apartment buildings people stretched, divided the Sunday Times, poured coffee into glazed mugs, but in the street it was a different scene: A bum covered by soggy shopping bags huddled in a closed storefront; a woman in a brown coat held a paper over her head and ran; a pair of cops whose walkie-talkies blared distorted voices listened to an old woman weep in front of a pink enamelled building. What, the man wondered, was he, a decent and respectable man, with a well-heated apartment, good books to read, a coffee maker, doing out among these people, out in the street on a cold Sunday morning?*

Well, I'm not to the end yet but I'll stop before you fall asleep. The point is this could have been written by any hack Creative Writing student. It has no "signature," no real authorial personality. And here, by contrast, is the openning of Dennis Cooper's *Safe:*

> *Mark had just opened a beer when he noticed an ad in the Advocate. It asked for someone like him to write a "beautiful, blond, twenty-eight year old lawyer with very specific ideas of love-making." He did, with a short, but exhaustingly rewritten note: "Dear Tony, if you're the hunk you claim, I'm in the mood for your body. Prove it to me." He clipped a photo booth*

*self-portrait onto the upper right corner. It hid what
he felt was his worst feature, shiftiness. The "Mark" he
dropped into the mailbox that evening had already got-
ten "his" shit together.*

Before Cooper, there was no American writing like this anywhere. Hopefully I've proved Cooper writes more succinctly, more beautifully, more originally, and with more wit than Leavitt. But what about his subject matter? What about all this drug use, s/m sex, this facination with hustlers and boy killing? That's not gay life, is it?

To be honest, I think we must admit that transgressive eroticism constitutes the very essence of gay life (or at least did before AIDS). Straight society gives a mixed message about sex: It's okay if domesticated or used to sell liquor, soap, and cars, but it's bad if enjoyed for its own sake or if linked to a passionate, spiritual quest. Church, state, and commerce have always viewed the ecstatic with suspicion because the ecstatic is transcendent. It's out of control. Since we, as gays, were defined as "bad" to start with, we jumped into the bad with both feet. What other options did we have? Either that or celibacy.

But we do have other options, one of which is art. I don't for a minute believe that Dennis Cooper (or Robert Glück, William Burroughs, or John Waters for that matter) would *literally* advocate the extreme behavior their characters indulge in. Quite the contrary. Instead it's the imaginative act of the art, or of love itself, that becomes the cathexis of transcendance. Or in the words of George Bataille, "With the death of religion, the novel becomes the bloody sacrifice." It's the same sort of sacrifice, I might add, that Catholics celebrate in their Mass.

This, then, is what makes the difference between serious writing (Dennis Cooper) and formulaic writing (David Leavitt). The former is socially disturbing but spiritually transformative; the latter is socially reassuring but spiritually dead. With this in mind, it's no wonder that *The New Yorker* prefers David Leavitt over Dennis Cooper. Happily, their conclusions needn't be ours.

# REDEFINING REDON

Odilon Redon, a sick child, was born in 1840 and raised by an aged uncle in a haunted mansion in the isolated, swampy region of Medoc, France. One hundred and twenty-five years later I discovered his art as a closeted freshman at the University of Nebraska. Redon's impact on me—both his "black drawings" and colorful, floral still lifes—rocked me more powerfully than did my first LSD trips.

What I loved about Redon then I still love—his ghostly androgynous profiles, the dark phantasmagoria of his lithographs, the brilliant yet eerie color juxtapositions of his flowers, which seem to breathe with an inner life of their own. Everything the 19th Century tried to repress bursts forth with a vengeance in Redon, unleashing an erotic spirituality. But now, viewing the Woodner Collection of Redon at the Berkeley University Art Museum, I see even more.

First, with the exception of some tree drawings, it's more apparent to me than ever that Redon simply can't draw. His copies of earlier masters are pedestrian and his earliest original figures (e.g. "Woman with Outstretched Arm," 1860-70) are even more stiff and awkward than William Blake's, which they resemble, hemmed into geometric patterns as they are. Yet this defect becomes the key to Redon's genius and originality.

"Art does not render the visible but makes visible," as Paul Klee later wrote in his diary. But how can one draw what's beyond form? Anatomical exactitude eluded Redon throughout his career. His figures forever melt, evaporate or blur into a yearning formlessness. But perhaps it's the Egyptian, Greek and Renaissance draftsmen who were wrong. Animal and plant bodies do not stop at the limits of their shape or skin. We breathe in, breathe out. We perpetually mutate, not only physically but emotionally and spiritually, in a lifelong rhythm of expansion and contraction. Moreover, in this mutating dance, we continually merge and interact with all the organic and inorganic life forms that surround us.

Leonardo Da Vinci hinted at this insight but Redon alone gives witness to its dual or paradoxical nature: ecstasy and death, transgression and transcendence are inextricably linked. The marriage of heaven and hell Blake aspired to, Redon achieves. For form must fall into formlessness if it is to re-emerge transformed as a phoenix on it funeral pyre.

Redon's "Ophelia" pastel (1905-10) is especially telling in this respect. As Hamlet's girlfriend sinks into her watery death, flowers burst forth from her breast. A preternatural bright blue (water or sky?) forms a crescent halo around her limply arched torso. Blue then bleeds into a pale, formless, mottled pinkish-gray at the top of the drawing. The whole creates a kind of gnostic cosmology.

Redon's earliest champions were the symbolists Mallarme and Huysmans who opposed the realism of Zola. They loved the velvety blacks of his charcoals and lithographs, the "morbid genius," as Huysmans put it, of his shadowy anthropomorphic creatures. Redon himself observed (as if a prophet of today's New Wave fashion): "Black should be respected. Nothing prostitutes it. It does not please the eye and does not awaken sensuality. It is the agent of the spirit much more than the splendid color of the palette or the prism."

In this phase of his work, Redon illustrated texts by Poe, Baudelaire, Bulwer-Lytton and the Belgian satanist poet Iwan Gilkin. Don Larson's weird "Far Side" cartoons might be said to echo the Redon of this period.

But then Redon suddenly embraces color in a turnabout as astonishing as Van Gogh's when the latter entered a mental hospital. And the colors of both artists are brighter than life as if in protest against the impoverishment of daily life under Industrial Capitalism.

Whereas Van Gogh encased every object in heavy outlines, Redon's objects, figures and flowers merge into their surroundings. The gold cloak of "The Druidess" (1910), for instance, hovers about the figure like a shimmering mist, while the back of her head melts into a rich purple twilight. As in Giorgioni's paintings, the time of day is as indeterminate and mysterious as the subject's expression. Redon's figures and flowers alike give off a last gasp of luminous light (an aura all the more haunting and orgasmic for its finality) like that of the departing soul of someone just deceased.

Yet when so much of life is stuck in the rut of class, category and commodification, Redon's indeterminacy can also be seen to function as a herald of radical social change. The blurring of boundaries, which seemed so eccentric and marginal in Redon's day, has since become a central feature of all postmodernism.

Indeed, we can see echoes of Redon today in the most unlikely places, such as in Robert Frank's realist photos, also on display in the Berkeley museum. Frank's gritty Welsh miners, for instance, look oddly mystical with the smoldering white highlights on their blackened faces. A 1952 photo of London mimics Redon's "black drawings" while "Mary, Provincetown" (1958) has the same profile and water above Mary's head as does Redon's "Ophelia." Finally, Frank's 1958 bus series, shot from moving buses in NYC, blurs boundaries much as Redon did in his paintings. I'm not suggesting that Frank was consciously influenced by Redon: only that the coincidental juxtaposition of these two shows reveals how pervasive Redon's "mad and morbid" vision has become.

Finally, a note of interest for gay viewers. Although Redon wasn't overtly homosexual, as far as I know, many of his symbolic motifs (e.g. butterflies, unicorns, snakes, spiders, etc.) have long emblemized gayness. Even his favorite colors (greens, purples, violets, magentas, pinks, etc.) have often functioned as secret codes of our sexual identity. Sheer coincidence? Perhaps. But just as Redon was drawing and painting figures of mutating gender and species, German doctors were coining the term "homosexual."

# ABOUT FACE

An artist I know arrived at a party wearing a t-shirt emblazoned with Jack Kerouac's face. Whereas the young Kerouac's face was idealized in rapt attention, my friend's face looked heavy, weary, dull. This set me thinking.

Moving up the evolutionary ladder, nature puts increased emphasis on the face. Protoplasms don't have them. Fish have mouths and eyes, but their faces are rudimentary—not yet separated from the body by a neck. Bird and reptile heads sit on necks, but their faces show no expression. A cat or dog, however, catching the master's gaze, may look away as if in guilt. Dog lovers argue that their pets respond more expressively than cats, but neither cats nor dogs match the grimaces monkeys make. "Monkey face" is a fond nickname parents often give to their children.

But if the expressive visage is a sign of upward mobility, why do adult faces show less life than children's? Or why are faces of wealthy urban dwellers frozen in contrast to the rural poor? Even city youth affect mask-like gazes. Death-rockers wear expressionless pancake white, while punks sport a makeup of the lurid wound.

The face is the most intimate sign of human identity. "I'd recognize that face anywhere," says the lover. Or a cop: "Here, look through these mug shots." It's as if we were reading a map. We are, for the face is also a primal landscape. No wonder "face" and "place" rhyme. After blindly groping for mom's breast, her face is the first territory infants recognize and reach toward—not only a memory but a complex, unconscious machine hooked into the present. It constitutes not only a primal site of desire; it generates potentiality. For the rest of our lives we will yearn for a face not merely human, but divine.

But in the face of cataclysmic social crisis, the face itself becomes a site of crisis, an ideological battleground. The recent movie *Brazil* illustrates this. While every social institution crumbles around Kathrine Hellman, the hero's mom, she wants only to have her face yanked, stretched and lifted until it resembles a starlet's.

We can see this struggle even more clearly in the history of Western painting. Giotto moved the face from icon to image. Although still a pious Christian, he freed the face from the cold, universal abstractions of church dogma and illumined it with the more rounded individuation of emerging national and mercantile interests.

Today the face is again problematical. Picasso and the Cubists deconstruct it; Francis Bacon and Ralph Steadman explode it; Andy Warhol duplicates it in a series of endless images reflecting almost no depth or external reality. As the value of human uniqueness erodes, the face becomes either pure spectacle or an empty gaping wound.

This power struggle is echoed in the language of daily life; chin up, face off, about face, follow your nose, face the music, face down your opponents (but up to your responsibilities), save face. And lastly, as Chinese say, don't lose face. But we have. And manipulating our craving for what we've lost, advertising moves into the void. The face becomes the new marketplace, the port of entry for interior colonization. The "faceless-crowd" is barraged with faces on billboards, posters, TV and movies, magazines and record covers and, finally, on t-shirts.

I recall a billboard at the corner of Divisadero and Haight a few years back. "A pretty face isn't safe in this town," read the caption under a woman's attractive face. Sure enough, the billboard was soon defaced. And why do punks purposely damage their faces with crude tattoos, pierce their ears and noses, shave their bleach-tortured hair in asymmetric patterns? Ritual sacrifice? Or do they seek safety by making their face commercially useless. (Think of the faces in Giotto's day smeared with soot during Lent).

But because even the most beautiful face is still limited, even the most vapid face still unique, advertising has moved further. The most popular "talking head" in 1986 was not Dan Rather or David Byrne but Max Headroom—a computer face designed to sell Coke. By 1988 he had mutated into Ronald Reagan in the *Doonesbury* comic strip.

Mutating faces—which brings me back to my friend and his Kerouac t-shirt. Kerouac's face is shown turning to profile, the idealized lines of its features were like the outline of a key. What matters is not its unique characteristics, but the effectiveness with which it unlocks a code: writer = glamour = power. Kerouac's face signifies what my friend wants but feels he can never have. He can only wear Kerouac's face on his shirt like the coat-of-arms of a dying aristocracy.

But this t-shirt face is also a shimmering nexus of possibility. Kerouac's head turns. His face is torn between two positions. In this gesture the code can be read writer = spontaneity = freedom, or writer = warrior = a call to arms. What the code heralds cannot yet be deciphered. Like Christ's face on the Shroud of Turin, the messages of the human face are so subtle and fluid that even our defeats offer signs of hope.

# BOB KAUFMAN: HIDDEN MASTER OF THE BEATS

I was visiting a North Beach friend one cold February night in 1975 when she suggested we go around the corner to the Coffee Gallery to listen to music. The club seemed full of basket cases and I wasn't surprised when a thin ragged Black man wandered in, took a swig from a bottle, and jumped up on stage spouting some haunting words that were barely audible to most of the audience. The MC, an attractive blond wearing a medieval pageboy costume, then took the microphone. "That was Bob Kaufman, founder and greatest poet of the Beats."

Kaufman! The Beat movement was founded in his blood and vision while others got the fame and money (when San Francisco columnist Herb Caen coined the term "beatnik" by writing of a "beatnik screaming Sputnik, Sputnik!" it was Kaufman he was writing about). I dimly recall reading Kaufman's "Abominist Manifesto" in the first City Lights *Journal For The Protection Of All Beings* in the early '60s. Although Kaufman's work has now been anthologized some 70 times, he was excluded from some of the most important: Don Allen's *New American Poetry*, Seymour Krim's *The Beats*, and LeRoi Jones' *Black Fire*. Why?

"They all knew Bob," Eileen Kaufman told me, "but they didn't take him seriously as a writer. That's probably why he was left out of the Gallery Six reading too." Raymond Foye, who, along with SF poets Neeli Cherkovski and Kush, has been pushing to get wider American recognition of Kaufman's work, had another viewpoint. "Ginsberg's extremely uncomfortable around Bob, even now," Foye told me. "He thinks Bob's work is confused. He's embarrassed by him. I think Ginsberg and his contemporaries are somewhat jealous of Bob's uncompromising commitment to lyricism whereas their own work has become increasingly pragmatic and safe."

One of the few well-known writers who's been upfront about Bob's great influence is Ken Kesey. Kesey called Kaufman "the first far-out person I ever saw" and on March 16th, 1976, gave this testimonial to Tony Seymour:

> *We headed up Grant Street. It was a Sunday after-*
> *noon just when the whole beatnik thing was hitting*

200

*and a lot of tourists were driving through to look it over. The cars are moving very slow, warm sunny day and the windows were open. All of a sudden, down the road, here comes this guy! He was Black but he wasn't quite a Negro. He was loud but he wasn't quite offensive. And he had these crosses of tiny white bandaids all over his face in a pattern to make them look a little like Crosses on a leatherbound Bible. He was going down the road (& I realize years later, probably wired as hell) and spouting poetry into the window of each car according to the car and the occupants. He came by our windows and ran off some stuff. I can't remember what he said, all I can remember was the effect. I knew this guy was talking the truth straight off the top of his head about us and he wasn't being insulting because nobody took it amiss. Everyone was greatly shocked. Later I came to know this was Bob Kaufman and I'd see him hanging around the Bagel Shop with (his son) Parker and a little clarinet case. I didn't really appreciate him as a poet until much more recently, within the last four of five years. In rereading his stuff I could trace back and see how— "Yeah, yeah! That's where Ginsberg got that riff, here's where Kerouac picked up that thing, and that's where Cassady picked up..."*

Like many, I too came to Bob Kaufman the legend, the personality, before I finally came to Bob Kaufman the writer to be studied on the page. I was struck by the work's incredible power, music and originality, especially when I read it aloud. Unlike so much of American surrealism, a personal urgency drives each word forward. What reveals itself is a voice; each image nailed to the cross of personal experience. For instance, in the poem "Unhistorical Events" when the poet says: "Apollinaire / never slept all night in an icehouse / waiting for Sebastian to rise from the ammonia tanks / and show him the little unpainted arrows," Kaufman's referring to a time a white lynch mob hung him by his thumbs all night in an icehouse when he was just thirteen. Or in the poem "Early Lovers," when he writes: "Dying love, hidden in misty bayous / Red love, turning black, brown / Dead in the belly, brittle womb / Of some laughing crab / A father. Whose, mine? / Floating on seaweed rugs / To that pearl tomb, shining / Beneath my bayou's floor," he is speaking of his father who drowned when he was nine years old.

More than most American writers, Bob Kaufman reflects the "gumbo of multi-culturality" Ishmael Reed speaks about. Born of a German Jewish father and a Native American Martinique Black Roman Catholic mother in New Orleans, April 18th, 1925, Kaufman grew up speaking Cajun as well as English. His maternal grandmother, who'd come to America on a slave ship from Africa, used to take him on long morning walks. These early experiences and influences constantly appear in this work, informing it with a deep empathy for minority cultures, as well as with a wider range of voice than is evident in most American poetry.

At the age of 13, Kaufman shipped out as a cabin boy and was befriended by a first mate who introduced him to the Classics: Shakespeare, Melville, T.S. Eliot, Hart Crane, and Lorca. Much of this work Bob memorized and even recently he astonished strangers in North Beach bars and restaurants by reciting long works by these and other authors from memory. Kaufman went on to become active in the Seafarer's Union and sailed around the world nine times. He's remembered by fellow shipmates not as a poet, but as a man who was fearless, who always undertook the most dangerous jobs, such as tying down loose rigging in the midst of a storm. Foye, who has interviewed several of Bob's old shipmates, says he's also remembered as a man who was extraordinarily kind and quick-witted, as well as politically active. Many of the crazy names in Kaufman's work, such as Riftraft Rolf and Rotgut Charlie, refer to these shipmate heroes of his youth. Because he was an active Communist labor organizer, Kaufman was debarred from shipping out during the McCarthy Era.

After WWII, Kaufman began taking classes at the New School for Social Research, in New York City. He studied Sociology and Communist Labor practices, and went on dangerous forays into the South, organizing

Black mine workers. More than once he was brutally beaten by police. Eileen Kaufman, his wife, first met him in May of 1958, just after he'd returned from Austin, Texas where he'd been arrested for vagrancy and kicked in the stomach all night by police. "Bob could hardly eat anything for six months," Eileen Kaufman says. Bob moved to San Francisco in 1954, having heard of the poetry scene there while working as Second Caterer at the Beverly Hills Hotel in LA. Although he was making good money, he walked up to his boss one day and said: "I'm quitting. I want to be a poet again." Kaufman never did anything halfway. He drove out of LA in his new Buick but abandoned it on the road when it developed a minor malfunction. He then decided to live in Big Sur.

The late 1950's were a time of tremendous creative energy in San Francisco, as well as the time of Bob Kaufman's own greatest poetic output. Jazz clubs flourished. Lenny Bruce, Mort Sahl, and Phyllis Diller appeared at The hungry i, Diller often reciting poetry herself. On Blabbermouth Night, Jack Spicer, John Wieners, Jack Kerouac, and Kaufman held court at The Place. But the Co-Existence Bagel Shop was Kaufman's special turf. The police hated the Beats and tried to pin every neighborhood crime on them. They singled out Kaufman for their special wrath since, in addition to being a self-proclaimed Beat, he was also an uppity Black living with a white woman. In the space of one and a half years, Kaufman was arrested 35 times. Bob Kaufman Defense cans were an omnipresent item at all Beat hangouts.

Kaufman was dauntless in his own satirical counter attacks. In response to the gawking tourists flocking into North Beach, he chartered a Greyline Bus "Tour of Bourgeois Wastelands," exchanged bagels with David's Delicatessen on Union Square, and read poetry from a megaphone in front of the St. Francis Hotel. The Beats won national media attention largely because of Kaufman's constant street theater. In May of 1959, Kaufman, along with Bill Margolis, Allen Ginsberg, and John Kelly, started *Beatitude* magazine, where many of the famous Beat poets first appeared.

For a while, the Kaufmans lived on Harwood Alley across from the Shooting Gallery, a junkie hangout where, for a few bucks, you could stick your arm through a hole in the door for a quick fix. In October, the night before Eileen gave birth to their son Parker, Margolis went into a frenzy, throwing all his belongings out the upper story window, finally jumping out himself, which paralyzed him for life. Kaufman writes of this in "Harwood Alley Song" and "Sullen Bakeries of Total Recall" ("A Wounded Margolis in his suit of horror, his eyes of elevated Brownsville, that taste of gas in his smile, I could hear him when my ears were Mexican weed"). Having no money to pay the doctor, Kirby and Lawrence Ferlinghetti helped distract the head nurse at St. Mary's Hospital so the Kaufmans could get their son.

In the spring of 1960, Kaufman was nominated for the prestigious Guiness Poetry Award. Harvard University sent Kaufman a round trip plane ticket so he could come to read. After kicking in all the windows at the bagel shop, Kaufman flew to NYC two weeks before he was to go to Boston for the big event. Tragically, in a misguided attempt to kick his alcohol habit, Kaufman got hooked on speed and the reading was postponed. He stayed in NYC however, reading and singing at the Gaslight and other East Village clubs. One of his songs, "Okay Dokey Soda Cracker / Does Your Mamma Chaw Tobacco" was picked up and recorded by Chubby Checker. The New Christy Minstrels recorded another one of his songs: "Green, Green Rocky Road." Kaufman also met and shared a stage with Bob Dylan at the Gaslight during this time. That Dylan was much influenced by such Kaufman work as "Dear John" and "Does the Secret Mind Whisper" is evident in the new turn his own lyrics took and in his novel *Tarantula*.

During this time, Kaufman was hanging out a lot with Kerouac, Ginsberg, and Timothy Leary. On March 11th, 1976, Ginsberg recalled one episode to Tony Seymour:

> *I remember being upset that Bob was there. I didn't know him so well then...his surreal style poetry, yes, much appreciated by Simon Watson Taylor, translator of Jarry and other pataphysicians...Bob and I and Peter were seated on a bed in the middle of the room...Bob looks at me anguished, tender, trusting, honest, tears in his eyes. "I love you" and puts his arms around me,*

*holds me close. I'm amazed. Then I thought I heard him*
*say "I'm depending on you. You're a soul captain, show*
*the way—courage. Where's the way? I'm lost. You know*
*the road. I'm trusting you." Well, that couldn't have been*
*what he said but that was the message I thought I got.*
*And he kissed me. And I felt like a fink 'cause I hadn't*
*known who he was. What an Innocent! An Innocent!*

In the spring of 1963, Kaufman was to return to SF with Eileen and Parker. Although she deeply loved him, her devotion had been sorely tried: rent money squandered, appointments missed, the time he and friends had spray-painted absolutely everything in their apartment, including the typewriter with a half finished poem still in it. When Bob didn't show up for their ride home, Eileen returned to SF without him. What she didn't know was that he'd been arrested for walking on the grass at Washington Square Park. He was taken to the Tombs and then to Rikers Island. Doctors termed him a behavior problem and began giving him forced shock treatment. He was not released and allowed to return to SF until October whereupon he gave Eileen, oblivious to what he'd been through, the following poem:

BLOOD FELL ON THE MOUNTAINS
BLUENESS, THE COLOR OF LOVE, BLUE
SLANTED TO A CRACKLING AND BLUE
COLOR, THE COLOR OF COLORS AS SWEET
BLUE
NOCTURNES OF THE VOID
SOLITUDES FILLED WITH LONELINESS,
BLACK RAIN,
TWISTED HAIL, WOUNDED SNOW.
THE MOUNTAINS CRIED DRY, TEAR OF
STONE AMONG
THE TALL TREES
THE SLEEPWALKER WALKED THE BRIDGE
OF EYES

AMIDST COLORS OF THE DAY.
IN THE LEFT HAND IS THE DREAMER
THE BALLAD AT THE SOURCE
THE SINGER AND THE SONG,
POEM FOR EILEEN ON MY
RETURN HOME.

I AM A LOVER
BOB
ME TO YOU

But tragedy for the Kaufmans wasn't over. When John Kennedy was assassinated, Bob took it especially hard, as he'd once met Kennedy and greatly admired him. "When a President gets shot, it's gone too far," he said. Walking home up Grant Avenue, he knelt down every two or three steps. Great visions of devastation came upon him. For the first time he insisted that Eileen and Parker go to Peter and Paul's Church with him. The weekend after, they saw Oswald gunned down on TV. It was then that Bob took his famous vow of silence. Except for a rare greeting, he neither spoke nor wrote for the next ten years. Raymond Foye believes the germ for this was sown when Kaufman met Peter Orlovsky's catatonic brother Lafcadio. "Lafcadio can speak but doesn't want to," he often had mused. An emphasis on silence was also prominent in his poetry. Unable to live with this silence, Eileen moved out with Parker. Bob slept in parks and sleazy hotels. Old friends thought he'd gone crazy.

His first book, *Solitudes Crowded With Loneliness,* was published by New Directions, in 1965. Eileen had sent them the manuscript from Mexico the year previous. It included his favorite poem, "Would You Wear My Eyes," as well as "The Abominist Manifesto", and the amazing prose poem "Second April" which is centered in the Whitmanesque vision that "We are each other's members." The poem begins:

> *O man in inner basement core of me, maroon obliter-*
> *ation smelling futures of green anticipated, comings,*
> *pasts denied, now time to thwart time, time to frieze*

> *illusionary motion on far imagined walls, stopped*
> *bleeding moondial clocks, booming out dead hours—*
> *gone...gone...gone...gone on to second April*

The poem continues to build energy with eerie, intricate patterns in which the word "thing" gongs with increasing background force as a symbolic motif of both death and resurrection:

> *Session zero in, is diluted, they watch, diluted that's*
> *a thing, we have not now or ever been a member of*
> *diluted, the spoon is a cop, the door is closed, I hope*
> *Rimbaud bleeds all over my stolen pants, pants, that's*
> *a thing, they watch...*

> *Session ten... burning burns on burned hand, that's*
> *a thing a thing, down to ten thousand wounds...they*
> *watch, we swap watches, we chew time, they chew us,*
> *chewing, that's a thing, a new thing, chewing, every-*
> *body chew somebody; everybody chew a dog, cats*
> *exempt, numbers too...they watch, a dusty window,*
> *hell my eyes, bell my tongue, we are attacking our*
> *hair, it waves to neighbors in skies, kinky relatives,*
> *wrapped in comets, a thing, comets...*

Kaufman recited his poems aloud for years, variously altering them before writing them down. Even when he wrote poems down he frequently lost them, so that much of what we have of his work is due to the vigilance of others. If "Second April" alone were better known, Kaufman would perhaps have the recognition he deserves as one of America's most original poets.

In 1967, City Lights published a second Kaufman book, *Golden Sardine*. The jewel of this book is the long prose poem tribute to Caryl Chessman. Perhaps because of Kaufman's silence, and the fact that he did not take a careerist stance, his books went largely unreviewed. Only in France, thanks to the efforts of Kaufman's French translator Claude

Pilieu, was Kaufman's work acclaimed. Features and reviews appeared in leading French journals such as *L'Express, La Quinzaine, Jeune Afrique, Jazz,* and elsewhere. France hailed Kaufman as an American Rimbaud. Even today his name is known to shopkeepers as well as French literati. But in America, outside of the Black community, he continued to be ignored.

Meanwhile, another tragedy struck the Kaufmans. While in Europe, Eileen had left Parker with friends to go overland to the East. They became separated, and for two years she didn't know where her son was. Finally he was located, trapped in the winter snows of the Khyber Pass in the middle of the Pakistani-Indian War. NET'S Soul Series was planning a 90-minute program: "Coming From Bob Kaufman, Poet." With money Eileen received from some old photographs she allowed the NET to use, she was able to bring Parker, now aged 13, home on March 31st, 1972. The family reunion was emotional and occurred April 1st, the day of the NET broadcast of Bob. Surrounded by friends and a son he had not seen in so long, Kaufman finally spoke his first words.

Not until the Vietnam War ended, however, did Kaufman completely end his vow of silence. "We were on our way to see Miriam Patchen," Eileen recalled. "Kenneth had just died and out of respect for Miriam's grief, Bob was silent during the visit. Afterwards, we went to a friend's photo exhibit in Palo Alto. We were listening to this beautiful harp music. I remember, when Bob stood up and started reciting poetry":

> *All those ships that never sailed*
> *Today I bring them home and let them sail forever*
> *All the flowers that never grew*
> *Today I bring them home and let them grow forever*

Shortly afterwards, a big reading was held at Malvinas' where Bob was honored. It was his first real reading in 11 years.

Bob Kaufman never sought fame and has often said he'd prefer to be anonymous, a simple member of society, a man among friends. He's always preferred the company of working people, musicians, painters, and filmmakers, to the self-serious stuffiness of any literary establishment. In 1973 he started writing again, and New Directions published *The Ancient Rain* in the spring of 1981. This book, with its brilliant, long title-poem was widely and favorably reviewed, and Bob won a NEA grant that same year.

After a long illness, Bob died on January 12th, 1986 at the age of sixty-one. Hundreds attended a January 17th memorial at San Francisco's Sacred Heart Church. Dwarfed by a huge baroque alter, which featured trumpeting angels and a painting of Christ Resurrected, Lawrence Ferlinghetti read a message from Allen Ginsberg ("We're blessed by the ghost of Bob Kaufman who's spirit exists ever breathing in the earth"), as well as a poem of Eugene Ruggles and Bob's: "I am a Camera." Michael McClure read a short Shelley poem. The priest quoted Bob's poems in his sermon, and Bob's brother George read a message from Ozzie Davis.

Looking up at the ceiling I saw a painting of the angel staying Abraham's hand as he was about to sacrifice Isaac. Isaac means "laughter." I was reminded of Bob's "Small Memorium For Myself":

> *Beyond the reach of scorn, lust is freed of its vulgar face*
> *No more blanch of terror at reality's threat of sadness*
> *No blend of grief can cause the death of laughter now.*
> *In remembrance of certain lights I have seen go out*
> *I have visualized pathetic rituals and noisy requiems*
> *Composed of metaphysical designs of want and care*

Instead of the usual church organ or choir, a jazz trio played.

As poets, artists, musicians, friends, and family poured from the church for a party at Le Mirage bar, Jack Micheline gave a stirring rendition of "All Those Ships That Never Sailed" on the church steps. Other poets followed. Friends mingled and conversed. Bob would have loved it.

From Baudelaire to Kaufman, the social role Western society has accorded serious poets and artists is that of visionary outcasts. The Beats were the last American literary movement to accept this sacrificial role. More recent movements—feminist, language-centered and New Narrative—have redefined the writer's function. Avant-garde writers today are more apt to work in dialogue with a particular non-literary community and to help strengthen alternative communities, while critiquing language systems that preserve existing power structures.

This doesn't deny the Beats' major contributions. The Beats, as well as the Black Mountain, and Spicer circle, freed poetry from the bourgeois social and literary forms of academia. They recharged poetry with a sense of the sacred and regrounded it in the actual human body. They began a critique of capitalism, sexism, racism, and homophobia that still continues. This is the context, not in the context of his personal legend, that Bob Kaufman's poetry can best be appreciated.

# THERE GOES THE NEIGHBORHOOD

Riding the bus down Haight Street one afternoon I see graffiti sprayed on the side of a building. "Eddie's neighborhood's moving." A vision flashes through my mind—seven Victorians and a corner grocery tiptoeing down the street. Is that a baby outhouse running to catch up? Then the darkside to this Disneyesque joke. If I was Rip Van Winkle and fell asleep on this bus in 1976, and I just woke up today, the only store I'd recognize would be Uganda Liquors.

The graffiti, which at first seems metaphorically outlandish, turns out to be literally true. The Italian neighborhood of North Beach is turning Chinese while the inner Mission goes Beatnik. The Castro has changed from Irish working-class to gay to a mishmash of condos, chainstores and boutiques. The Haight looks increasingly like Union Street, which looks increasingly like Ghiradelli Square. And Ghiradelli Square looks like shopping malls and tourist traps everywhere.

San Francisco is becoming homogenized at a dizzying speed; each neighborhood with its own McDonald's, its own Round Table, its own Gap. Even Terminal Drugs, across from the Transbay Bus Terminal, has been terminated.

When I first came to the city, I changed apartments six times in five years. But the apartment building I've occupied since 1979 has changed owners five times. The first owner bought the building for $35,000; the current asking price is over $300,000. (One owner tried to evict me Christmas Eve, then sold a month later.) "Landlords are the worst capitalists," Karl Marx wrote, "because they speculate on what everyone else needs—a place to live." Lest I sound un-American let me add Walt Whitman railed against real-estate speculators too.

Nor are the poor the only ones to suffer. I know of someone who paid over $300,000 for a home with a view on Diamond Heights only to have his view blocked two years later. Those in the Marina are gouged by skyrocketing rents just as are those in the Western Addition. Whose quality of life, if anyone's, improves? Theaters and artist's lofts disappear one by one. Are we headed for a future as described by J.G. Ballard—one wherein we'll all be living in broom closets?

Bruce Boone, a writer whose keen insight and vast knowledge never fails to amaze me, tells of a supposedly true story he read in the memoirs of Saint Simon. In pre-revolutionary France, a certain Count was irritated by a peasant's cottage blocking his view. He tried to buy out the peasant to no avail. He threatened but the peasant wouldn't budge. So one day, while the peasant was working in the fields, the Count ordered his servants to move the peasant's hut.

The house was carried, stone by stone, some fifty yards back from the road. Every chair, every table, every pot and pan was put back exactly where it had been before only fifty yards away. When the peasant returned from work that night, he was exceedingly perplexed. And well he might be. He felt all around but his house wasn't there. When morning came he finally found it, exactly as he'd left it, only in its new location.

"Some sorcerer has done this," the peasant cried, and ran into town to tell the news.

But the townspeople, having been informed of the Count's mischief by the Count himself, only laughed at the peasant's credulity. With this humiliating insult added to his injury, the peasant appealed to the King. But the King, too, only laughed. Saint Simon concludes by saying that the King declared if this were the worst that the Count had done he would not have him put to death.

One might draw several morals from this story. First, it would appear that even before their deathblow from without (i.e. the French Revolution), the French aristocracy were defeated from within by their growing love of bourgeois trickery. Why just rob or abuse a peasant when you could make a fool of him at the same time?

Second, consider what this says about the art of storytelling itself. One steals a story from another and, by retelling it, alters its meaning by a new context and vocabulary. (Arab terrorists are "outlaws who must be punished"; CIA funded Contra terrorists are "freedom fighters like our own founding fathers.") But what happens when you take a story and move it, word for word, 200 years from its original site?

The plight of the French peasant in the 18th century is the common dilemma of all urban dwellers today. Some of us came to San Francisco for gay freedom only to wake up in a city where gay bashings are more frequent than in the rural communities from which we fled. Others came to be hippie artists only to discover the preppie's credo back in. All of us came for the beauty of San Francisco's unique neighborhoods only to return from work and find, like Eddie, that our whole neighborhood has moved. Who can even find their front door anymore for the scaffolding, street drilling, double-parked cars?

Two weeks ago I ran into a Berkeley friend in Cafe Flore. He was sitting with his cup of tea in a kind of daze.

"What brings you here, Bob?" I asked.

"I came over to get a sauna at Finnila's," he said. "only, I can't seem to find it."

Of course he couldn't. A half-finished cement monstrosity, due to become still another mall of boutiques now, stands in its place. But when I told Bob this, his anxiety only increased. What might he find when he returned home? Might not the same sorcerer be busy there too—and if not today, tomorrow?

Meanwhile, Mayor Feinstein plots on how she might legally overturn the people's will on Proposition M, the initiative to limit San Francisco's growth. If this was the worst our elected officials did.

# VISITING STONESTOWN

If Liz Smith could take Liberace to his first visit to the Metropolitan Opera, I reasoned, then I certainly could introduce my friend Felix to the wonders of Stonestown. "Jonestown?" Felix asks. "No, Stonestown," I reply. "It's where we inner city gays go for a change of pace. Stonestown boasts San Francisco's only bona fide parking lot, for Christ's sake. And that's only one of its virtues."

It was a perfect day—warm, sunny—and I began, as usual, by reading *The Chronicle*. Former homecoming queen Kathy Miller, who shot a Walnut Creek minister, had "strange things going on in her head," her mother says (don't we all?). Henry Kissinger and Jeane Kirkpatrick visit Sarkharov (together?). Still another SF landlord's offed by angry tenants and Berkeley's Hare Krishna Temple has fought off a hostile takeover bid by a rival swami in West Virginia. ("Hey, I went to college in Virginia," Felix says.) I could see it would be one of those days.

Across town, my friend Ron was serving breakfast to Anita Bryant at the St. Francis. "Do you want fruit on your cereal?" Ron asked. But Anita declined the fruit and the orange juice, too. "She looked like a cross between Lyndon LaRouche and Jerry Falwell," Ron tells me. "Oh Ron," I reply, "Don't be mean. None of us gals look good when we first get up in the morning."

"Anita Bryant—isn't she the one who took orange juice to Jonestown?" Felix asks. "No that was Jim Jones and he took Kool-Aid," I reply. These young ones just have no sense of San Francisco history.

I was hoping we might take a leisurely bus trip to Stonestown but Anne Hamersky picks us up in her LeMans Safari wagon. Don't kill anyone with the car, Anne, I think as we cruise out 19th Avenue past the Islam Temple. "Look at those bungalows on top of that hill," Felix gripes as we stop for a light at Noriega (not the Panamanian general, the street). "You think they'd want to hide things like that."

Then Stonestown, its familiar squat building stretching four blocks, set off by a skeleton of new construction. "Business As Usual During Construction" proclaims a big sign.

214

"Look at that little fountain," Anne cooes as we turn in. "Mary Magdalene can wash our feet," Felix giggles. My heart pounds as I see the Emporium. "Petrini's at Jonestown?" Anne murmurs.

"STONESTOWN, STONESTOWN!" I holler, "How come no one can get it straight?"

"Let's go to Mrs. See's Candies," Anne says, changing the subject. A little cardboard house stamped "Quality without Compromise" presses against the window. "Compromise without Quality," Felix quips, then: "Hey look, they have a meatslicer in there to cut up the chocolate." We go in and Anne asks if we can have samples. "Well, I guess so," says a thin blonde in white. She looks like an extra on *General Hospital*. She kinda backs away after leaving three little chocolates on the counter for us.

"Let's visit Petrini's," I say. We enter on the parking lot side, turn left past Le Petite Fleurs, and behold! A plethora of ethnic fast-food counters: Chopsticks, Foods of Mexico, Chicken Höfbrau, Italian Pasta. "This is incredible," Felix enthuses rapturously. "I wanna live here." A 250 lb. chef with a red beard glowers at us from behind the Hofbrau counter.

Next we hit the Vienna Cake Box. Hundreds of little cakes and pastries beckon but my attention focuses on the plastic brides and grooms for the wedding cakes. Suddenly I feeling mushy and I ask Anne to take our picture.

Walking on into Petrini's, Felix decides to xerox a tuber and a couple of round fruits. (You can imagine how I arranged them on the glass.) Meanwhile, I discover a letter someone's left behind.

> *Sirs: I'm confused. In the Smithsonian two months ago, you advertised three compact discs for a dollar as an inducement to join your society. Today I got a card saying these recordings are a 10 day free audition. This seems a misrepresentation. If so, I must request you immediately cancel my subscription.*

Another disgruntled consumer. But above the xerox is this quote from Fred Petrini: "Kindness is the one thing you can't give away." And later in the milk and butter section: "We should never allow ourselves to disappoint those who believe in us."

"But if you don't believe in us, fuck off," Felix adds, shivering in his shorts and tee shirt. Then, "It's becoming winter over here." Off he goes as I ponder a Dr. Pepper display that says "Trail Cans" on the sign but "Trial Cans" on the tiny silver cans themselves. I'm slightly dyslexic so it doesn't take much to confuse me—especially with Felix around.

Now we walk across the street to Doktor Pet. Anne's in a snit because Felix wouldn't moon the convex mirror in Walgreens and I'm miffed because the old Walgreens soda fountain is gone. I wanted to show everyone the elderly ladies with blue hair and the waitress who looked like Flo on *Alice*. A handwritten sign on the pet shop door says: "Rated PG. Parental Guidance Requested."

Inside, Felix says, "Oh look! A de Chirico landscape in the tetra fishtank." Sure enough, little Greek columns protrude from black gravel on the floor of the tank. But now Felix has got his head down by the hermit crabs. "Hey, I can hear parakeets," he says. A suspicious clerk asks if we need "help."

Next we go to Judy's, which is having a temporary closing-out sale. I buy a pastel paisley tie and a tube of Chocolip Pretzels for Bob Glück's 40th birthday (Petrini's didn't have his favorite Russian liqueur). Bob's a writer, so I know he'll appreciate The Chocolip Story on the side of the tube:

> *It was destiny. They were meant to be together. A classic case of "opposites attract." One sweet, white smooth. The other crisp, thick, slightly salty. They brought out the best in each other. But the lovers faced a rocky road. There was prejudice from all sides. So in a bittersweet moment, they decided to run away. . .*

"To Jonestown?" Felix asks, wrapping a scarf around my neck as I check out a wide-brimmed straw hat in the mirror. "You look like Minnie Pearl," he giggles.

"Well at least I look better than Anita Bryant," I grump. Anne snaps pictures of Felix amid the wedding gowns. Unlike Petrini's or Doktor Pet, Judy's patrons enjoy our cavorting.

Back on the mall, we notice most shops have closed because of construction. Malm's refused to let Anne take photos of its empty store. Casual Corners looks like the stage of a Beckett play. "Sorry you guys couldn't have seen Stonestown in its full glory," I apologize.

"But it is glorious," Felix says. "It's like the fall of Rome."

"The critic Guy Davenport says every building in the United States is an offense to invested capital," I lecture. "It occupies space which can always be better utilized."

"And Dawn Davenport says in *Female Trouble,* 'These are not my cha-cha heels,'" Felix retorts.

At the mall's end we follow a long winding corridor that points to "The Spa." It's like those Italian neo-realist flicks till you go down some stairs where it turns Fellini: orange tiles, big mirrors, a window full of plastic ferns, and lots of weird looking bodies. On the wall someone's written: "BX is your life now."

The Spa is full of humorless old folks and a few very handsome, young Asian guys. "I feel like I'm in Miami," Felix says. As we mingle among the sweaty bodies, a Spa clerk asks what we want. "I'm just here with my Dad," Felix says, making me wish now I had bought that Minnie Pearl hat.

Last stop the Emporium, its aisles reeking of perfume. Felix notices "Swiss Performing Extract" at the Estee Lauder counter and wonders if a handsome Swiss man will come out of the bottle if you rub it. "We're the Performing Artists here," I tell him but he's off again, this time to fondle the mannequins.

"So much for Gonzo journalism," Anne says as we head for the parking lot.

"You mean Gonzo-With-The-Wind journalism," Felix replies.

Felix laughs when I show him the first draft of this but later objects. "You've cheapened me," he says. "That's not really me." He's right. No writing (or photography) can really "capture" reality. But I sense something more in Felix's complaint. I felt drained after our Stonestown visit, as if we had pushed ourselves into a decentering hysteria.

Gonzo journalism, as first practiced by Hunter S. Thompson, attempted to parody journalistic distortion through exaggeration. But where does the hype of caricature and ego-inflation end. As image piles on image, joke on joke, we swirl into an endless vortex. I think of Darth Vader spinning into space at the end of *Star Wars*—an emblem not only of mass culture but of us who critique it. I don't want that anymore. Like Felix, I want to be real.

# DIALING FOR SEX

It's a rainy Wednesday morning. You have the day off and feel bored, horny. Paging through *The Sentinel*, you see phone sex ads where bathhouse ads used to be—eleven to be exact.

"When one just is not enough!" teases a blue banner headline above four photos of attractive nude guys. "Only 95 cents...conference call...976-BODS (not a recorded message)."

Staring at the phone I feel silly. I want to see a guy's eyes, face, how he moves his hands (80% of all communication lies in body language, psychologists say). If I'm calling someone I really like, I sometimes stare nervously at the phone for 20 minutes before dialing.

Like Dean, a guy I met last summer whose phone voice was hypnotic. Just as certain opera singers can hit a pitch that shatters glass, the timbre of Dean's voice automatically gave me a hard-on. Or was it how he'd start to murmur? Is language innately sexual with some words carrying extra voltage? "Murmur," for instance, or "spank"? (All "sp" words turn me on actually—speak, spark, sperm.) If I heard Dean's voice on the phone now, I'd swoon.

Screwing my courage to the sticking place, to steal Shakespeare's metaphor, I dial 976-BODS. A scratchy, rapid-fire recorded message says, "Welcome to the gay conference line. You'll be connected up to eight other guys. Start talking and enjoy."

"Hi," I began hesitantly. "I'm Steve and I'm looking for someone. Is anyone there?" Dead silence. I babble on inanely a minute more before hanging up, feeling foolish, irritated, relieved. I hang up and smoke a cigarette.

Then my phone rings. Is BODS calling me back? No it's Stan, a friend I can make a real date with. We chat. I relax; smoke another cigarette. When our conversation's over I return to the phone sex ads.

Some turn me off right away. Sleazeline offers trucker, bikers, B&D. On the opposite page a smaller ad catches my eye. Is that my heartthrob Lou Cass on the couch? "My girlfriend's gone and I'm horny," says the headline. So I dial 976-RODS. A young voice answers.

"I was on my way home from the gym when I see this hot punker get off the bus. He was carrying a skateboard and I could see he had a big, hard dick. He followed me home to my apartment and...."

A recorded message but the script's well written, actually believable, and the narrator gets breathy and excited as he builds up steam. I can imagine I'm right there....

Voyeurism lies at the heart of all good storytelling. You haven't really had the experience until you've shared it. So porn, like gossip, confirms our human identity. We need it to exist like we need air to breath because we're social animals. Repress it and it will pop up in your dreams. (What does Ed Meese dream about I wonder?)

...So I'm just getting into this hot story when an adult voice breaks in: "Ron's fantasies change with every call, so call back soon." Click.

Silence—there's the rub. When the State wants to break a person, they throw them into solitary confinement. When the New Right wants to break our community, they try to silence all our porn outlets. Control the airwaves (including phone lines) and you control the nation. About 40% of the 976 numbers are for "adult services" and Pacific Bell claims to get 100 complaints a month—mostly from parents. Phone sex calls generate about $12 million a year for the phone company and Ronald Thompson is suing Pac Bell for $10 million for corrupting his twelve year-old son who molested a four year-old girl after listening to $50 worth of phone sex chatter.

Who can I sue for the contradictory sex messages that were stuffed into my head as a child: "Sex is bad—unless used to sell Coke or new cars... Sex is playful, but should be carefully regulated and controlled...Only the young are sexy: only the old are wise and nurturing...Homosexuality is an illness." Can I sue the Church, the government, my parents?

I ask friends about their phone sex experience.

"I used to work for a phone sex outfit," Jeff tells me. "I like talking on the phone and I like talking dirty so it was great. But exploitative. I got $5 for every $35 my company got. Phone sex is safe but it's not healthy."

Not healthy because we're driven to it out of loneliness, or because it reflects our fear of intimacy? Jeff doesn't say.

"I called the Connector," *Sentinel* rock critic Don Baird tells me with a laugh, "every guy I talked to said he had eight inches." Marc Geller says it's great if you get the right message but just when you spring a boner, your call is over.

Chris complains that his ex-lover ran up huge phone bills making 976 calls to NYC. "Some of the recorded messages are a real hoot," Chris says. "The conference calls are more interesting. You can listen to other people before joining in. The hard part is getting the right guy to call you back."

I don't want to dump on anyone's pleasure, but what I wonder is how much real satisfaction phone sex gives. If I want to masturbate, I can come up with some pretty good fantasies on my own and to disembody the sexual experience by talking to strangers on the phone strikes me as the height of absurdity. And yet a lot of people seem to enjoy it. Are we becoming addicted to the tension of dissatisfaction?

"Intemperate language wreaks havoc on the heart," Matthew Arnold wrote in *Culture and Anarchy*. Does intemperate dialing, do the same?

# ON THE SIGNIFICANCE OF 'SIGNIFICANT OTHERS'

*Lady Windermere: "Why do you talk so trivially about life, then?"*
*Lord Darlington: "Because I think that life is far too important a thing ever to talk seriously about it."*

          - Oscar Wilde, *Lady Windermere's Fan*

"Guess what I have for you?"

An ironic edge in my editor's voice boosts my anxiety level ten decimals. Are we talking a pay cut here or an assignment (perhaps a particularly bloody hatchet job) more dreadful than any arts editor has ever before imagined. I hold my breath as my editor hands me a promo folder on... ARMISTEAD MAUPIN!

"But I haven't read his earlier novels."

"Then say that," my editor continues. "Try to explain *why* he's San Francisco's most famous gay writer and have fun, too. Be playful."

"Is that all?"

For a brief moment, I feel like I've been locked in a room by Rumplestiltskin and asked to spin gold from straw. Actually, I read *Tales of the City* when it was first serialized in *The Chronicle* in 1976. Both the author and I had only recently moved to San Francisco from the South (he, from Charleston; me, from Atlanta). Like the flood of other gay immigrants, I delighted to follow the whacky exploits of gays — and in a major daily newspaper! Free at last, free at last! God Almighty, it felt like we were free and *accepted* at last.

Times have changed and so have the characters in Maupin's fiction. We've all aged some and AIDS has thrown a bucket of cold water on our Teddy Bear's Picnic (the lyrics of which opened the Big John and Sparkie radio show in the '50s and which Maupin quotes at the beginning of his latest novel, *Significant Others*). But much of what I liked about Maupin's writing to start with I find I still like.

First, even though many of his characters are wealthy, Maupin's writing retains a grassroots community quality. He continues to project a "family" feeling about gay life, about San Francisco life, about life in general. No character is too old, too eccentric, too fat, etc., to be excluded from this generous human family in which gays and straights, men and women, old and young can find bonds of true warmth and friendship.

In *Significant Others*, for instance, Wren Douglas, a beautiful fat woman, finds herself in a local talk show waiting room with a latchkey kid named Ikey who's actually a 17-year-old midget. After a bit of tension between them, Wren lets the kid stick his arm between her breasts. At this point, the talk show host walks in on them.

*"I've done shows on child molestation, but I never thought...."*

*"That child," said Wren, "is seventeen years old!"*

*"....Who told you that?"*

*"He did."*

*Thrown, the anchoroid thought for a moment, then said: "And I suppose that makes it all right."*

*"No," Wren replied evenly, "That makes it none of your business."*

Class conflict between boss and worker, or sexist conflicts between lesbians and gay men, likewise melt in this warm glow of family feeling. When a lesbian greenhouse clerk asks for time off to go to a lesbian retreat, this dialogue ensues:

*"....C'mon, Michael, don't make me miss this opportunity."*

*He smiled at her. "Thousands of half-naked women going berserk in the redwoods."*

*"No!" she protested. "Some of them are* totally *naked."*

*He laughed. "You don't sound like somebody looking for a wife."*

*Actually, she reminded him of himself years ago, relishing the prospect of a weekend of lust at the National Gay Rodeo in Reno.*

For Maupin, humor and camaraderie both of place and bodily pleasure are the magic keys to utopia.

*The worst of times in San Francisco was still better than the best of times anywhere else. There was beauty here and conspicuous bravery and civilized straight people who were doing their best to help. It was also his home, when all was said and done. He loved this place with a deep and unreasoning passion; the choice was no longer his.*

As in the writing of Oscar Wilde or Quentin Crisp, Maupin's writing often sparkles with witty one-liners. "I hate being a whore," says one character. "There are too many responsibilities." Or, says Mrs. Madrigal: "I tried growing my nails long. I wasn't man enough for it." Or, says Wren Douglas to the make-up man who'd camouflaged her chins for TV: "Sweetie, my chins and I are not of different races. If we were, I'd call them The Supremes or something."

In these desperate, anxious, and career-driven '80s, it's easy to see why Maupin's so popular, not only with gay but straight readers as well. He creates a world where social contradictions are leapt over with a persistent kindness and a buoyant, slightly subversive sense of humor. But close reading reveals a darker side to Maupin's world. If separatist ghettos like Bohemian Grove and Wimminwood can't keep death and nastiness at bay, neither can Maupin's humanist philosophy of creature comfort. To some extent, Maupin seems aware of this, to some extent not. Chaos and violence hover at the edges of Maupin's world threatening to engulf it, as early as the opening paragraph:

> *Brian's internal clock almost always woke him at four fifty-six, giving him four whole minutes to luxuriate in the naked human body next to him. Then the Braun alarm clock on the nightstand would activate his wife with its genteel Nazi tootling, and her morning marathon would begin.*

Something bothers me here. What kind of characters can be so superficial as to make flippant jokes about Nazism as if kindness or joking could ameliorate fascist evil? The coffee machine, too, is described as a Nazi grinding its coffee beans. Indeed, references to fascism and terrorism run rampant in *Significant Others*: Reagan's tasteless, cynical visit to Bitberg, plastic "fascist" wristbands at Wimminwood, the coming home party for two San Francisco gay hostages of a terrorist hijacking.

I recall that homecoming party on 18th and Castro well. I was there, standing in the street, and Maupin himself spoke to the crowd that evening. But what did the two gay hostages feel? What were their names? What did this trauma do to their lives? Maupin never once delves into such issues. News events, the AIDS epidemic —all these matters which should evoke deep feeling — are only briefly touched on, glossed over. Good, evil, tragedy — all are reduced to an ironic, cartoonish level and feeling is blocked or denied with a clever quip. Here, for instance, is a paragraph on AIDS introducing a character (Michael) whose lover has died of the disease:

> *It wasn't just an epidemic anymore; it was a famine, a starvation of the spirit, which sooner or later afflicted everyone. Some people capitulated to the terror, turning inward in their panic, avoiding the gaze of strangers on the street. Others adopted a sort of earnest gay fraternalism, enacting the rituals of safe-sex orgies with all the clinical precision of Young Pioneers dismantling their automatic weapons.*

Michael then recalls trying, unsuccessfully, to have sex to a porn video at a JO buddy's house. Their timing is out of synch and the fast-forward button blurs Al Parker into the Keystone Cops. The question Michael asks at the end of this section never quite gets answered: "What was to stop you from abandoning human contact altogether?"

Real human contact requires occasionally going deeper than camp repartee. Maupin's characters seldom do. Even Maupin's descriptions swathe his world in a kind of toxically cloying glue (e.g., a navel is "miraculously *aerobicized* into a tiny pink seashell," a potentially handsome Victorian is "hideously *eisenhowered* with green asbestos shingles"). With all this denied, bottled-up feeling, no wonder one character confesses: "I wanna lie around and be a total slug."

Because of this avoidance of feeling (and its reverse, a grandiose, sentimental excess of feeling, such as a Pre-Raphaelite funeral at Bohemian Grove), I found myself losing interest in Maupin's characters around page seventy. How can I care about people who hide in a Never-Never Land of childhood or '70s nostalgia? How can I care about people whose connection to life is so persistently trendy, minimal, and vapid?

Serialized in a daily newspaper, Maupin's stories delight for the same reason Herb Caen or a soap opera does. In the space between episodes,

I can fill in the character's lack of depth with the emotions of my own life. (Reading "Tales of the City" with my morning coffee in the '70s, for instance, was a pleasant transition from the dreaminess of sleep.) But in an extended novel, I desire something deeper — Don DeLillo's *White Noise*, for instance, which covers much the same territory but which documents and plumbs the horror of modern urban life down to its core. Charles Dickens, to whom Maupin has been compared, managed to accomplish a similar in-depth analysis of his society *despite* his serialized format. This was difficult for Dickens, and for Dostoyevsky too, but they did it.

Armistead Maupin is a social satirist whose utopian yearnings run deeper than P.G. Wodehouse or Ronald Firbank. His virtues of community, kindness and humor are indeed welcome and, in this respect, I consider his project superior to the privatized visions of David Leavitt and many New York gay writers. But to heal the crisis of the human spirit today, we need more than flattery and wit. If we are to reimagine and create a better world, we need greatness. That means we need to face the full range of human emotion, and it also means looking at the social contradictions that block our full integration and fulfillment as human beings. It's time we begin to demand the very best of our artists and writers, not only in the gay community but in the world at large.

# WIENERSCHNITZEL

1.)

Piercing the air "like arrows tipped in fire" (Dante) yet with the "simplicity of an ax blow" (Bataille), the cry shimmers like a strobe light, an oscillating/oscillating of both horror and eroticism. Indeed the oscillum, a little face of mask hung from a tree and swaying in the wind, could be John Wieners' emblem. The face appears obsessively in his early poetry: "waits for the face to spell out the numbers of letters in 'I love you.'" "Scenes for a Film," "Drawing the face / and its torture" "A Poem for Painters," "I am / done with faces / I have seen before" "A Poem for Early Risers," "let no ache / screw his face" "A Poem for the Old Man," and culminating in the most horrific of faces, Munch's *The Scream*, "with Munch the most / obsessed. His face / carved by knife blades."

Accompanying Wieners' face, horror if not kisses (sometimes both) and a cry: "Oh come back, whatever heart / you have left." "A Poem for Painters," "Oh Johnny, women in / the night moan yr name" "Act 2."

2.)

As intensely focused, vulnerable and "sincere" as these early poems are, their lyricism is not monological. Paintings, older literary or biblical phases, jazz and the underworld street culture of drugs and prostitution are not quoted so much as witnessed, interrogated, extended. More remarkable, Wieners' heteroglossia—while important to note at this early date—grows out of the most rudimentary and unmediated of utterances, the cry. Even the cry is dialogical. Someone's implored, an answer's called for. And the climatic coital gasp or death scream? Here too someone is "hooked" or indebted by the gift/sacrifice of vocal expenditure. Merely to hear is to be irrevocably and sexually implicated: spit, spark, sperm, speak.

3.)

Whose cry?

Ginsberg begins *Howl* in past tense, as witness. "I saw…" His rage, a linear response to his friend's pain. Only as the catalogue of horrors lengthens, and adjective piles upon adjective, does the bottom fall out into an apparent madcap heteroglossia. Wieners, in "A Poem for Painters," mixes tenses and voices from the start. The stately, almost classical generality of "Our age bereft of nobility / How may our faces show it?" is abruptly answered by the urgent "I look for love." "I" and the various others addressed or heard (roommate/painter Bob LaVigne, America, etc.) change shape in the discourse like amoebas. Wieners' "I," for instance, shifts almost line by line, from aristocratic, to romantic, to painterly, to philosophic, to biblical, to landscape-identified, to childlike and so on. But the cry that "boils over" is not merely Wieners'. It is primal, unconscious, collective. "Oh come back, whatever heart / you have left" is Wieners' own desperate cry on one level, the generic lover's on another, and on still another a Job-like reverberation of the earlier more metaphysical and scatological "Oh stop up / The drains / We are run over."

Unlike Ginsberg's howl, Wieners' cry (and his faces too) function as one of Guattari's "concrete machines," a matrix organizing modes of subjectivation. Memory enters effecting a mysterization, thus combining de-territorialization and re-territorialization. Wieners' cry thus becomes our own. It propels us into a future, dislodging us from our past by deepening and darkening it. Like a bloodstain on the hotel carpet, it spreads, sinks in.

4.)

Dear John,

I'm so tired of being serious now tho the '80s writing scene increasingly demands it. And where's all my fancy French crit vocab gotten me? Into *Poetics Journal*? Fat chance! I'm too apt to interject SEX into my discourse, or a working-class bluntness, like the pics of boys getting blowjobs in yr *Behind the State Capitol* (yr only book not in the SF Public Library I noticed). Thus sadness covers our work like a shepherd's tent of night the earth or as if God (bless his excruciating absence) were Christo wrapping us all in mummy white.

*Or mommy white. Virgin blue? "What Happened to the Mind of Jennifer Jones" and "Hong Kong Boasts a Hotel for the Dead," my 2 fave titles of yrs, esp. as they apply to the sentences introducing paragraph above. So let poetic license grant the bearer of these words all the rights and privileges thereunto appertaining: "I'm only asking that I shall be shot with him, said Claretta Petacci, his mistress."*

*much love,*
*Steve*

5.)

As for Wieners' glances into the abyss, isn't it time to call to account those for whom they have only been the object of an eclectic curiosity? Many realities are subject to the law of all or nothing. This is the case with Wieners. The Spiritual Exercises of Saint Ignatius of Loyola would be nothing if they were not mediated in the greatest silence (and mediated, they are a prison without an exit). What Wieners shattered can only be opened to those carried forward by the need to shatter; the others do to Wieners what they do to everything else: nothing has meaning for them, and everything they touch decomposes. It is a law of present-day life that an ordinary man must be incapable of thinking about anything at all, and be tied down in every way by completely servile occupations, which drain him of reality. But the existence of this man will end up crumbling into dust, and one day he will no longer be astonished when a living being does not see him as the ultimate limit of things.

*[from Bataille's "Nietzschean Chronicle" with Wieners' name replacing Nietzsche's]*

6.)

When Tomasco dragged Eva back to our table his sweatsoaked shirt was unbuttoned to the waist. His eyes gleamed and his tongue wagged when he laughed. Eva was laughing. Tomasco fell into the chair next to me squeezed the back of my neck smelled like everything I ever wanted.

"Betcha never saw anything like this before." I could feel the heat of his body pulsating wanted to lean over kiss him leaned over he pulled me away. "Whatdaya think I am, Queer?"

[*randomly chosen from my novella* Holy Terror]

Curiosity: from sun up to sun down, sound, behold this day of days to which is given tension. A find or fugued place. A torsion as in Loyola who set his days on edge by emptying them out. No conceptual body but this body which forgets itself.

One month ago, in Boston, I made love to a man on a roof. It was as if some giant hand grabbed us up and emptied us out. Dangerous nights stars spilling over a city. And below us, a poet whose works I admire dying of drugs on Joy Street.

[*from my poem "Days" extracted from journal entries 7/31 to 8/12/79*]

7.)

A human being is dissociated when he devotes himself to a useful labor, which has no sense of itself; he can only find the plentitude of total life when seduced. And just as virility is tied to the allure of a nude body, full existence is tied to any image that arouses hope and terror. THE LOVED ONE in this broken-up world has become the only power that has retained the virtue of returning to the heat of life. If this world were not ceaselessly traversed by the convulsive movements of beings who seek each other, if it were not transfigured by the face "whose absence is painful," it would still appear as a mockery to those it causes to be born:

human existence would be present there, but only in the form of a memory or of a film of "primitive" countries. It is necessary to exclude fiction, with a feeling of irritation. The lost, the tragic, the "blinding marvel," possessed in one's innermost being, can no longer be met anywhere but on a bed. It is true that satisfied dust and the dissociated concerns of the present world also invade bedrooms; locked bedrooms nevertheless remain, in the almost unlimited mental void, so many islands where the images of life reconstitute themselves.

Her reality is as doubtful as a gleam that vacillates, but which the night makes violent.

*[from Bataille's "The Sorcerer's Apprentice"]*

# PASSING STRANGERS

I'm standing in front of the B & K Bargain Market talking to a friend when a Chinese boy of about fifteen leaves carrying a brown ceramic coffee mug balanced precariously on top of a styrofoam take-out dinner container. He's laughing. Chris laughs too (about something else), throws his head back and squints. At the same instant, an ex-boyfriend named Carl, whom I haven't seen for some time, walks up from behind with his wife Pat.

"Hey Steve, let's get together."

Even the most banal day overwhelms me if I don't keep some distance. But how much? I last saw Carl at the Democratic Convention. He said he was moving back to San Francisco from Tennessee. Carl's legs look strong, if slightly bowed, in loose grey cotton trousers that flap in the wind. He moves energetically. Suddenly I recall how terrific it felt to be in bed with him, how big and powerful his body was. Not until later do I remember the tattoo on his shoulder, an unfinished tiger climbing a half-drawn mountain.

Carl and Pat pass on into the pedestrian tangle like an odor of bread. People move out of my life like that. Before I can reach out, they're gone. I told Dodie over brunch two days ago that I wished I could think of my skin as connecting me to the world instead of separating me from it.

Most of my writing is published in obscure magazines. I like to write on unusual topics: the history of rubber stamp art, avant-garde poetry, tv commercials, horror movies. I want to make connections.

Someone I briefly wanted to be boyfriends with said, "I can't accept the idea that Jesus died because God wanted a blood sacrifice."

"But that's the best part," I replied. Ted later said he got angry when I said that.

Last night I felt lonely so, after a sauna, I went to a couple bars. This was foolish because I don't drink or smoke anymore and I was too tired to dance. Even so, there's something delicious about a roomful of young men, their necks flitting so close to one's lips. I say delicious; I mean unattainable. I say unattainable; I mean I just walked in, cruised the bar and left. It was just something to do before going home to read.

Later, I pass a blond on Haight Street. After a couple of steps I turn and look back. He does the same. We keep walking but turn to look at each other again twice. By the time I decide I'm really interested he turns the corner. I go back and look up the street. Empty darkness! Well, not entirely. The street he's turned onto separates two rows of cars, houses, trees. How the streetlight splashes down on top of the trees contrasts with the black emptiness of the sidewalks.

I would like to call Carl but something inside me freezes.

My ex-lover Joe dumped me for a $1000 a month coke habit. For the past eight months he's had all the sex he wants; I've had none. He sings joyously at work; I'm miserable. Joe says he isn't "denying" reality, merely "selecting" which reality he wants. It's not that he can't stop doing drugs; he's engaged in "scientific research."

I think of Dr. Mengele and his "scientific research." He wasn't denying reality at Auschwitz either, just selecting it. He thought it charming to sew three-year-old twins together without benefit of anesthetic. Yet if *I* were honest, I'd have to admit I don't care about Dr. Mengele or even Joe so much as myself. When I don't get what I want, I clutch resentment to my bosom like a brilliant military banner.

"See, this is what Joe did to me!"

"Heil Steve, you poor thing!"

"What you need, Steve, is to be spanked and fucked!"

"How soon, O Lord! How soon?"

In the summer of 1964, the Japanese novelist and playwright Yukio Mishima, flew to New York for sex. The friend he visited, Faubian Boyers, did nothing for him. Mishima's fame and writing weren't enough so he built a beautiful body. That wasn't enough either. What *can* one do?

After seeing a movie one afternoon, I spy a pair of red, high-heeled shoes on top of a yellow *Examiner* newspaper box. I think of taking the shoes for my fourteen-year-old daughter but the newspaper box is on fashionable Union Street so I don't. A few minutes later, a young man with close-cropped hair and a moustache stops and picks up one of the shoes to examine it. After glancing around furtively, he slips the shoes under his sarape and walks on.

Later that evening Sam calls. He says he dreamt he had two sets of eyebrows, one above the other. Even in his dream he knew this was monstrous, he said, but he didn't feel monstrous, just odd.

These events remind me of how I like to lie in bed naked and read, holding my penis in my right hand. When it starts to swell I feel secure. "Now I have a grip on my life."

On the darker side, my favorite painter when I was in high school was Hieronymus Bosch. I loved the grinning devils who shat coins and humans. Perhaps then I began to see the anus as something magical, holy. The upper mouth, made for eating, drinking and talking seems too public; but the lower one, the anus, gnostic lips all puckered and quivering, waits for a more persevering, private lover—my tongue. Sticking my tongue up Joe's ass drove him into frenzied paroxysms of ecstasy. This was my greatest pleasure.

Joe's transgressions were of a different order. Once when we were returning from three horror movies at The Strand, he confessed he felt like a monster. He'd stolen some coke from me.

"But I thought you'd broken all your needles?"

"I had, but I found one in the street around 18th and Castro last night."

Another time Joe showed me ugly puncture wounds on his arms. He'd used needles so big the cocaine wouldn't stay in his veins. He was shamefaced but perversely proud. That his drug behavior and his promiscuous sex practices put my life in jeopardy didn't bother him. Irresponsibility, Joe felt, was his sacred, inalienable right.

The night Joe kicked me out of his apartment he was at the end of a three-day coke run. He was bouncing off walls and his skin had a greenish tinge. Even then I thought I could help him.

"Maybe I could do heroin for awhile," Joe mused. "Maybe if I was careful I wouldn't get hooked." He said Eddie, one of his fuck buddies, suggested speedballing. "I didn't," Joe said, "but it's not that dangerous." At this he looked up and smiled. It was the most trusting smile I'd ever seen.

Then the light in Joe's kitchen changed. It got denser, more yellow. This happened quickly, like the click of a camera. Suddenly I felt loaded myself. I heard a buzzing, seductive hum, and I saw – squatting behind Joe and about a foot taller than he – a beautiful, diaphanous insect. The creature, an iridescent emerald green, materialized slowly. I guessed immediately that it was the spirit of the drug. Its eyes were black and shiny. It seemed neither good nor bad, just there – vague, relentless, like a hologram between Joe and the stove.

As Joe laughed, the demon spun a kind of web before his eyes. It sparkled and glistened. That's why Joe was so happy. He didn't notice that the insect's proboscis thrust deep in his skull.

"ASSHOLE!" I screamed. All I could think was to blast the bug away or make Joe jump away himself.

"YOU ASSHOLE! WHATEVER YOU CAN SAY ABOUT SPEEDBALLING, ONE THING YOU CAN'T SAY IS THAT IT'S *NOT DANGEROUS*! WHAT DO YOU THINK FASSBINDER AND BELUSHI DIED OF ANYWAY? I'M TIRED OF PEOPLE I LOVE DYING. YOU STUPID SHIT, WHADAYA MEAN IT'S NOT DANGEROUS!"

The insect vanished but I couldn't stop yelling. Joe jumped up and rushed over to me, jutting his chest out like a rooster's.

"Get the hell out of my apartment," he sputtered. His lip quivered and he clenched and moved his fists as if he'd like to hit me.

"HOW MANY OF YOUR FRIENDS APPROVE OF YOU SHOOTING COKE? HOW MANY EVEN *KNOW*?"

"Almost none," he whispered.

"Almost....*ALMOST*?"

"Okay, *none*!"

I hit the street sobbing and crying. Everything in my life had collapsed. I felt *I'd* screwed up, that *I* was to blame. I felt this for two months.

When a lover of Sam's OD'd on quaaludes, Sam wrote several poems and a story to exorcise his grief, maybe his guilt too. Jim Carroll sings about all his friends who've OD'd.

As for me, I feel guilty merely to be attracted to someone. No good can come of this, I think. When I met Sam, for instance, I avoided coming on to him because I was reviewing his book. If I see attractive men in the street I avert my eyes. One night Joe got angry because I didn't notice a guy cruising me on Market. I got pissed that he should think I should care. I get a lot of junk chain letters too.

Lonely and horny, I go to Lands' End. Monterey cypresses twist and slope towards the shore, as in fairy tales. I enjoy the cubby holes under these trees, the ocean's roar, gusts of wind filled with negative ions. Maybe it's more negative ions I need.

A few naked men stand in the bushes, some lazily masturbating. Others mill around, give each other blow jobs. This makes me nervous. I've made it outdoors with Joe before but here I feel threatened. I pick an isolated spot in the sun. Taking off my shirt, but keeping my pants on, I lay down. Suddenly a man in his mid-thirties is upon me, his eyes dark and wild.

I don't think Joe ever said no to anyone who wanted to have sex with him. He wanted many centers in his life, he said, not just one. The more fleeting and shallow an encounter, the prouder he was! Joe once insisted I should have at least two other boyfriends besides him. Could he maintain this morality if not on drugs?

After our blow-up, I peruse my journal to see how often I'd expressed unhappiness over Joe's drug use. Twenty times in three months. His mood swings are more extreme. He's more irritable, unreliable, inconsiderate. But he makes me laugh too, get outside of myself, love nature. He's mentally stimulating without being too intellectual. My favorite entry is this:

> *October 3, 1984 – Joe meets me at the courthouse where we've come to see Francisco. He's been charged with the murder of a street kid and I'm glad to see solid support for him from the Chicano community. Afterwards, Joe and I have a mocha at Cafe Flore, then climb to the top of Corona Heights. A sunny morning! Joe scampers about like a mountain goat.*

*As we look out over the city, more beautiful than the one with which Satan tempted Christ, Joe points to a blue and grey house with gables. "We'll have to live there sometime," he says. It's the first time, even whimsically, he's suggested we live together. Later we walk to my place in the Haight. Joe's loving and flirtatious. I'm turned on. When I push him against the wall for a deeper, more lustful kiss, he holds me back. I relax, drop my head on his shoulder. Happy now, he strokes my hair and neck.*

When I'm not upset, I like to sit in cafes and watch people. I try to guess where they're going, what kind of parents they had. In college, I sat next to the entrance of the student lounge. Watching how the door opened, I tried to guess what kind of person was entering. I had only fifteen seconds to do this.

For a different perspective, I watched people from the window of my dentist's office. It was ten stories up.

Now I sit and do zazen. I don't do zazen to attain enlightenment, I do zazen just to do zazen. You sit in an erect posture, with your hands in a mudra position over your abdomen, and you observe your breath. I observe my breath by counting exhalations: 1, 2, 3, and so on till 10. If thoughts come I let them but I keep counting. If I lose count, I start again. Sometimes I doze off and almost fall over. Then I straighten myself up again and resume counting. I'd like to be able to let go of everything, to let things pass through me, but I've build up certain mental habits or resistances. Who would I be without them?

When I first met Joe I never imagined that we'd become lovers. I was drunk and he entered The Stud with someone I liked. When the bar closed, we happened to be standing next to each other. I let him come home with me and we had hot sex.

Months passed before I saw Joe again. I was walking to a bus stop and he followed me. I didn't like him much then. His clothes were dirty and ill fitting. He'd start talking mid-sentence and I couldn't understand what he said. Later I remember feeling embarrassed when he stopped me at the Castro Street Fair. But during the '82 Christmas Season, when I was lonely, Joe started coming over a lot. He'd phone and say "Can I come over and fuck?" "Sure," I'd reply. "Why not!" Joe was the first person in several years I felt like having sex with more than twice. But never in a million years did I think we'd become boyfriends. It just sort of happened. We were together a lot and then, during sex on our first acid trip together, he looked me in the eyes and said, "It's okay if you want to love me."

Joe told me he loved me too though any commitment or declaration of feeling scared him. He was always feeling trapped. I feared abandonment.

"We're incompatible," Joe explained.

"I know," I replied, "That's why we *had* to become lovers."

What's more pleasant after a harrowing day than to come home and listen to messages on the answering machine. Jim wants me to hear his band. Jason wants to return a book. Frank wants to see a movie. Jack wants to thank me for something. Jerry wants to renew a past I'd rather forget. Joyce wants help on *Poetry Flash*. Alysia, my kid, has lots of calls and puts weird announcements on the machine ("We can't pick up anything right now...the phone I mean.") Harold says it could mess me up if I get any business calls. As I rewind the tape, messages overlap:

> *BEEP-Jim-Jac-BEEP-Jasper-BEEP-BEEP-Sam!*
> *Sam has a new boyfriend. He gave no indication, aside from intimate late night phone calls, that he seriously wanted me but, infant that I am, I feel hurt. When I feel hurt I withdraw – except from Joe, that is, although lately I'm withdrawing even from him. When I had dinner at the Four Seas with Mario the other night, the message in my fortune cookie said: "He loves you as much as he can. But he cannot love you very much."*

December 16, 1984 – I attend my first drug recovery meeting. About twenty-five guys sit in chairs or on cushions against the walls. One lies on the floor with his hands under his head. I don't recall much else but the reading of the steps. These are merely suggested but addicts in the group claim that they work.

1) We admitted that we were powerless over our addiction – that our lives had become unmanageable.

2) We came to believe that a Power greater than ourselves could restore us to sanity.

3) We made a decision to turn our will and our lives over to the care of God as we understood him.

The first step I can fully accept. Since getting kicked out of Joe's six days earlier I was hysterical. I couldn't read, watch a movie or sit still. I felt so helpless, in such intense pain I would have done anything for relief. Only the idea of vengeance soothed me. What if I got a gun? I didn't know what I might do and I was scared.

Other things about the group bug me. I hate saying: "My name is Steve and I'm an addict" and having to wait for the chorus, "Hi Steve," before going on. The second and third steps bug me too. For a queer to embrace any of the major Western religions would be like a German Jew joining the Nazi party.

"But your higher power can be anything," replies a handsome man with a crewcut. "It can be your deeper self or even what people say here at meetings." Another addict said a cigarette lighter was his higher power. There were no "musts" but "turn it over" was a phrase I heard a lot. It meant we were powerless over people, places and things, as well as over drugs and alcohol. So I started saying the "Serenity Prayer" and, thinking of Joe, following it with this prayer of my own:

> *Dear God, look after this man I love. Don't let him die. I don't understand your ways but if anyone can help him, you can. He's a stubborn, self-righteous bastard, like me, so please let him open his heart and stop the disease he's in before it's too late.*

I'd say this several times a day. It was all I could do. I knew that as I got well, my life would become an affront to Joe as it already was to his addict friends. We share this characteristic with lobsters. When lobsters are caught in a net one tries to escape, the others pull it back.

Gradually my mind cleared, my body stopped hurting and my skin glowed with new health. I even had glimpses of serenity. "This is what I used to take drugs to feel like," I joked. Then the other shoe fell. It was the night I got my three-month chip, a recognition that I'd stayed off drugs this long.

I decided to take a sauna afterwards. While I sat in the gray, cracked plaster steamroom at Finnela's, sweat dripping from my body, I remembered all the people I'd fucked over when I drank and used. There was my wife Barb and daughter Alysia, my lovers – British, John, Ed, Joe – but what was worst was the long string of guys whose names I couldn't remember. All these passing strangers – how could I make amends?

At the same time I felt enraged at my unbearable loneliness. I couldn't take the clarity of sobriety anymore. Either I had to go out and drink and shoot heroin, or kill myself; suicide was the only dignified option. But did I have the courage? As I left Finnela's, I saw Joe.

"Pray for me," I mumbled. He gave me a funny look.

"I'm surprised you think I still do that," he joked. I put my hand over his.

"If anything happens to me tonight, I want you to know it's not your fault. No one's responsible but me." Joe looked more serious now.

"Take care Stephen," he whispered.

Though I was far too angry to be social, the addict in me craved a drink. I felt insane with craving. As I walked by Cafe Flore I thought about my "Higher Power." Had I been duped again? If I couldn't see, hear, smell, taste or feel this power, what good was it? To pray for Joe was one thing – but for myself? I decided to go home although it was only 10:30 p.m.

As I walked across Duboce Park, not even the mist from the park sprinklers relaxed me. "Okay," I said at last. "If you're out there God, show yourself! Show me why you're putting me through all this pain and shit."

When I arrived home, I got in bed. Ten minutes later the phone rang.

"Daddy, I'm scared. There's a guy trying to get into the house here and I don't know what to do."

Alysia was babysitting across town. I pressed for details. Carol, the woman she was sitting for, had warned Alysia to watch out for a kook from upstairs who'd once tried to burn down the building. Alysia said this guy tried to get her to let him in to leave a note for Carol. When she wouldn't, he comes back wearing dark glasses and a wig saying he has flowers to deliver. Still later he phones to ask when Carol will be back.

I told Alysia to call Carol at work and I called the police. I'd never heard Alysia this upset before. Her voice was shaking. Moments of our life flashed through my mind: how she babbled on the phone to me when she was two; pony rides after Barb died; her first day at school with her Snoopy lunch pail. Recent resentments about parenthood lifted as I dialed Yellow Cab. Then it hit me. This was God's answer. If I hadn't been so miserable I wouldn't have come home early. And if I hadn't come home early I couldn't have helped Alysia. Don't two and two make four?

"Coincidence!" my mind answered. But in my bones I knew it was more. I phoned Alysia again and we talked until the cab arrived. "Don't worry," I said. "I'll be there soon." When the cab honked, I bounded downstairs.

"Thank God," I murmured, rubbing a knuckle over my cheek.

Dear Joe,

I wish I could give you unconditional love. Unfortunately I can't. Neither of us is perfect but we developed little God complexes. In my script love lasts unto death: Gilgamesh and Enkidu, David and Jonathan, Achilles and Patroclus, Alexander and Hephaestion, Jesus and John, Rumi and Shamsuddin – then there's the suffering of saints! You told me that when you were little you wanted to be like St. Adrian who had all his bones crushed. I thought of this when I saw you at The Stud last Saturday. Maybe that's why you can only love guys like Tommy. And the excuses you invent for yourself and your friends.

Today *I* feel so obnoxious! You've destroyed my life. I've had to spend over $1000 on therapy. I've lost $1500 because I'm too paralyzed by depression to write. My relationship with Alysia has hit an all time low. I hate change. I hate not having sex and I'll probably never have sex again. Most of all I hate my feelings. I hate facing reality and I refuse to, even though it's tougher without booze and drugs. We're addicted to pain. It pains me to admit that the only thing that makes me happy is to see you getting fucked over by your lousy friends. No one deserves misery more than you.

I hope this letter makes you furious. I hope you get so pissed you come over and beat the shit out of me. Wimp that you are you won't though; you'll just withdraw and pout. Well, I'll just write another story and then another and another. I'll tell about the time you broke the thermometer by "testing" it in a cup of hot coffee and how Tommy bawled you out till you almost cried and how Tommy laughed then and thought that was real funny. I know you intend to keep practicing your drug addiction and do everything possible to spite me till you die. So, if not lovers or friends, let's be enemies, okay?

his Royal Majesty,
BIG BABY

ps – If you thought you could keep me from getting "emotionally charged" just by refusing to have sex with me, *boy were you wrong!*"

\* \* \* \*

Dear Baby,

We hear you're feeling blue cause you're not getting enough hugs. Of course it's hard when you push people away. Remember the Kenegge sisters? You'd visit them when Mommy and Daddy didn't give you what you wanted. They'd dote over you and give you milk and cookies like Wilber's wife next door did. You were so cute in your little sailor suit you must have thought you'd be the center of the world forever.

Well, some shit you have to do more than "turn over." You have to scoop it into a bag and throw it out. Unless you like the smell, that is. If you like the smell you can wallow. Joe won't care and I won't either. If you want to create a hell for yourself, fine. If you want to empty your head of Joe, that's fine too. Hang in there, baby!

> lovingly yours,
> your Higher Power

\* \* \* \*

Dear Dad,

No one's more a stranger to me than you. I didn't meet you till I was four and you, just home from war, weren't affectionate like Mom and Grandma. I must have given you a pretty cold eye too. Who's this stepping between Mom and me? So there was always a distance. I had to run to keep up with you and you yelled at me a lot, especially when I had trouble with my multiplication tables. Damaged relations go back long before us -- you and your Dad, he and his, Abraham and Isaac.

You read me the story at bedtime along with the rest of the Old Testament. I could see Isaac laughing, wearing short pants like I had, and running along the dusty road. Then he notices something's wrong. "Hey Dad, here's the fire and wood but where's the sheep?" And

243

Abraham, not wanting to lie, says: "Oh, don't worry. God will provide." So Isaac skips along trustingly till suddenly Daddy grabs him, gags him, throws him on the alter and lifts up this flashing knife which the Angel holds back only at the last second. And God *blesses* Abraham.

I wonder about you after that. Later I learned about Cronos who ate his kids, about the Aztecs who sacrificed thousands of theirs, and about war – blood sacrifice on the grand scale. But it was that first image, duplicated in the erotically crucified Jesus, that marked my imagination. So I put myself on the altar for cold men, even to the point of death. Could it be that if you scratch a gay drug addict you'll find a terrified Isaac, or a despairing Peter Pan?

In your last letter, you asked how I am. Sometimes I'm happy, sometimes I'm sad, and sometimes I'm hanging over a cliff's edge and kicking at it with both feet. Maybe that's how the tiger felt in Carl's unfinished tattoo. When we die, maybe then we'll know why we've lived and loved.

your son,
Steve

# WILL WE SURVIVE THE 80's

Never has evaluating the present and future of gay politics and culture been so problematic.

The 1986 Supreme Court ruling (Bowers v. Hardwick) was a setback, but AIDS has become our greatest challenge. And yet we've made great gains over the past 20 years. Before the Stonewall Riots in 1969, our existence was virtually unspeakable. The phrase "corruption of morals past all expression"—used by European colonists about Native American sexual practices—was America's prevalent attitude toward homosexuality. More liberal, educated citizens merely considered us "sick." So out of fear we hid—from America, from our families, from ourselves.

*Coming Out*

The first step in our liberation was "coming out." Even before Stonewall, a brave handful of individuals had done so: poets such as Robert Duncan and Allen Ginsberg, activists such as Harry Hay, Frank Kameny and Barbara Gittings. But after 1969, this process mushroomed. Antiwar activists paved the way saying "Make love, not war," and hippies by saying "Do your own thing." Feminists challenged sex roles. New underground and gay newspapers proclaimed: "Gay is good." Gay bars played the role for us that black churches played for the black civil rights movement. They were our meeting places.

I still recall the first gay bar I attended in Atlanta, Chuck's Rathskeller. On weekends, over 1,000 gays and lesbians attended. I never imagined our numbers were so great, and the thrill I felt in seeing so many same-sex couples dancing together cannot be described.

But coming out publically was a different matter. Friends and jobs could be lost. So the first wave of us who came out were political radicals. We'd marched for other causes; now we marched for our own. At first the older "hidden" gay community felt threatened, but our numbers grew. And as we came out, America noticed. First in curiosity, then in growing respect.

Now national TV networks, magazines, and newspapers discuss us on a daily basis, often in regard to AIDS but in other contexts too. ABC News recently did a segment on parents of gays and Cleve Jones was its "Person of the Week" when the NAMES Project went to Washington. Gay leaders, such as Ken Maley, have been profiled in the *Examiner*, and Issan Dorsey, of the Hartford Street Zen Center, in *The New Yorker*'s "Talk of the Town." Openly gay journalists, such as Randy Shilts and Edward Guthman, have won awards for their writing in the *Chronicle*.

We've won numerous political battles as well. In 1974, the American Psychiatric Association decided we weren't mentally ill. During the course of the 70s, half of the states eliminated sodomy statutes and many large cities included us under civil rights protections. In the 80s, gays in professions and academia have come out as well. Dear Abby and Ann Landers now advise Middle America that our sexual orientation is a valid option.

Culturally we've done well too. Never have there been so many good books, plays, and films on the gay and lesbian experience: witness the increasing size of our film festivals, major studio films featuring gay love stories, and *Newsweek* featuring gay writers in its book section. Gay bands, choruses, square dancers, and performance artists tour the country regularly. Gay playwrights, such as Harvey Fierstein and Harry Kondoleon, have been praised in *The New York Times*. And if Lou Reed felt a need to tone down his "walk on the wild side," many openly gay pop singers from Sylvester to Morrissey remain popular.

*The Impact of AIDS*

But while we defeated the Briggs and LaRouche initiatives and survived Anita Bryant and Jerry Falwell, AIDS has taken a terrible toll. In 1981, 225 cases of AIDS were reported in America; by the spring of 1983, 1,400 cases; by summer of 1985, 15,000 cases; and two years later, 40,000 cases.[1] We've lost many of our most brilliant political leaders. America has lost many of its most promising and prominent cultural figures. Meanwhile, with the exception of Surgeon General C. Everett

Koop, the Reagan administration has just twiddled its thumbs. Let us call this cruel indifference by its right name—intentional genocide.

Now the upwardly spiraling statistics—450,000 American cases of AIDS projected by 1993—have goaded even Reagan's conservative AIDS commission to call for major action. It's not, I suspect, that they care about the lives of gay people; they're just worried about the coming insurance and health care crunch. I read recently that one in every 152 San Franciscans has AIDS; by 1993 it will be one in every 42.[2] No cure appears to be in sight. What this means is that in five to seven years the gay community may be depleted by three-fourths its present size. Can anything save us from political and cultural extinction?

San Francisco's gays won political power only because we became a large, well-organized voting block. What will happen when this voting power shrinks? Culturally too, our films, plays, novels and music sprang to national attention only because a large core gay audience was hungry to hear its stories told. By 1995 this voting power, this cultural audience, this political and cultural leadership, will be largely gone.

Our history, even when we've been strong and well-organized, has not always been happy. The first Christian emperor of Rome, Justinian, believed we caused earthquakes, and massacred us as a matter of state policy. During the Inquisition, we were the "faggots" used to burn "witches." Hitler crushed a rising gay movement in Germany and sent 200,000 of us to death in concentration camps. In the past year, sparked partly by AIDS hysteria, antigay violence has risen 42% in America.[3]

Nor does this persecution come only from ignorant street thugs or emotionally unstable assassins like Dan White. In 1984, two prominent American poets—Ed Dorn and Tom Clark, the latter who now teaches at New College and reviews books for the *Chronicle*—published a satirical "AIDS Awards for Poetic Idiocy" in Dorn's literary newspaper, *Rolling Stock*. In this, they join intellectual fag-bashers such as William F. Buckley, William Gass, Midge Decter, and Norman

---

[1] D'Emilio, John and Estelle Freedman, "The Contemporary Political Crisis," *Intimate Matters: A History of Sexuality in America,* Harper & Row, New York, 1988, p. 354.

Podhoretz. They mock us as we die, knowing full well that antigay humor leads to antigay violence. Language and ideas can kill just as surely as viruses, clubs, and guns. Indeed, there's more of a connection here than is generally realized.

*Language, Capitalism and Disease*

What feminism, gay liberation, and the philosophical research of Michel Foucault contributed to an understanding of sexual identity is this: they showed us that sexuality is not simply "natural" as Aristotle thought, not just a biological urge as Freud thought, but a social construct that evolved through history to enable power to regulate and define social behavior and thought at both the level of individuals and groups.

Overthrowing earlier social formations, the ideology of heterosexuality used sexism to subjugate women and homophobia to keep this system intact. Industrial capitalism (ownership of other's labors, bodies, and sexuality) embraced this ideology even more fervently than did feudalism. The body was now considered a little machine to do power's bidding. Nor did Marxism fundamentally challenge this ideology, since its main focus was economic.

But facing successive crises, postindustrial capitalism (like a clever virus) mutated. It incited a division of sexualities so as to internalize, intensify, and yet disguise its control. Now power could be almost liquid in the games it played. It could make us feel free even though the only choices we were allowed to make were increasingly superficial, even though we were really only free to participate in what Guy Debord called the "society of the spectacle" (welcome to the spectacular abundance but increased manipulation and impoverishment of "TV reality"). Capitalism could even encourage us to be gay while twisting tighter the screws of internalized homophobia (e.g., good to be gay only if young, pretty, rich, hip—in short, a good consumer).

---

[2] Jeffrey Amory, director of US Public Health Department's AIDS Office, testifying to US Senate's Governmental Affairs Subcommittee, *San Francisco Examiner,* June 7, 1988, p. A-18.

[3] As reported by the National Gay/Lesbian Task Force's Antiviolence Project (1987 study) *San Francisco Examiner*, June 7, 1988.

Non-Western medicine (that of the Chinese, Sufi, native peoples, etc.) has long recognized that physical disease results from spiritual disharmony. To obsess about sex, for instance, throws one out of balance. To do this and feel guilty increases stress, causing internal conflict and eventually mental or physical collapse.

Consider the new diseases that have come to flourish under postindustrial capitalism: cancer, heart disease, AIDS, drug and alcohol addiction. All are caused by excessive stress, bad diet, or a toxic external environment. The first two are epidemic only in advanced capitalist countries. In fact, cancer—in which some body cells go out of control in their desire to overwhelm and dominate surrounding cells—might be seen as a miniature paradigm of capitalism. Addictive behavior, on the other hand, is a response to feeling psychically helpless in a hostile world that one can't, but nonetheless tries to, control.

And AIDS attacks the immune system, that part of the body that preserves the body's identity and repels foreign invaders. If one is attacked, a healthy response would be to fight off the attacker. But if one has internalized the oppression (as in internalized racism or homophobia), if one consciously or unconsciously agrees, "Yes, I am sick. Yes, I am bad," then one either tries to escape this realization via excessive drug and alcohol use, or else one simply begins to internally self-destruct.

*Fighting Back*

Our community has always been cross-class, cross-race and cross-gender, and we have suffered divisions based on these differences. But whenever we were attacked—by the Briggs initiative, for instance—we came together and fought back. In many ways we are doing this now. Gays and lesbians are working more closely together on a personal level, on new magazines such as *Out/Look*, and on the recent March on Washington.

In the Bay Area especially, where a strong support network already existed, we have done heroically well in caring for each other. We have worked in Shanti, in the AIDS Foundation, in setting up hospices and, perhaps most brilliantly and creatively of all, in the NAMES Project. The NAMES Project Quilt showed America, the world, and ourselves how deeply and beautifully we care for each other—not just in the sense of *eros* but in the even deeper and more spiritual sense of *agape*. The NAMES Quilt stands as one of the most glorious accomplishments of our history. However, the division between sick and well, and the problem of how to preserve our culture and community cannot be bridged by a quilt alone, no matter how large it may grow.

The majority of those uninfected in our male population are young. And youth—struggling to build its own identity, to find housing and work—is not renowned for compassion. Playful, energetic and lustful, yes; patient, wise and loving, no. Moreover, youth wishes to imagine it can live forever and generally seeks to avoid such depressing topics as illness and death. I could cite many notable exceptions—indeed, gay youth today are probably more serious than ever before—but, overall, we cannot expect youth to be anything but what it is.

So "Boy Clubs" are flourishing with all the happy frivolousness that the phrase implies—dress-up, go-go dancers, moderate drinking and drug taking. And while a new seriousness is evident artistically and spiritually, political maturity is often lacking. Rights so painfully won are often taken for granted.

The generation that would normally provide education and leadership to gay youth has largely turned inward. Some are providing daily health care to lovers and friends, care not provided by society at large. Others have admirably devoted themselves to anonymous 12-step programs such as AA, NA, and Al-Anon to recover from their own addictive excesses of the past. Still others have turned away from political and social concerns for an inward personal and spiritual evaluation.

In some ways this turning inward may be positive, a leadership of quiet example—not who's on stage but what's on the page. Several marvelous books on what it means to be gay have resulted: Judy Grahn's *Another Mother Tongue*, Edmund White's *The Beautiful Room Is Empty*, Robert Glück's *Jack The Modernist*, and *Gay Spirit* edited by Mark Thompson, to name a few.

Many publications within the gay media and organizations such as the Gay Sierrans, the San Francisco Gay and Lesbian Historical Society, Black and White Men Together, and Act Up also play a crucial leadership role. Gay playwrights and filmmakers, in particular, have taken the lead in teaching us how to cope with AIDS and with our grief. But gay leadership today is not so simple as it was 10 or 20 years ago. A dollop of good cheer, or burning anger, may be useful but it's not enough. Who can provide easy answers if there aren't any?

*Revisioning Who We Are*

To fight AIDS and the conditions that threaten us, we need more than scientific research, more than money, more than leadership. We need to rethink America's spiritual, political, social, and cultural systems at the most fundamental root level. How do we use power? How do we use language? It is clear that what we are doing now—as bosses and workers, as men and women, as gays and straights, as whites and non-whites—is killing us all. And as we project these attitudes onto other species and towards the Earth's ecological system, we are jeopardizing our very planet. I would argue that today we can no longer afford to see anything—not even "gay liberation" or our survival—as a separate issue needing a separate cultural, political or spiritual agenda.

This does not mean I intend to renounce my sexual orientation, far from it. Even in times of sadness or loneliness, it remains my greatest source of strength and joy. But if my sexuality is a social construct, I can change how I think about and act on it.

"Gay is good" doesn't have to mean what I used to think—that I need a lot of sex or a lover to be happy. Nor need it mean the opposite—stoic celibacy. It can also apply to how I center and balance myself, how I choose and nurture friendships, how I support my community. And when I consider or have sex, can I change how I think about it—to admire, share, and enjoy beauty without trying to use, own, or consume it? Pleasure is good but we are not objects. And contrary to what fashion, ads and some songs suggest, neither are we just images or toys.

In work and play, how can I free myself from the hype of competitive stress? Can I learn to accept and find joy in the present moment, even when it's not what I might prefer? Can I continue to take risks, to redefine myself? Can I wake up from sexism, racism, ageism, and careerism

251

without becoming obsessed about being "politically correct?" Can I set and fulfill goals, while still allowing spontaneity? In short, can I take my energy glue out of the worry/fear/consumer trap?

These are some of my questions. What are yours? What do you hope for?

Each of us must take more responsibility for our own lives as well as for our collective life. Instead of doomsaying, we must participate more fully in social and cultural institutions, and change them—as indeed, we are. We have achieved what we have because we dared to dream and to risk acting on those dreams. This must remain our commitment.

*Sitting with My Friend*

AIDS is neither a curse nor a blessing; it just is. I see its inexorable progression in a 24-year old friend whom I've been sitting with every Friday for the past nine months. I got to know J.D. in a healing workshop. He came up to me one night and gave me a hug because, he said, he just felt I needed one.

J.D. is such a beautiful person I found it hard to believe at first that he was sick. But last fall he became bedridden. I wasn't sure if I could cope with helping care for him—I'm not trained as a nurse—but it was just something that needed doing, so I did it. I felt awkward at first but he encouraged and gave me confidence.

Words can't tell what I've learned from J.D.—about myself, about life. Sitting with him every Friday and watching his courage and dignity in the face of this disease has been one of the most intimate, inspiring experiences of my life. It's not always been easy, certainly—not for J.D., his lover, his parents, or for any of us—but it's been real. Often we've sat for hours together and said nothing, yet said more than most people ever do. His hands flutter like butterflies. He sometimes suffers delusions. But don't we all?

Because I'm antibody positive, I know I may be in J.D.'s position myself someday—still alive but fading, with little control of body or mind. We all die differently, just as we all live differently. I don't know what it will be like for me but I'm no longer afraid. I still feel angry, frustrated, or self-pitying sometimes—often over the most trivial incidents—but when I'm with J.D. these feelings drop away. And I'm filled with such a profound gratitude to be alive, to be gay and to have the friends I have and have had, that I cannot explain it.

It's a simple fact that someday all of us will die. Maybe our entire planet will. But I also know now, more deeply than ever, that our lives, our culture and our world are too beautiful to throw away.

# MY KID

*How does it feel to be a single gay father?*

When Alysia was small I said it was like living with a lover who won't leave you. Now that she's fifteen it's more like living with a messy roommate who holds the lease.

But I lie. Parenting necessitates this. I don't mean simple hypocrisy such as bragging about one's kids or unwritten rules such as "All parents must feel guilty that they're not doing enough for their kids", though this too enters in. I mean many of my deepest feelings around or "for" Alysia shock even me. So we must consider two orders of lies embedded in the postindustrial institution of parenthood: lies of the tribe and lies of the soul.

Perhaps all parenting models practice terror and torture. Primitive societies, such as studied by Gilbert Herdt and others, condense this into initiation rites. The horror is over quickly and society as a whole takes responsibility. Modern patriarchal families derive from Rome where the father has complete life and death rights over the children. I can be a benevolent dictator if I choose but if Alysia robs a bank society will hold me responsible. I always rejected these models—mirroring and reproducing the repressive State as they do—yet in times of stress I fall back on terror's worst excesses (e.g.—yelling: "Shut up!"; threatening violence). So I am torn, forced to live a lie. How can I be a parent? I've always hated parents and avoided their company. I don't want responsibility. *I* want to be the child. Denials or displacements of parental selfishness constitute lies of the tribe.

This said, parenting can be—indeed, was and is—quite different than I anticipated. While I imagined I couldn't relate to a child before it began to speak for instance, I found my richest, most rewarding time with Alysia *before* she talked, or to be more precise, before she spoke the English language.

When Alysia was born a psychic channel of communication immediately opened up between us. There's no way to say in words what it was like, this telepathic participation in nonverbality, except to say it was incredible. Wrinkled, red, helplessly writhing in my hands, Alysia nonetheless exuded an overpowering aura, as if she were an emissary from outer space come to raise me more than I could ever "raise" her. I was amazed that I could sometimes calm her, communicate to her in ways even her mother couldn't. But there were troubling, scary episodes too.

When Alysia was eight weeks old I took some LSD and went into the bedroom to play with her. Her eyes rolled uncontrollably, her arms and legs flailed. I was confronted with a monstrous id. It takes an incredible, rapacious ego just to focus one's eyes or bring one's arms under enough control to reach for a ball. If I entered into or shared Alysia's consciousness at this point I, the adult, would have become more monstrous than Charles Manson. I had to leave her presence because I was too psychically vulnerable. I understood too the biblical phrase "They stiffened their backs against us." How little we adults let ourselves feel. When Alysia got angry her whole body turned beet red and her back arched like a bow.

Then sex. Incest is a forbidden topic. Its causes are even more unsettling because it's not just a matter of "evil" parents. I remember holding and kissing Alysia when she was a few months old. Impulsively, unthinkingly, I put my tongue in her mouth. She giggled with delight and wanted to do it again. I felt suddenly appalled at how sexual we were and I felt guilty and afraid Barb would come in and see us like this. After that I was careful to hold myself back. But I could see how easily incest could occur. Infants are polymorphously perverse. They have no morality. It is exceedingly dangerous to fall under their spell. Denials and displacements of true infant consciousness and its attendant powers are lies of the soul. All societies discipline and punish children, I think, out of fear.

*Did anything else embarrassing occur during Alysia's early childhood?*

More before she was born. Barb and I continued fucking until a few days before Alysia's birth. Maybe we were monsters but we didn't even mind fucking during her period. I had no hangups about menstrual blood. The odder situation is that I was "coming out" during Barb's pregnancy—and with Barb's wholehearted encouragement. She liked the guys I was attracted to and didn't want me relating to other women, not even as friends.

At first, the guys I knew were all straight, mostly students or friends between the ages of 18 to 21, though a few were younger. I was 27, Barb 23. These guys had a close emotional fondness for me but never would have made it with me alone. I suffered thinking I was the bad one so Barb instigated three-ways. After dinner she'd say "Let's go lie down" and it would start from there. She had this way of making sex seem really wholesome and innocent because she was such a joyful, vivacious, and uninhibited person. We had several hot sessions with a highschool kid who turned his friends on to us. It's a miracle we weren't busted for corrupting minors.

My main love was a college sophmore named John. He was the only one Barb didn't get on with. John was cold, competitive, and aloof towards Barb but extremely seductive towards me. Even though he was straight, supposedly, he would lie back on the couch and adopt langorous poses. Yet John was so sensitive towards Barb's pregnancy that he once got symptoms of morning sickness.

The night Alysia was born was the first night John let me screw him. I'd waited over two years. So when I visited Barb and Alysia at the hospital the next day I felt ecstatic and guilty at the same time. I was supposed to be ecstatic because I'd had a baby; instead I was ecstatic because I'd fucked John. Barb was so ecstatic over Alysia she didn't care. She was just happy I was happy. So we were all ecstatic but me for pseudepigraphal reasons (note: the pseudepigraphal books in the bible are the gnostic texts almost nobody accepts as valid).

That day I also held Alysia for the first time. She was about the size of a large frog. The first thing she did was pee on my arm. This was my anointment into parenthood. The pee and shit of newborns has a sweet rather than noxious odor.

*Wasn't your wife at all upset about your gayness?*

Quite the contrary; I'd told Barb I was bisexual when I met her. That turned her on to me more because it meant: "I could love the whole human race, not just half of it," as she put it. I suppose I represented added mystery, challenge. Also, early on, Barb had an indispensable role to play. Later, when I got into tricking at gay bars, it was a different story. Barb always wanted the phone number of where I'd be and she'd call at 7 am to ask when I was coming home.

We were very political at this time and, in theory, gay liberation was seen as supporting women's liberation. It was the most direct way for men to confront and fight sexism or "phallic imperialism"as Sue Katz called it. I say "in theory" because I later came to see such thinking was overly utopian. But it did soften my macho viewpoint and made me much more sympathetic to women's social role and viewpoint.

At the same time, because I had a wife and kid, no one could question my "manhood." I obviously wasn't gay just because I *couldn't* relate to women sexually.

No doubt this allowed me to "come out" much more publically and aggressively than I would have otherwise. Even so, I paid a price. I lost friends. What was hardest for Barb, so she claimed, was her straight friend's "sympathy." "How can you stand it?" they'd ask. They refused to accept that it didn't bother her all that much. She had other boyfriends and at least one other girlfriend herself. What she loathed was others seeing her as a poor suffering victim of my gayness.

*But you said Barb was jealous of John and guys you picked up in bars?*

Well I was obsessive about John. It's pretty sick now that I look back on it. I even left Barb and Alysia to live with him for six months. There were some fights and suffering around that which, naïvely, none of us expected. Sex with John signified cosmic transcendence, whereas my relationship with Barb meant long term commitment, especially since I'd cared for Alysia during much of her early infancy as a "househusband." Barb and I pioneered what John Lennon and Yoko Ono wouldn't do till much later but Alysia was the glue holding us together certainly.

Barb was more upset, jealous if you will, about the mansion we lived in for a year. We lived with between 8 to 12 people in this 20 room Spanish

Mediterranean mansion. It was cold and gloomy and Barb couldn't stand sharing a kitchen with other people. So she withdrew a lot and actually moved out on me before I moved in with John. Ironically, Barb ended up in an even weirder commune. She became houseparent of a cottage in this retardation center where we worked. Alysia was doted over by hippie staff and played with retarded 18 year olds, some of which were the size of pro football players.

As for John, he finally couldn't stand my craziness. I was fiendishly possessive, smothering in my solicitations, and I wanted to fuck him two or three times daily. When he finally left I flipped. I'd sit catatonically in a closet or go into crying jags that would last hours. The only reason I wasn't psychotic, Barb said, is that I was too neurotic. But I was definitely pushing the edge. Barb became much more sympathetic to John when he returned from Florida and she even scolded me when I treated him badly.

For a few months I went to Santa Fe, then San Francisco, but I began to miss Alysia and John too much. It's funny how I could talk to Alysia on the phone even though, at age two, she was barely verbal. We talked about ducks. I'd taken her to a lake to see ducks and she remembered that. Barb said I was the only one Alysia would talk to on the phone.

Upon returning to Atlanta I entered therapy, which didn't help much because I was constantly on drugs: alcohol, speed, coke, Quaaludes, Valium, hallucinogens of various kinds. Meanwhile Barb entered into a relationship with one of her patients. She'd changed jobs to a mental hospital and Trip was a beautiful 18 year old who'd attempted suicide after being raped in prison. He was on Thorazine so he wouldn't kill people. Anyway, when Barb could get him out on a pass, the three of us would shoot MDA and have orgies. They introduced me to needles, which I'd so far avoided. In-between orgies, I was hearing cosmic voices telling me to kill John and myself so we could be reincarnated. Barb was about to have me committed when she died in a car accident after going to Detroit to get Trip out of jail. I sensed our excesses would lead to death, only I assumed *I'd* be the one to die, which I longed for.

*What happened then?*

Barb's death shocked me out of my insanity. I'm holding the phone and my head starts spinning. Ordinary, banal moments come to mind first; trivialities I took for granted such as walking into an anti-war meeting with Barb, greeting friends, and sitting down. The longer I knew Barb, the more deeply I loved her. This may sound strange after what I've said but I increasingly respected her for her mind. I don't know how she put up with me for so long. I mean I'd take her money and give it to my junkie boyfriends—stuff like that.

I knew if I wanted to keep Alysia I'd have to stop being crazy. I didn't know if I could but I had to try. Alysia was all I had left in the world and I was all she had too. Not one of my friends thought I could do it. They all thought I should give Alysia to Barb's or my parents. But I pulled it together.

I took Alysia to her daycare center at 6 am, drove to my job by 7, worked till 3, drove back and got Alysia at 4 (or later if I took a nap), fixed dinner and played with Alysia some, read her a story and put her to bed, napped again, hit the bars between midnight and 3 am, napped, and was up again at the crack of dawn. After a couple months I went through Rolfing, a body restructuring therapy recommended by my Tai Chi teacher. That helped a lot. I also found time to make several children's books for Alysia including one that helped her get over her fear of monsters. And I wrote a novel.

*What was the novel about?*

Why people get into impossible relationships but refuse to let go of them. It was very gothic and took place in the Yellow Mansion. Lousy writing, but at least a start.

*How did Alysia take Barb's death?*

For two weeks she was real calm, cheerful even. Then one morning she went hysterical, screaming: "I want mommy, I want mommy." I'd already explained Barb's death with the aid of Alysia's Babar book and I demonstrated the accident using her toy cars. But I doubt she fully understood. Despite Alysia's freakout, I dressed her and took her to her daycare as usual. That was basically the end of it except that she'd occasionally say things like: "Let's go to the store and get a new mommy." She was a child of consumer society after all (laughs).

Because Alysia was only 2½ when Barb died, she doesn't remember her. So she's always wanted to see photos, hear stories of what her Mom was like. That's painful because I don't have a clear memory and what I do recall isn't entirely pleasant. I'd say Barb always had a big smile and liked to help people. And I'd say Barb loved her very much, which is true. Alysia went everywhere with us: marches, parties, you name it. Barb breastfed her in restaurants or on the steps of the Emory library, which shocked some people. People who weren't at all bothered by the Vietnam War were shocked to see a mother breastfeeding her child.

Alysia also asks what she was like as a child. She was happy, buoyant, didn't cry much. She had winning big bright eyes and intense flashing eyes when she was angry. I once caught her practicing her frown in a mirror. "Daddy gets angry, John gets angry, Alysia gets angry," she was saying. But she wasn't angry often. She sang a lot.

After Barb died, Alysia started pissing standing up. She always hit the toilet but when her grandmother corrected her she stopped. Then there was the typical father/kid stuff. Once I hid behind a tree and pretended to be the tree talking. Alysia talked to the tree for a while but, impatient for my return, pulled down her pants. We had a lot of fun together. I especially enjoyed skipping with her, which I wouldn't have been able to do if I was alone. Society frowns on adults skipping down the street unless they're with children. So, in a way, you get to be more of a kid if you have one.

*Was gay parenting easier in San Francisco?*

Not really. We didn't know so many people in San Francisco though early on I met a single mother who was pretty far out. M. wasn't what you'd call beautiful, but she always looked classy. She worked in a massage parlor, dealt grass and picked up young guys at the Stud. She'd get these boys to stay with her, then get them on GA and foodstamps that she'd take for their room and board. After she got them hooked on pot she'd make them ply their asses to pay for it. But M.'s little girl and Alysia got on like a couple water sprites. M. and I were friends till one of her boyfriends left her for me.

Later I became friends with an actress who had a little girl in Alysia's daycare center. J. knew folks in Warhol's circle, as well as Sam Shepard and some English women who went to school with Doris Lessing's son. So maybe I met more interesting people in San Francisco. But then Tim Leary and Mark Rudd stayed at my place in Atlanta, and I met Robert Kennedy and LBJ in Nebraska, so I guess you can meet famous people anywhere. The only time Alysia was impressed by my contacts was when I introduced her to William Burroughs, Richard Brautigan, and Nina Hagen in Amsterdam. We were in a poetry festival together. But Alysia wasn't much impressed to meet Robert Duncan, Judy Grahn, or Kathy Acker because she hadn't read about them in *Rolling Stone*. Fame is so fatuous. My favorite writers and artists have always been more obscure: Redon, Huysmans, Laure, Bataille, or Bob Kaufman or Irving Rosenthal to name contemporaries.

As for the gay scene, some were jealous of Alysia stealing their limelight; others feared she'd break their antiques. It got better after I helped found the gay fathers organization. I felt less isolated and weird then. The first group of us was mostly welfare fathers. When a more Yuppie crowd took over—real estate speculators or Doctors who'd "come out" at age 50—I felt somewhat outcast again. I mean, I was on AFDC and they sat around talking about their yachts. But I did make one good friend who became my next-door neighbor. Will had two kids and was even poorer than I. He also turned me on to the poetry of Jack Spicer and wrote a poem that I put on the back of my first book. When I got into the poetry scene things got a lot better because now I had a reason to live in addition to Alysia. I didn't want to end up like those parents who live *only* for their kids. It's bad for them and the kids both.

*How has Alysia reacted to your being gay?*

From babyhood she's seen me in bed with guys. I've never hid this. She assumed we were playing, which is of course correct. She liked John and she particularly liked a San Francisco boyfriend named Ed who lived with us for several months. She called him Eddiebody. He picked her up from daycare in drag once, which freaked out the staff.

When Ed and I were on acid once, Alysia came over and said very solemnly: "Daddy, you can be a boy or you can be a girl. You can be whatever you want to be." It was hard on us both when Ed left. Then, when Alysia was five, I mentioned to her that I was attracted to one of her new daycare teachers. She embarrassed the hell out of me by marching over to him and saying, "My Daddy really *likes* you." A week later I saw him in a bar and we got it on.

Around 3rd grade there was a shift. She was in a very proper French American school now and walking home with a friend one day they saw a "No on Prop. 9" poster in a window. That was the Brigg's Initiative regarding gay teachers. "My Daddy has one of those," Alysia said proudly. Her friend, with a sort of horror no doubt picked up from her parents, replied: "Do you know what *that* means? That's when boys like boys and girls like girls." Since then Alysia's been more cautious, or ambiguous, about letting her friends know I'm gay. She may have even lost some high school friends over the issue; I'm not sure. But I don't think she minds personally. In fact, her uncle, Barb's brother, is gay and she likes to hang out with him and his friends, as well as with some gay guys in their late 20s who she's met through me. It's safe flirting. On the other hand, she's made a couple sharply critical comments of late, when she was mad. Once about "the whores" I take to bed and once about how I didn't care about (or ever notice) women. Actually, I pretty much stopped tricking when she was in 4th or 5th grade. Although it's partly the result of getting older, I toned down my life a lot because of Alysia.

A resentment on my part is that she's disrupted some of my relationships. All single parents have to put up with this, I'm sure, but Alysia's very clever and manipulative. She knows how to push people's guilt or insecurity buttons—mine included. She can charm anyone's heart away, when she wants to, but she can be a rude witch too. One friend said we seem more like brother/sister than father/child. Another noted that we sometimes bicker like an old married couple. Basically I feel there's a very deep mutual love and respect between us, one that many parents (or children) might envy.

*How does Alysia feel about your drug addiction? Has this affected her?*

When I denied it was a problem, so did she. Of course, she's grown up to be very independent in a unique environment where a bit of craziness was always ready to irrupt. So she's extremely alert to social nuances. Learning to live in so many different environments—mine, her grandparents, her friends, schools, the woman she babysits for, tv world, etc.—has made her very creative, fluid, imaginative. She loves to draw, act, and write stories. She also tends to procrastinate, be disorganized, and her room's a mess. What that means, if anything, I don't know. When I first got clean and sober I was very irritable. Alysia and I quarreled a lot. Lately we're both much happier and get along quite well.

Alysia doesn't tell me everything about herself but, when she was in 8th grade, she asked me what taking LSD was like. A friend of hers had taken some and gotten into a roaring fight with her mother. So I told Alysia how it affected me, the hallucinogenic effects and all, and added that it might break chromosomes. Recently Alysia asked if I'd approve if she took ecstasy (MMDA) with her girlfriends. She'd read that some psychologists advocated its use. I told her I knew it must be hard to resist peer pressure but that I never knew anyone to do a "fantastic" drug just once. I hear she asked some other older friends what they thought too. I think she decided against it, for now anyway.

I think Alysia knows that because of her mother's and my background she might be genetically predetermined to addiction. It's a disease you can harbor latently before you ever use. I took Alysia to a couple NA meetings once and she has a friend whose mother is in AA. Alysia's reaction to the meetings is that they weren't dramatic enough.

Also she's an agnostic and doesn't go for the higher power stuff. She wants to run her life her own way. I can share my experience with her, and I'm glad she sometimes asks me to, but I don't try to butt into her life too much because, at this point, I really have no control. If she's "damaged," I can't "fix" her. I'm doing well if I can take care of myself.

*What does Alysia want to be when she grows up?*

What do any of us want to be when we grow up? (laughs) Seriously, she doesn't have any firm ideas about that at present. She's variously said she'd like to be a painter, a writer, or a psychologist like her mother. She's much more clear as to what she *doesn't* want, namely to work in an office. She wants to return to Europe when she graduates from high school and she plans to go to college. During the past year she's earned $80 to $100 a month from her allowance and babysitting. The woman she babysits for has also given her a lot of nice clothes. Like all of us, she likes the independance she feels when she has some money in her pocket. She spends a lot of time figuring how much she'd have to earn to go in on an apartment with her friends.

*Why haven't you written more about Alysia?*

We're too close. It would be too scary. Also, I tend to write out of my obsessions and she doesn't fit into them very directly. When Alysia was younger I did get some poems out of things she said, especially when she was still learning and exploring the language. She'd say things like: "Why is the moon following us?" or "Open these flowers or beware." I can't do that any more because she talks and thinks too much like I do now.

*What is the earliest memory of your own childhood?*

The first time I go out into the yard by myself. It's absolutely exhilarating. I can still smell the fresh grass. But the yard is so big, so vast. It's as huge as a battlefield. I've been told Dad's away fighting a war, so I suppose that's why I think of this.

Then, far away across the street, I see a little blond girl about my age. She just stands there gazing at me. Neither of us speaks. I'm too terrified to either move or speak. This must be what war is like, I think. Staring into the eyes of a total stranger. Total freedom. Total death.

*And your earliest childhood dream?*

I'm in the yard naked; my friends Randy and Marsha are across the street. They're naked too and call for me to come over for Marsha's birthday party. I want to go but when I step into the street, fire engines shriek by. Then Dad comes out. He's naked too. "Come on," he says and crosses the street. I really want to go but when I step in the street again, more fire engines roar by. "Run," Daddy calls. But I'm too scared.

I had this dream several times between kindergarten and 2nd grade. It was worst when I was sick with a fever. No one could protect me. Ever since, my nightmares have all involved sex or being in cars which go out of control. Before leaving Santa Fe for San Francisco, for instance, I dreamt the highway narrowed into a weird house with a long dark hallway. A weasel in the hallway tried to bite me. The dream made me anxious and I considered postponing the trip but didn't. About fifty miles from Flagstaff, my Toyota hit a patch of ice. I was going 60 when the car skidded off the highway but the speed had slowed to 30 or 40 when the car started rolling. "This may be it," I thought and I just totally relaxed. Amazingly the only damage was a cracked windshield and a flat tire. I wasn't even scratched.

On another occasion, I was hit by a speeding car in Rome. My life flashed before my eyes as I flipped into the air. This time I only cracked two teeth. But it dawns on me; the feeling of being in an out-of-control-car is not unlike the feeling I had when Barb first told me she was pregnant. You see, I thought she was using an IUD. What I first felt was panic. Then I relaxed. Whereas the idea of fatherhood in the abstract terrified me, I found I could cope if I just took it one hour, one day, one step at a time. So far, despite all the craziness and unorthodox parental situations I've found myself in, that's worked. When I let go of fear, life works.

FAMOUS LAST WORDS

Dear Mother,

Dim jerky stars are blowing away across a gleaming empty sky. Tonight I shall meditate upon that which I am. I'm like I was back then, really. Well, almost always...designing the elements of my own car crash. I have not come to since and I never shall.

I am now discovering that reason, unable in the first place to prevent our misfortunes, is even less equal to consoling us for them. Was it conceivably for this piece of knowledge that I journeyed so far? Alone I cannot carry this burden of joy and doubt. You my double, my witness... there, lean over with me...let's look together...does it emit, deposit...as on the mirror we hold before the mouth of the dying...a fine mist? Who knows but that, on the lower frequencies, I speak for you. So against you I will fling myself, unvanquished and unyielding!

(So it goes in the world. "Well, I shall have a cup of tea." A voice interrupts the words of what has already been said. But it is difficult for words to say that which it is their purpose to deny.)

Lord, how quickly it gets dark here. Night and the deafening racket of crickets again engulf the garden and the veranda, all around the house... leading to this page, this sentence, this full stop, by the old pen frequently and mechanically dipped into the blue-black ink. But let's return to the subject.

There are many things to be done towards the business of living but I decided I no more know what to do than if I was just another lousy human being. Pity the unbeliever who would feign believe or the galley-slave who goes to sea alone at night, beneath a firmament no longer lit by the consoling beacon-fires of ancient hope. They're just waiting for you to try something stupid like that. But now each time I read your letter I feel confident again. Do you think I could ever have spoken to you in this fashion if I wasn't some little supernumerary in a play?

The supersensuality has lifted now, and no one will ever make me believe that the sacred wenches of Benares or Plato's rooster are images of God. This temple was built by neither Semiramis nor the Queen of Sheba, but they say that on its stones are engraved the principal secrets of Nicholas Flamel more enigmatic even than those of

Paraceleus. For instance, "The care with which there is incredible justice and likeness, all this makes a magnificent asparagus, and also a fountain." Or, "An addition of information must fly." But however passionate, sinning and rebellious the heart hidden in this tomb, the flowers growing over it peep serenely.

It was only after daybreak, after all the dancers had left, that Sir Stephen and the Commander, awakening Natalie, helped O to her feet, led her to the middle of the courtyard, unfastened her chain and removed her mask and, laying her back upon a table, possessed her. I saw no shadow of another departing from her. She was alone. The next day, I left the bathroom. So it's not a question of suicide; it's only a question of beating a record.

(O all these gold ribbons, blowing with the rhythm of breathing, breathe in, breathe out, the light falls quite gently now, breasts heaving, red blood become milk! Beauty will be CONVULSIVE or it will not be at all.)

What then? I don't know. Who can tell? Surely the reader cannot be so stupid as not to remember what happened next.

P_____ was sitting downcast and mumbling something incoherent and senseless. He was withered, wrinkled and loathsome of visage like a gigantic whirligig beetle which has had the left half of its brain extracted. "You understand," said the old man. "People repeat what they've been told, a misfortune for instance, they say it's a testing time or just something you have to put up with, they don't look any further, but misfortune has no date, it does not arrive one day and fly away the next, it's there, it doesn't budge, we experience it or not according to unknown laws." That is what he tells me.

"Like a *lizard*!" he said; it was as if the shame of it must outlive him. "Forever," he said. He told Grace he'd rather just be effeminate. He only hopes his hat may not have given you a headache. And the dog too gave up then, and lay down, his eyes bloodshot, his head flat along her knees.

The argument that next develops is one in which various explanations on widely different scales interact, forcing language to a new scale of discourse that includes all these possible conflicts—and the motivation behind them. (*Why can't lizards go to heaven?*) Unfortunately, they agreed about nothing at all. I lingered around wondering how anyone could ever imagine unquiet slumbers for the sleepers in that quiet earth.

Then she saw him moving farther and farther away, farther and farther into the darkness until he was a pinpoint of light. As he caught his footing, his head fell back, and the Milky Way flowed down inside him with a roar. That was the last thing he ever saw.

The man did not stir. He was so tired. He died with a whimper. After the autopsy, all our medical experts rejected any possibility of insanity. He was soon borne away by the waves and lost in darkness and distance. And wherever he may have disappeared to, I wish him luck.

Then I fled, my face in my hands. A plague of confusion has followed me ever since. No...it all happened. Go and see for yourself if you do not believe me. We want no proofs; we ask none to believe us! Someday I shall write about all this in greater detail.

(So that is why music and dancing come from Guinea, God sent it there first—A way a lone a last a love a long the *lickety-lickety-lickety-split*—the tune was "My Heart's in the Highlands.")

In a little while I shall place these written pages in an empty oxygen cylinder and throw them into the deep. I leave it to be settled, by whomsoever it may concern, whether the tendency of this work be altogether to recommend parental tyranny or reward filial piety. For me, it will be an act of piety for everything that lives is Holy...and the dark and dank tarn at my feet will close sullenly and silently over the fragments....

...and among the forms in my dream are you, who like myself are many and no one. Because you thought you were special — (Her same eyes, her same mouth, open in surprise to see, at last, her long-cherished wish. We must have looked at each other like two blank crossword puzzles confronting themselves. And that was the end of us.)

Then we walk out into the polyped street and in some miraculous manner are transformed into passersby. The miracle at last! The light went out; is going out. It is in the future that we must see our history.

Trust me.

God goes with thoughtless people.

Smell the flowers while you can.

A story like this can have no happy ending...or can it?

Toward us, singing, came eleven little blind girls from the orphanage of Julius the Apostolic. For the first time they had done something out of love. Matter of fact, I think this was the youngest we ever felt. It was our best time. But we couldn't find a single mention in the press of this turning point in our lives.

# ILLUSTRATED POEMS & COMICS

BEFORE & AFTER. LAUGHTER. A MALEBOLGE OF MISTAKEN IDEAS (SHE WENT TO BED WITH AN IDEA & THE IDEA HURT. SWELLED UP, A PURPLE GRAPE. "PUT THIS RING ON FOR SIZE & YOU'LL BE MINE FOREVER.") THE CALIPERS (MR. & MISSUS)...

COOLIDGE? McNAUGTON?

BRING IT ASHORE COUCH

EXIT

COULDN'T NUANCE WHERE ANYWHERE WOULD BE TOMORROW (LOSING THEIR METAPHYSICAL PREDICAMENT) & MAPS OF MARRAIGE FALLING DOWN LIKE LONDON BRIDGE. NOW MOVED TO A GHOST TOWN IN ARIZONA. NO CHILDREN. ANYMORE. OR VERY FEW. TROLLS UNDER ALL THE BRIDGES.

RIBBONS IN HAIR YOU COME UPON THEM. SMILING MARVELOUSLY. "PEEL ME A GRAPE," YOU SAY, WISHING THEY WOULD WEAR IDEAS MORE SERIOUSLY ("PLEASE... PLEASE"). THEY GIVE YOU ANDROGYNOUS CANDY & A BIG THUMP ON THE BIBLE. PLAIN. TO SEE THEY WILL ALWAYS BE IN PAIN TO BE.

QUICKLY PASSING.

AND NOW TO HACK MY PUNK COUCH TO BITS... CALL IT "FLUX-CORRECTIONISM"... A NEW CRAZE... AH...

THE END

277

# JACOB'S ANGEL SEEN AT CAFE FLORE

I think I see another angel there.
Hovering over coffee as in prayer
His wings enfolded, shielding him from care
The sun falls harp-like freshening the air.

In all the morning seems so crisp and clear
That Beauty's magic now is understood~
Still, something troubles me, a monkish fear.
If I could believe in Innocence I would.

The angel turns now, politely stares at me
Wondering why, perhaps, my Faith's not free
I sit behind my table like a tree
Uprooted, looking down mysteriously.

For certain trees like melancholy coasts
Hang bleak with burdens like the sea its ghosts
And though fair angels promise to uplift,
I can't again accept such risk.

The angel pauses seeing me amiss,
His mission not to force me but to sift
Out what is lustful in my boasts
As diplomats read nuances in toasts.

And so the angel watches peacefully
My tortured wooden similes, his glee
Distending metaphysically
Until I also laugh. Discovery!

Wrenched, tossed, blown~ it's queer
This sudden sharing flash in angelhood:
As simple as relaxing over beer,
Yet rare as Power melded into Good.

So joyously I take the angel's dare
And wrestle with his eyes under the stare.
Not his arm subdues me but his hair~
The way he simply smiles and lets me care.

Stephen Abbott 1977

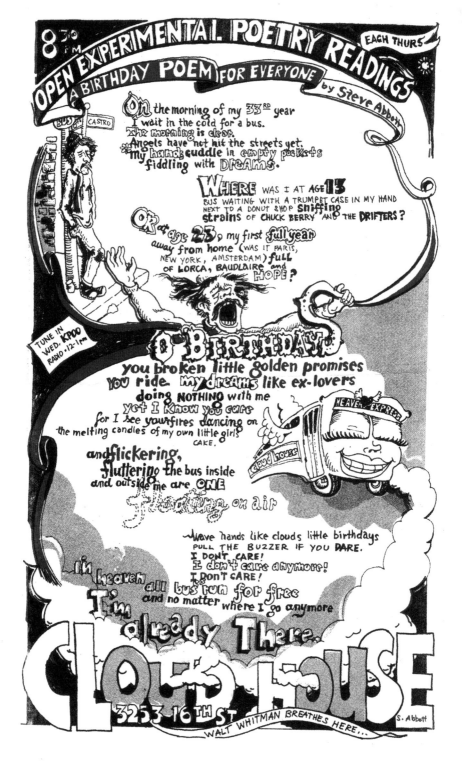

# COUNTING STREAMS IN THIS FOREST OF YOUR EYES

COUNTING STREAMS IN THIS FOREST OF YOUR EYES
I WAS VERY. I WAS BUBBLY TOO
WHEN UPPEST, CRAZIEST WATERFALL SPASMS SPRAYED
    OVER ME,
IT WAS SO CLEAN.
IT WAS SO CLEAN YOU COULD HEAR FOR YEARS
AND THE REDWOODS DID HIGHEST ALGEBRA IN OUR HAIR.

THIS POEM WILL NOT JIG A DISTANCE OF TIMES.
TREES COULD NEVER SING SUCH A SAD SONG.
WHAT MOTHER SAID LONG AGO
SCARES EVEN BULLDOZERS AWAY FROM OUR HORIZON. AND NOW
A COUNTING DANCES OVER OUR FINGERS.

ONE, TWO EYES IN THIS FOREST OF STREAMS. FOUR. FIVE
    MILLION.
WE ARE SO MORE. WHO CAN SAY BUBBLY NOW?
THE WEATHER OF MATHEMATICS HAS MADE THE REDWOODS LAUGH
AND THEY HAVE DROPPED CLEAN OUT OF SCHOOL.
IT IS SO CLEAN.
IT IS SO CLEAN YOU CAN STREAMLINE EYES.
THE TEACHERS OF LOVE ARE BULLDOZERS DIGGING FOR ROOTS
BUT THE UPPEST, CRAZIEST WATERFALL SEASONS SPRAY OVER US.
    SO SAID OUR MOTHER LONG AGO.

—STEPHEN ABBOTT, 1977

# HIPPIE HISTOMAP

A BRIEF CHRONOLOGY OF MAGICIANS & OTHER COUNTER-CULTURE ARTISTS, WRITERS & PHILOSOPHERS

**HARD/DARK TRADITION**

**SOFT/LIGHT TRADITION**

THRU 18th CENTURY

### EGYPT
Hermes Trismegistus (legendary)
The Emerald Tables

### GREECE
★ Pre-Socratics & Sophists (600-400 BC)

GNOSTICS:
Mythic & Mystery religions, Simon Magus, Orphites, Cainities etc (100 BC — 1700 AD)

### PERSIAN
Zoroaster (628-551 BC)

KABBALAH:
(Sepher Yetzirah-300AD
to Zohar — 1300 AD)

### HEBREW
Key of Solomon (before 100 BC)
Essenes & Jesus of Nazarus (100 BC — 33 AD)

Hieronymus Bosch (1450-1516)
Cornelius Agrippa (1486-1534)
Nostradamus

Albert Magnus (1206-1280)
Duns Scotus (1265-1306)
★ Nicholas de Cusa (1401-1464)
John Dee (1527-1608)

St. Francis of Assisi (1181-1226)

### INDIA
Buddha (563-483 BC)

SUFIS:
Ashati-as-Sata (623 AD) to Rumi (1273 AD)

### CHINA
I Ching (3000-1200 BC.)

Taoism: Lao-Tzu (600-500 BC ?)

7 Sages of the Bamboo Group (250-300 AD)

Li Po (8th cen.)

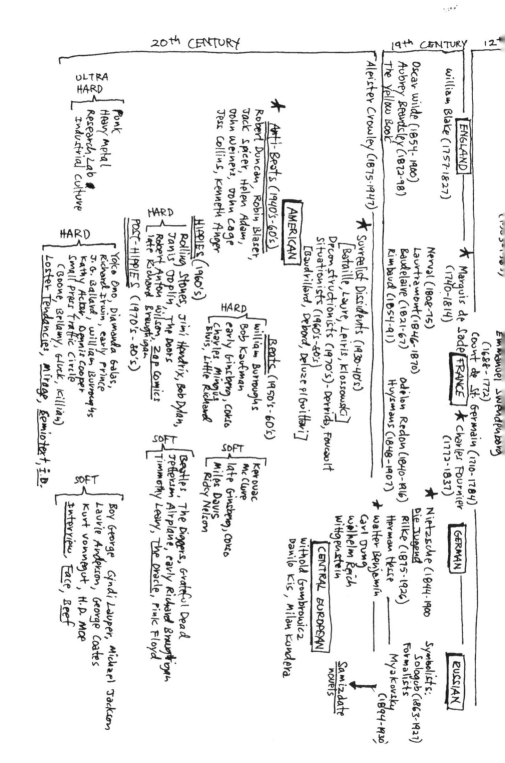

20th CENTURY    19th CENTURY   12

Emmanuel Swedenborg (1688-1772)
Court de St. Germain

**ENGLAND**
William Blake (1757-1827)
Oscar Wilde (1854-1900)
Aubrey Beardsley (1872-98)
The Yellow Book
Aleister Crowley (1875-1947)

**FRANCE**
★ Marquis de Sade (1740-1814)
★ Charles Fournier (1772-1837)
Nerval (1808-55)
Lautréamont (1846-1870)
Baudelaire (1821-67)
Rimbaud (1854-91)
Odilon Redon (1840-1916)
Huysmans (1848-1907)

★ Surrealist Dissidents (1930-40's)
[Bataille, Leiris, Klossowski]
Decon. structionists (1970's) - Derrida, Foucault
Situationists (1960's-80's)
[Baudrillard, Debord, Deleuze et Guittari]

★ Anti-Beats (1940's-60's)
Robert Duncan, Robin Blaser,
Jack Spicer, Helen Adam,
John Weiners, John Cage
Jess Collins, Kenneth Anger

**AMERICAN**

HARD
HIPPIES (1960's)
Rolling Stones, Janis Joplin, The Doors,
Robert Anton Wilson, late Richard Brautigan, Zap Comics

HARD
POST-HIPPIES (1970's-80's)
Yoko Ono, Diamanda Galas,
Richard Irwin, early Prince,
J.G. Ballard, William Burroughs
Kathy Acker, Dennis Cooper
Small Press Traffic Circle
(Boone, Bellamy, Gluck, Killian)
Loose Tendencies, Mirage, Semiotext, I.D.

HARD
Beats (1950's-60's)
William Burroughs
early Ginsberg, Corso
Charles Mingus
Elvis, Little Richard
Bob Kaufman

HARD
early Jimi Hendrix, Bob Dylan

SOFT
Kerouac
McClure
late Ginsberg, Corso
Miles Davis
Ricky Nelson

SOFT
Beatles, The Diggers, Grateful Dead,
Jefferson Airplane, early Richard Brautigan,
Timmothy Leary, The Oracle, Pink Floyd

SOFT
Boy George, Cyndi Lauper, Michael Jackson,
Laurie Anderson, George Coates,
Kurt Vonnegut, H.D. Moe,
Interview, Face, Beef

**GERMAN**
★ Nietzsche (1844-1900)
Die Jugend
Rilke (1875-1926)
Hermann Hesse
★ Walter Benjamin
Carl Jung
Wilhelm Reich
Wittgenstein

**CENTRAL EUROPEAN**
Witold Gombrowicz
Danilo Kiš, Milan Kundera

**RUSSIAN**
Symbolists:
Sologub (1863-1927)
Formalists
Mayakovsky (1894-1930)
Samizdate novels

ULTRA HARD
Punk
Heavy Metal
Research Lab
Industrial Culture

# Burning to Speak

A tension in the woods. The rest
we have forgotten.
Today is not so ~~easy~~ easy as fall-
ing into it.
Bullets felled my butter donkey target.
Dust to dust.
Hey a moody baby doom a yam?
I don't know
but tomorrow my emotions intercept
what you wanted me not to know.
(chorus)
Burning to speak. Burning to
speak. Been waiting on the phone for
nearly a week. Burning to speak.
guess you figure I'm just some
kinda half to.
Le ciel d'amour. Close the door.
Have you forgotten?
Today is not so easy as falling into
it. They're getting ready to send our
whole life up in smoke.
Some kinda joke. I think I'd laugh
but I'm in love
with the beautiful things your
eyes say when ~~you~~ you say nothing.
(chorus)
Burning to speak. Burning to speak.
Been waiting on the phone ~~you~~ for
nearly a week. Burning to speak.
Burning to speak. ~~The~~ beautiful
things your eyes say when we
say nothing.

Sylvan Woods 12/10/80

Sylvan Woods © Robert Pruzan

TOXIC SHLOCK

LIVING AN UNPLANNED LIFE

He had a dream, a nostalgia for sexuality. In this dream he goes to
a sex bar and sees Eddie who is talking to Steve Barton of *Translator*.
Barton asks Eddie what he thinks of the band. I make a mistake and
confuse Barton with another band member. I make a mistake because I
am not in this dream, let alone living
     in the future.
          The bar is made of wood and there's sawdust on the floor.
          The bar is *not* full of fashionable young men in skirts
            and there's no moon landscape on the walls. The
              bar is old fashioned, everything vague and
                comfortably confused. This is how
                  it is in the dream. He ambles,
                    rambles into a dusty back storeroom;
                  Eddie follows. When he turns
                    around, Eddie's lips float
                closer like a video of John Glenn
              walking on the moon. Their lips collide
            like two halves of a map of Africa. You
          can almost smell the jungle beat of
        their hearts. Nothing has ever been
      quite so sweet as the slow tender sucking
     and palpitation of this kiss. Someone
   else comes into the room just as Eddie
     is prepared to go down on his cock.
       A person entering breaks the spell and Eddie
         decides to go back and dance. The one
           entering is young, white but turns
             black (perhaps a blues
              musician) when he walks
                over to say: "I
                  was going to avoid you
                    when I saw those magik symbols
                  on your pants."
                  He awakes
                 now suddenly aware

he's wearing an old pair
of patched hippie jeans. On one
two figures kneel on a raft (or
flying carpet) while behind them
stands a white-robed holy man, arms upraised.
Five eyes are drawn across the holy man's back.

He awakes realizing he has just received a divine illumination. So why does he want to take revenge on his ex? Why should it matter that his ex-boyfriend lied and dumped him for another? He decides to tear his ex-boyfriend's photo into 4 pieces (in lieu of tearing out his eyes) and on the back of each, draw a curse to break their karmic bond. He'll mail this grimoire to his ex on his birthday:

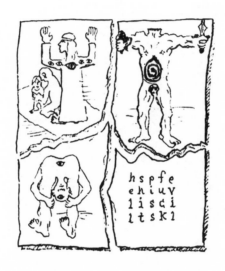

When he walks into the sunshine, everything changes. He feels he has just crawled out of a cave. He decides to let go completely which he has never done before. Light floods into his mind like air into a vacuum. Crossing the street, he's amazed at how joyfully life comes into focus...A woman wearing a red coat gets into a dark blue Buick...A dog urinating by a tree in front of The Deluxe is interrupted by the sniffing of another dog. A teenager pulls the second dog away...Wauzi Records...His ex-boy-friend rides by on a bicycle. The red of his headband stands out against a yellow school bus moving in the opposite direction...He is phased by nothing, by everything...a little girl in a blue stocking cap being tugged along by a woman carrying a bag of groceries...

<u>SKINNY TRIP TO A FAR PLACE</u>

# SETTING FORTH

Melancholy's an eternal traveler. When my daughter arranges a cut-rate trip to Kyoto through a friend's mom, I think "Why not? Some poets of old died traveling."

Our Supershuttle driver enlivens a ride to the airport with some chatter. To further lighten my mind I read Bashō and two issues of *Time*. Here's what I learn:

> Bashō praised Takekuma Pine.
>    Mr. T cuts down his
>       'cause he likes the buzz saw sound.

## OUR ARRIVAL

Landing in a foreign country, tripping over your tongue. As a cushion I took a crash course in Japanese before leaving. I can say "Excuse me" (*Sumi-mausan*), "Water please" (*O misu kudasai*), "Thank you" (*Domo*) and "Where's the bathroom?" (*Oteari wa doku des ka*). The words we hear upon entering Kyoto:

> Hankyu Dept. Store,
> Hankyu Subway,
> Hankyu very much.

# DAY ONE

We walk to a market where stalls reek of fresh fish. A cuckoo clock sound tells blind people when it's safe to cross the street. A cardboard collector announces his truck's arrival with a jaunty electronic tune. Then,

> 4 tiny pair of tennis shoes
> lined up off Kawaramachi-dori.
> "Paradise" — words on door.

Next we visit Kiyomizu-Dera, which means "pure water." Two wooden devas guard the gate while inside the little stone buddhas wear linen bibs. The temple is dedicated to Kannon Bosatsu, incarnation of mercy and compassion. Here, beside a waterfall, I write a postcard:

> In pure water I
> write this, now
> trembling in your hands.

In the middle of Kiyomizu-Dera is Jishu Shrine, dedicated to the Shintoist Cupid. When a rabbit got its way by deceiving others, it was forced to peel its skin. Okuninuski healed it and made it mend its ways. I successfully walk between the shrine's two love stones with my eyes shut, which means my love will be realized. In gratitude I write:

> Bugs Bunny — America's
> sexual panic. Whoopie!
> No Elmer Fudd.

## DAY TWO

Heian courtiers devised a poetic diversion called renga (linked verse) in which one person writes a triplet, another a couplet. A trip to the Tojiin Temple Sale reveals this:

> 2 old women walk to Tojiin,
> backs bent parallel
> to the ground.

> Doctor: "Calcium deficiency."
> Poet: "Looking for gold."

That evening I spend two hours searching for C'est Bon, a gay bar. Finally "the master" (bartender) sends someone to fetch me. After a year and a half, a night of sensual delight.

# DAY THREE

Exhausted after shopping, and in despair at having overspent my budget by ¥10,000, I smoke cigarettes when I don't want them. Billowy clouds cover the sun as we approach mamma-san bowing to her neighbor three times, very deeply. Alysia asks how to work the washing machine. Should I go the Golden Pavilion or cash Traveler's Checks? I turn on TV and see this commercial for a popular drink that replaces negative ions lost in perspiration:

> Beautiful blond
> on huge, fabulous bird —
> POCARI SWEAT!

## DAY FOUR

Floorboards squeak like nightingales at Niji Castle. This warns the Shogun of impending assassins. We're swarmed by school children in crisp blue and white uniforms.

> Giggling, you ask to trade
> coins. Alysia delighted,
> making ¥90 on the deal.

We pass this sign off Nagawa-dori as we walk back to our inn:

> Welcome to our Japanese dish restaurant.
> You will have Tempura and Osashimi.
> Other dishes will be served too.

## DAY FIVE

Visit Chion-in, main temple of Jodo Buddhism. This "Pure Land" sect advocates throwing away human intellect, which I unwittingly do when, to the amusement of a temple monk, I stamp Buddha Amitabha in my pilgrim book:

>"Return to ignorance," Honen taught.
>"Become illiterate."
>I stamp Buddha upside down.

Alysia and I then stroll up "The Poet's Walk" in a neighborhood she calls the "Pacific Heights" of Kyoto. We pass a Most Wanted poster. Alysia doesn't hesitate to remove it from its glass case but later, at a teahouse, I forget the poster, leaving it rolled up by my chair. When I return for it, the proprietor grins at me like I'm a nut. And the Silver Pavilion?

>"Where's the silver?"
>Alysia asks. A bromidic batrachia
>plops into a pond.

## DAY SIX

Lost again. Tourist Information Center puts me on wrong bus to Ryoangji. I ask the driver where to transfer and he cracks a joke in Japanese. The passengers laugh but a student named Haruhiho (meaning "Spring Man") springs to my rescue and walks me to the temple.

"Learn only to be content," says the inscription on the temple's washbasin. I am, once I reach Ryoangji's famous rock garden. Only 14 of the 15 rocks in this white gravel ocean can be seen at one time from any but an aerial view. For three hours I gaze at it.

> Cool garden of stone
> *Athwirrrr...*
> Piercing bird cry.

# DAY SEVEN

Murderous heat, tired feet. I'm tired of walking, going to temples, eating yakasoba, writing postcards, reading, watching TV, Alysia's grouchiness, and my own. Mostly I'm tired of myself. Is this what I came to Japan to discover?

> Staring at the ceiling —
>      is there a poem
>         here too?

Then I go out to eat. It's dark. Traffic and shop lights glisten like a Rajah's sleeve in the cheap restaurant three flights above Higashiorji-dori. "No future," sing the Sex Pistols on the radio. But eating curried mussels and rice pilaf, I suddenly recall how free and glorious I felt traveling through Europe when I was twenty-two. Poor then, poor now. Yet for 20 minutes, I feel happier than a king.

# DAY EIGHT

I meet someone special at The Gie, a Jazz Club near our inn — Anna Kristina, a 23-year-old Norwegian dancer. She's left family and friends, her school in Amsterdam, and traveled through Russia and China to study Butoh dance in Tokyo. This dance is dangerous, painful, physically self-destructive. Exhausted, Anna's traveling south to find — what? She isn't sure. Yet even in her confusion she seems calm.

"Why do you shut yourself off from people's love?" Anna asks at the end of our conversation. Then she shares a poem by Zong Baihna, which she found on the Trans-Siberian Express, crossing from Russia into China on a Full Moon night, March 17th:

> A flower faded
> And fell upon my breast.
> It touched my heart
> Melting into this poem,
> A flower...

In the Full Moon Bodhisatva Ceremony, we let go of our "ancient, twisted Karma."

# DAY NINE

Anna asks if she can visit the poet Cid Corman with me, a visit I'd previously arranged. Cid greets us in front of his coffeehouse on Marutamachi-dori. He's portly and his eyes sparkle. We go in and sit at a table made from an old saki barrel.

Cid licks his lips as he tells of his immigrant Russian Jewish parents, his boyhood in Boston, his adventures in Paris and in Matera, Italy, a 4,000-year-old town of cave dwellers so poor even the mafia ignore it. Cid's as loquacious as his poetry is spare. Each story spawns several digressions, which branch out like labyrinthine tunnels.

This American poet has lived in Kyoto for 25 years. Anna says afterwards that he reminds her of her grandfather, a sea captain. I buy one of Cid's books, Root Song, which contains this poem:

> Always on
> the verge of
> returning
>
> only to
> find out one
> has gone on.

# DAY TEN

The train starts outside my window at five a.m. It's probably the beginning of a solipsistic novel, but no, it's just another haiku:

> Traffic below on Sanjo-dori,
>     waves of memory — like a vacuum
>         cleaner sound when I was 3.

To think, took ten days to notice. But it's starting to rain and the poem says nothing of this. Try again:

> Outside my window
>     is that bird getting wet?
>         Squeaky windshield wiper cry.

Impossible to write haiku in English.

Back to sleep. I dream I've arrived late for a benefit poetry reading. Robert Glück gives me a glowing introduction, says I've made a breakthrough merging the elegance of Versailles with the wit of Kevin Killian. But I've forgotten my poems. "Don't worry," says Bob. "You left some in this box."

I take out a book I don't recall. The pages are soggy, turn slowly, tear easily. They look like haiku; the print's difficult to read.

Awake again. Reach for Phil Whalen's *Heavy Breathing*, which lies next to my tatami. Opening at random, I read: "Japan is a civilization based on an inarticulate response to cherry blossoms."

## DAY ELEVEN

"These streets weren't made for cars," Haruhiho told me. Or Nancy Sinatra: "These Boots Weren't Made for Walkin.'" Alysia and I finally locate a street sign in English.

> "Oike-dori," Dad used
> to say. Alysia: "Does it
> intersect with Hunki-dori?"

Then rain. No money for a taxi or even a bus. As Bashō showed, even the worst moments can yield haiku:

> When summer rains fall
> smell their fragrance
> in these artless lines.

## DAY TWLEVE

Lady Murasaki's calligraphy brush no longer exists. Bashō's house is gone, as is Gojo bridge where Yoshitsune defeated the samurai monk Benkei who then became the bishonen's devoted follower. But the wooden Kurama train still creaks up to Kuramadera. Do its passengers have "the crookedest toes in the world" as a Phil Whalen poem maintains? I don't know. Both coming and going I fall asleep.

> One wooden train,
> two thousand stone steps —
> steep in Buddha's path.

# DAY THIRTEEN

Alysia and I set out for Nara to see the Great Buddha at Todaiji, which Emperor Shomu completed in 749 A.D. Anna was coming too but decided to move south. I think of a walk we took the night before:

> Walking on Mt. Nyaigadake,
> the evening ends
> amidst brumous croaking.

Most haiku express the sadness of partings, of seasonal changes, of emotions suppressed until the final moment. The *Hagakure*, an 18th Century treatise on samurai ethics: "Once love (for a boy) has been confessed, it shrinks in stature. True love attains its highest, noblest form when one carries its secret to the grave." Again I think of my friend in San Francisco.

But these thoughts vanish when I enter Daibutsuden, the largest wooden structure in the world. Looming up 53 feet in the darkness, Buddha sits like a mountain (500 tons of copper, 8-and-a-half tons of gold, etc.). Even Alysia is moved. She tugs the beribboned rope hanging in front of the altar, clangs the gong, and claps her hand three times. Enlightenment! To lighten up.

> If Buddha turned
> to look at us —
> laughter at last!

Sadness and joy, reverence and silliness. In Japan — with its layerings of Shintoism, Nihonism, Buddhism — moods shift constantly under an external blanket of conformity. Alysia wasn't interested in feeding the deer that approached us earlier but now seeks one who holds back.

> A fawn flickers its ear
> at Alysia's outstretched hand—
> Crackers!

"It's the challenge I like," Alysia says.

Returning to Kyoto on the Kintetsu Express, a clump of green bamboo flits past our window. Moments later I see this sign above a village shop: "New Light People."

# DAY FOURTEEN

Another dream: I'm given a private tour of a movie set, a fabulous but unused gold banquet hall. Then I'm in a stairwell with the comedian Robin Williams that turns first into an elevator, then a car. We look out the window and see we're in New York City. Williams wants to show me his house, a narrow three-story styrofoam job that collapses into a hook-and-ladder firetruck. In it we drive to an art opening in a new hotel. The furnishings are lavish but everything's upside down. Some black kids sitting in the bar ask for candy. It's all gone.

"Hell," gripes one.

"You can work your way up in hell if you want," I reply. "And I should know. I'm *Satan!*"

But I'm also an art critic, one who's expected to say something brilliant and incisive.

"So whadaya think?" The artist tries to sound nonchalant.

"These stairways are kinda busy," I reply.

What does the dream mean? That my life, like Kyoto, is too rapid, stressful? I walk to the Heian Shrine.

> One more temple:
> five green tiled roofs,
> 70 orange pillars,
> a white gravel courtyard.
> The yard is flat, huge,
> more so for endless grey sky
> hovering overhead.

What really hovers in my mind is Anna's absence. I feel like I'm lost in a watercolor painting.

> Now that you're gone
> your question floats
> in this silent room.

## DAY FIFTEEN

Kyoto's English bookstore won't carry my *Lives of the Poets* but I find Isaiah Ben-Dasan's *The Japanese and the Jews*, which Cid Corman mentioned. The author was never photographed. He never appeared in public, not even to receive a book award. Is his book a fake? On page 111, I read of a Christian missionary who sees an old man praying before a statute of Buddha.

"God doesn't reside in statues," says the Christian.

"Of course," replies the old man.

"Then why do you pray here?"

"First one sweeps away the dust, then one looks at the Buddha," says the old man. When the missionary doesn't reply, the old man mutters, "The Buddha is also dust" and walks away.

> Books fade from memory.
> Is anything "real"?
> Even Buddha disappears.

# DAY SIXTEEN

Walk from my room to the bathhouse, shower, dip into hot tub, brush teeth, and shave. When I come out I see Anna, rain drizzling down her cheeks and off her dark green plastic poncho. I invite her to my room, give her a towel.

"I was picked up hitchhiking by a 60 year old man," she begins, drying her hair. "He was very nice at first but later tried to rape me." We talk. Anna's angry for being so trusting.

"I sat zazen like you showed me," she says. "After an hour I felt someone hit my left shoulder. I felt scared because no one was with me. Then I felt the energy move from my left to my right side. Why am I so hard on myself? Is it guilt because everyone's always given me things? I want to do something for myself. But what?"

I reflect on my friend. I'm always wanting to give him things too. Whether giving or receiving, it's hard to act with clarity. "It takes a bodhisattva to graciously receive a gift," I say.

That evening, after exchanging messages, Anna and I go to The Lighthouse, a club near Nijo Castle. A taxi driver we met at The Gie is performing. Hisahiro became so fascinated with Leonard Cohen that he decided to study Hebrew. He shows us a teakwood tray into which he's carved a passage from Isaiah. "My father and grandfather were both carvers," he says proudly.

Although I seldom drink, I order a shot of absinthe, the favorite of Appollinaire and Rimbaud. This drink is now illegal in all but two countries. After one sip I know why. It burns with an hallucinatory warmth.

A 25-year-old car designer tries to pick up Anna, a transsexual with big earrings puts the make on me. Anna and I walk back to our inn together, stumbling in the back-way so as not to awaken mamma-san who's locked the front gate.

# DAY SEVENTEEN

Tomorrow Alysia and I return to San Francisco. Anna comes in, we chat. Then I walk to Nanzenji for one last time to sit and read. Giving up on haiku, I write a final poem:

> Anna says it's easy to change if you really want to
> The Airporter bus leaves at 9:46 a.m.
> A letter from Cid Corman in my Phil Whalen book
> is momentarily forgotten as I watch a Japanese boy
>     descend
> the temple steps. Down hard on those who disobey.
> Neck itches, scratch it. This temple's
> where I met a boy from Hong Kong my first day here.
> "Take a picture," he said. I did and still have it
> in my mind. Smoke from burning trash
> blows past. Then a group of schoolgirls:
> "What are you doing?" I say I'm writing
> this poem — a word they don't understand.
> Maybe that Hong Kong guy was trying to pick me up.
> Japanese schoolkids wear uniforms; public servants,
> white gloves. I bow my head
> to light a cigarette, listen to ducks.
> *Bishonen* are the Peter Pans of Japan.
> They say: "I love you" but don't mean it.
> What does "meaning it" mean?
> I woke up feeling I had a knife stuck in my heart,
> then went back to sleep and awoke again.
> Now I can enjoy the blue sky and white clouds.

# THE EVE OF DEPARTURE

Anna, the kids, and I attend a party in the Gion district hosted by The Gie's bartender. A band imitates The Rolling Stones fairly well but not Otis Redding. Afterwards, Anna and I meander along the Kamo River. Seventeenth century prostitutes draped their kimonos over balconies here. Now, teenagers set off fireworks on the riverbank.

> In this floating world
>     timeless light
>         pops effervescent mind.

# DAY EIGHTEEN

Shadows at daybreak
recall our journey.

So ends Cid Corman's book. After a final breakfast prepared by mamma-san, we leave Anna behind and taxi to the New Miyako to catch the Airporter to Osaka. Our flight leaves at 2 p.m., Kyoto time, and arrives at 8 a.m. in San Francisco.

How happy I am to see my friend again. But he's sick. He's returning to his parents. Will I ever see him again? The one thing I got for myself in Japan, a silk kimono, I give to him along with a poem.

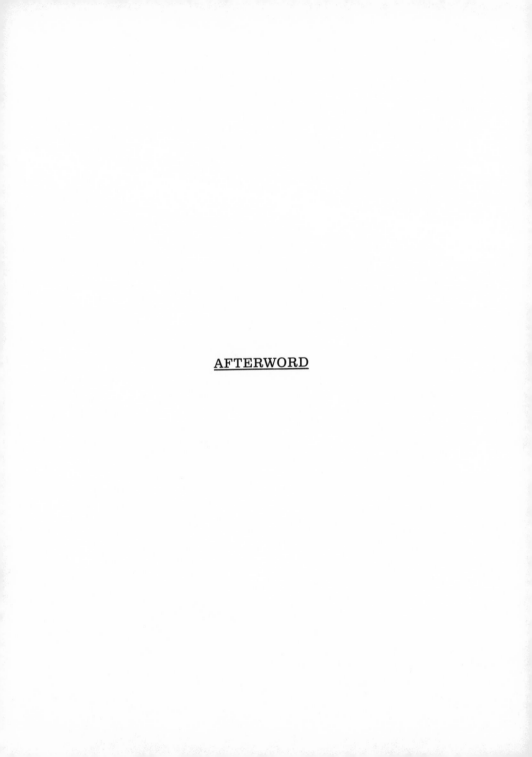

AFTERWORD

I've always had a complicated relationship with my dad's work. Growing up his only child, with him my only parent, I first saw his writing as my rival. Several nights a week he'd go to readings around San Francisco either taking me with him when I was too young to be left alone (and letting me fall asleep on his lap), or leaving me at home when I was old enough to make TV dinners on my own.

When he did stay home, his attention was frequently divided. I have vivid memories of him scribbling away in his spiral bound notebooks or typing on his typewriter and later his word processor, on deadline for another article or review. There was always a cigarette resting in his ashtray, one of his Carlton regulars, which would form a screen of smoke for me to cross. On those occasions I tried to cross, he'd sometimes let me in, ask about my day, or let me show off the clothes I'd purchased at Aardvark's, the thrift store across from our apartment on Haight Street. Other times, he'd outstretch his left hand, wordlessly clapping it open and closed to let me know that my talking was unwanted.

As a teenager, attending a private school with my grandparents' help, I was aware that his writing couldn't support us and I resented that. He took so many odd jobs—market research, temp work, adjunct teaching at USF, teaching out of our apartment, working the counter at the local bookstore, vacuuming the building to get money shaved off our rent. The columns and reviews he wrote for *The Bay Guardian*, *The Sentinel*, The *B.A.R.*, and *SF Weekly*, as trenchant and well-regarded as they were, (something I couldn't appreciate for many years), brought in small checks that didn't add up to rent. Nevertheless, it seemed like he was always working.

In 1991, I was living in Paris finishing up my Junior year abroad. By this point, my father had already gotten sick. He was taking infusions of medicine through a tube recently inserted into his chest. But he had downplayed his condition in his letters. When I saw him in person, he didn't look that different to me, but one night after dinner he finally disclosed that six months earlier he'd been diagnosed with pneumocystis, which meant he now had full-blown AIDS. The purpose of this visit to Paris was to ask me to move home and manage his end of life care. This being AIDS in 1991, that end of life could come quickly. He calmly detailed his possible life expectancy, and the personal effects he would leave me. I was by turns restless, short-tempered, in denial, and self-pitying. I was just 20-years-old at the time, and my dad was the closest person in the world to me, my whole family. I couldn't imagine, was in fact angry to imagine, a life without him. What could I do for him? How could I help and support him, in this state when I was so young and aimless myself? Remarkably, and this is something that really strikes me, neither these difficult questions, nor his difficult diagnosis defined his visit to Paris. He was still very focused on his work as a writer. I couldn't see this at the time, but looking back it's all I can see. He didn't know how many months he had yet to live, but he was still so determined to publish and teach, to create new work and conversation. Our letters from the time show that back in San Francisco he was in contact with an agent, hoping to find someone to represent his last work, a novel called *Lost Causes*. Now in Paris, between dinners planned with my French boyfriend at the time, and visits to cafes, he wanted to drop off several of his books at Shakespeare & Co. and wanted me to accompany him to a party at the Pompidou Center. He also wanted me take him to a meeting with Pascal Quignard, an editor at the French publishing house Gallimard, who would later win the prestigious Prix Goncourt. I would be Dad's translator.

I remember sitting in the book-lined office of this handsome balding man, confident and well-dressed, smelling of expensive cologne, as all cultured French men do. And there we were—this nervous young girl and her sick father. Dad spoke about the New Narrative writers—Kevin Killian, Dodie Bellamy, and Bob Glück, and about the intentions of New Narrative. I did my best to make him heard and understood but also felt uneasy. What did this editor think? Was he impressed? What did Dad hope would come of this meeting—that he or his colleagues' work would be translated and published? As far as I know, that never happened. But does it even matter? I helped him make this trip to the Gallimard offices. Eighteen months before he died, we went to the party at the Centre Pompidou and browsed the shelves at Shakespeare & Co. He was, for that week, experiencing literary life in Paris. He had a tube in his chest and he'd come all the way from the Haight Ashbury in San Francisco to this office of the Gallimard publishing house. What became of the meeting is less important than the fact it happened at all.

Since his death, I've had many opportunities to revisit these memories and to discover new facets of his life and career. In 2012, I was working on my memoir, *Fairyland*, which tells the story of my life with my dad. I would regularly consult his papers at the San Francisco Public Library downtown. It was there, sitting quietly among the boxes of his notebooks, clippings, drawings, and papers that I came across a stapled typed story he'd written for his MFA program at San Francisco State. *No Trouble, No Story*, he titled it. In it he wrote about our life, as reflected by "me." He even swiped bits of writing I'd sent him in college, repurposing it for his imagining of my memoir, much like I was doing with his old journals in writing *Fairyland*. I immediately thought of that famous lithograph by MC Escher—*Drawing Hands*—where two hands rise from a flat sheet of paper and the viewer is never sure which hand is drawing which hand. We were both wanting to tell our story, both wanting to author the other.

Another recent surprise came courtesy of one of my dad's friends, who let me know that audio of my dad's readings and workshops at the Naropa Institute in Boulder, Colorado have been made available online. I found a 1991 recording of a workshop he led called "Writing Against Death," which he described for me in a letter: "I read 'Elegy', then a poem about someone with AIDS, then some prose by someone who has AIDS. There were about 75 people in the class & things really began to get emotional esp. when I had students write about death & read their work." Then I listened to the readings he gave in July of 1991 and 1992.

I can't convey just how startling it is to reacquaint myself with my dad's reading voice, especially how it sounded that summer of 92, the last summer of his life. I listen to the recordings with my eyes closed, lying in my bed, computer next to my pillow. There's something so incredibly fragile, almost painfully present about my father's voice in these recordings. He's open about his illness and the gradual loss of his sight due to CMV retinitis. "If I stumble," he says, "it's because I'm trying to guess at the words with my remaining, half-good eye." He's not embarrassed when he does stop to wrestle with the text, or to read a line that he'd accidentally skipped. It's as though he has nothing left to lose—no status, no "face" that would make another writer, a writer like me, self-conscious. In this reading he gives to the Naropa community he just gives all of himself. It upsets me to listen—I want so much to protect that vulnerability, to beg that he hold more of himself back. But the audience at Naropa in 1992 just loves him for it. They sit hushed and laugh when appropriate and applaud heartily when he is done. "Everyone at Naropa kept saying how 'brave' I am," he wrote me. "But I don't feel 'brave.' Life is just one day at a time, that's all."

This last December 2018, would have been my father's 75th birthday. That same month I turned 48, the age he was when he died. Thinking about this, I realize just how premature his death really was. In the 70s and 80s when my dad was at his most productive, there was little interest in LGBTQ literature. The LAMBDA Literary Awards weren't instituted before 1988 and queer studies weren't yet taught in school. Today, however, the audience for queer stories and queer history is large and growing. Photos and stories are being pulled out of basements and dustbins and brought to light in popular Instagram accounts like the AIDS Memorial and LGBT History. There are queer memoirs, biographies, novels, and history books achieving critical and commercial success. Notably, many of these stories are being told by younger generations of queer writers and scholars, writers who want to claim and celebrate this history as their own rich inheritance. Kids who are the same age I was that summer my father and I met in France can now take LGBTQ classes and read queer literature in their core classes. They can cry along with Queer Eye or feel pride when movies like *Moonlight* and *Call Me By Your Name* win Academy Awards. My father would have loved to see this, and he would have loved to participate. Maybe, if he were still alive and working today, he would have received the recognition and financial stability that eluded him in life.

But then again, that was never the point of my dad's work. His engagement with and championing of queer literature was about far more than fame or money. The idea that they ever could be was preposterous at the time, which I imagine to be freeing in a way. For my dad, his work was about building community. It was about hand-illustrating posters for the readings he organized, copying then stapling them on bulletin boards all over town. It was about editing and publishing *Soup* magazine, on his own dime, so he could interview and excerpt the writers and artists who excited his imagination. It was about going out and engaging young men and women in classrooms but also in the cafes, bars, and bookstores around San Francisco, sharing his vast knowledge and encouraging them to add their voices to queer culture, in whatever way they could, even if that culture wasn't getting mainstream attention. He knew how important it was to support voices on the edge, writers that were pushing boundaries and weren't interested in keeping their readers comfortable.

Although I once felt jealous of my dad's work—and often it was his generosity with others that took him away from me—I know now how lucky I am to have loved and been loved by a writer. Friends who'd lost lawyer-dads have legal briefs to read in their absence. Accountant-dads might leave tax returns. Yet I have this marvelous wealth of his poetry and prose, criticism—*and cartoons!*—as you can see in this beautiful collection. In the more than 25 years since he's been gone, I've had time to truly sit with this work he'd shaped in the compromised privacy of his home office (which was really just a corner of his bedroom) and I can read it as an adult, a fellow writer, instead of as his daughter.

My favorite of his work is published here in full: *Lives of the Poets*. The book feels at once timeless—comparing the arcs and bizarre details of unnamed famous artists' lives—and also rooted in time, referencing people and places in San Francisco that no longer exist and are long forgotten, including Café Picaro and Finnila's Bathhouse. Of all of my dad's writing I think *Lives of the Poets* best captures his unique blend of erudition, curiosity, revelation, and playful wit. Listening to him read from this work at the Naropa Institute moved me to tears.

His essay *Dialing for Sex* —really any of his essays speaking frankly about sex—would have repelled me as a teen. Who wants to consider their dad's urges? The idea that any "sp" word turned him on—*speak, spark, sperm*. But reading it now I can appreciate his humor, his vulnerability, and his searching intellect. His observation "Voyeurism lies at the heart of all good storytelling. You haven't really had an experience until you've shared it" resonates as much, if not more, in our social media distracted 2019 as it did when my dad first published the essay over 30 years ago.

The essay *Will We Survive the 80s?* is a lament, a cry, and a call to arms. The "we" he speaks for is the LGBTQ community—how will *we* survive homophobia, sexism, AIDS—but it ends with the personal, as my dad considers his own death. He speaks with an honesty and forthrightness I don't think I could have handled during his lifetime——it was too much for me as a teenager and 20-year-old—but which I've come to appreciate and admire, now that I'm also a parent, and now that I've reached the age of 48, as old as he will ever be.

"We all die differently, just as we all live differently," he writes. "I don't know what it will be like for me but I'm no longer afraid...And I'm filled with such a profound gratitude to be alive, to be gay and to have the friends that I have and have had that I cannot explain it."

Alysia Abbott, March 2019

# ACKNOWLEDGEMENTS

First and foremost thanks to Steve's daughter Alysia Abbott and Steve's literary executor Kevin Killian for their generosity, time, and support of this project. Thanks to the staff at SF Public Library's Special Collections for their help and care toward Steve's archives. Many thanks to Lindsey Boldt, Stephen Motika, and the rest of the staff at Nightboat Books for their dedication to making this collection a material reality. Special thanks goes to Milo Gallagher for all their help and attentiveness in transcription work for the manuscript. To Joseph Bradshaw, Nick DeBoer, and Marissa Perel for providing much needed feedback. And to Ivy Johnson, for her thoughtful critique and endless support throughout the entire process of putting together this collection.

Much of the work included in *Beautiful Aliens* originally existed in the rich, fluid and beautifully expansive space of small press publishing in the 1970s and 1980s. It contains work previously published by number of magazines, periodicals, and independent presses, including Black Star Series, Dancing Rock Press, The Crossing Press, Androgyne Press, e.g. (a literary press), The *San Francisco Sentinel*, *Holy Titclamps*, and others. Many thanks to the editors for their support of Steve's work, and for their role in creating a vital legacy of queer independent publishing

# LIST OF PUBLICATIONS AND IMAGES

*Lives of the Poets* was originally published by Black Star Series (San Francisco: 1987).

The selection from *Lost Causes* is previously unpublished.

"How Michael The Archangel Was Fooled," Walking This Abandoned Field," "Lines for Chairman Mao," "Big Boys Don't Cry," "To A Soviet Artist in Prison," "Most Streets in Vallarta", "After Reading Catullus," "The Disturbing Painting," "The Departure," "Counting Streams in the Forest of your Eyes" were originally published in *Wrecked Hearts* (San Francisco: Dancing Rock Press, 1978.

"The Malcontent" is previously unpublished.

"The Politics of Touch," "It's a Strange Day Alysia Said, A Green," "Some Boys," "Al(Most) (Subject)ive Love Poem," "Wild Knots," "Transfiguration," "Days," "Body Language," "Do Potatoes Want Sex After High School?," "Mercury in the 7th House," "The Surprise on Venus," "Giving Witness," "Hit by a Space Station," "(Running) (Graves)," "Elegy" were originally published in *Stretching the Agape Bra* (San Francisco: Androgyne Press, 1980).

"An 'Educated Queer' on Hearing David Bottoms Read at Callenwold," "For Reza Baraheni, Tommi Trantino and Gennady Trifonov" "Sebastian," "Poem of an Epileptic Student Caught in the Watts Riot," "Poem in St. Paul," "Poem for Joe Mauser," "The Modern Relationship," "Sonnet to Bless a Marriage" are previously unpublished.

Selections from *Holy Terror* were originally published by The Crossing Press (Freedom: 1989).

"Notes on Boundaries, New Narrative" was originally published in *SOUP*, no. 4, ed. Bruce Boone (1985) and reprinted in *View Askew* (San Francisco: Androgyne Books, 1989).

"Diamanda Galas: If the Dead Could Sing" was originally published in the *San Francisco Sentinel* and reprinted in *View Askew* (San Francisco: Androgyne Books, 1989).

"Gay Lit's Bad Boy" is previously unpublished.

"Redefining Redon" was originally published in the *San Francisco Sentinel* and reprinted in *View Askew* (San Francisco: Androgyne Books, 1989).

"About Face" was originally published in the *San Francisco Sentinel* and reprinted in *View Askew* (San Francisco: Androgyne Books, 1989).

"Bob Kaufman: Hidden Master of the Beats" was originally published in *Little Caesar*, no. 12 (1981) and reprinted in *View Askew* (San Francisco: Androgyne Books, 1989).

"There Goes the Neighborhood" was originally published in the *San Francisco Sentinel* and reprinted in *View Askew* (San Francisco: Androgyne Books, 1989).

"Visiting Stonestown" was originally published in the *San Francisco Sentinel* and reprinted in *View Askew* (San Francisco: Androgyne Books, 1989).

"Dialing for Sex" was originally published in the *San Francisco Sentinel* and reprinted in *View Askew* (San Francisco: Androgyne Books, 1989).

"On the Significance of 'Significant Others'" was originally published in the *San Francisco Sentinel* (1987).

"Wienerschnitzel" was originally published in *Mirage 2* (1985) and reprinted in *View Askew* (San Francisco: Androgyne Books, 1989).

"Passing Strangers" is previously unpublished.

*Skinny Trip to a Far Place* was originally published by e.g. (a literary press), (San Francisco: 1988).

"My Kid" is previously unpublished.

"Evil Literature and a Forgotten Classic" is previously unpublished.

"Will We Survive the '80s" was originally published in the *San Francisco Sentinel* and reprinted in *View Askew* (San Francisco: Androgyne Books, 1989).


IMAGES


p. i originally printed in *Transmuting Gold*

p. x originally printed in *Transmuting Gold*

p. xxiv originally printed in *Lives of the Poets*

p.22 originally printed in *SOUP* no. 2

p.36 originally printed in *SOUP* no. 2

p.48  originally printed in *SOUP* no. 2

p.80 originally printed in *SOUP* no. 2

p.108 originally printed in *Transmuting Gold*

p.124 originally printed in *SOUP* no. 2

p.138 originally printed in *SOUP* no. 2

p.162 originally printed in *SOUP* no. 2

p.266 originally printed in *SOUP* no. 2

p.274 originally printed in *SOUP* no. 1

p.282 originally printed in *SOUP* no. 2

p.287 originally printed in *Living an Unplanned Life*

p.290 originally printed in *SOUP* no. 2

p.316 originally printed in *Transmuting Gold*


ILLUSTRATED POEMS


"The Vertigo of Loss" originally printed in *Stretching the Agape Bra*

"Reborn in Bat Town" originally printed in *Holy Titclamps* issue no. 17

"The Further Adventures of &" originally printed in *SOUP* no. 2

"A Birthday Poem for Everyone" originally printed as a flyer

"3 Dimensional Poem for 6 Senses Read Magically 4 Ways" originally printed in
*Ins & Outs* issue 4/5

"Jacob's Angel Seen at Café Flore" originally printed as a broadside

"Counting Streams in the Forest of your Eyes" originally printed as a broadside

"Toxic Shlock" originally printed in *SOUP* no. 2

"Hippie Histomap" originally printed in *The Lizard Club*

Photo by Robert Giard; Copyright Estate of Robert Giard

*Steve Abbott* (1943-1992) was a poet, critic, editor, novelist and artist. Abbott was raised in Lincoln, Nebraska, graduated from the University of Nebraska, and attended Emory University where he was an organizer for Atlanta's Gay Liberation Front and the gay lib editor at the underground paper *The Great Speckled Bird*. Abbott moved to San Francisco in 1974 where he became was a frequent contributor to local publications, including *The Advocate*, The *San Francisco Sentinel*, and the *Bay Area Reporter*. He was also one of the founding editors of the literary arts newsletter *Poetry Flash* and the publisher/editor of the literary journal *SOUP*. Steve wrote a number of books of poetry and prose during the 1980s and early 90s including: *Wrecked Hearts*, *Stretching the Agape Bra*, *Lives of the Poets*, *Holy Terror*, *Skinny Trip to a Far Place*, and *View Askew: Postmodern Investigations*, a book that collects Steve's essays from The *San Francisco Sentinel*, *The Advocate*, and the arts journal *Mirage*. He was active in various reading series and discussion groups in the Bay Area, including Cloud House and Small Press Traffic, and, in 1981, he co-organized the historic Left/Write conference. Steve was also a respected critic and the first to use the term "New Narrative" to describe the work of contemporaries including Bruce Boone and Robert Glück. Abbott died of complications due to AIDS on December 2, 1992. His novel *The Lizard Club* was published posthumously.

*Jamie Townsend* is a genderqueer poet and editor living in Oakland. They are half-responsible for *Elderly*, a publishing experiment and hub of ebullience and disgust. They are the author of several chapbooks as well as the full-length collection *Shade*. An essay on the history and influence of the literary magazine *SOUP* was published in *The Bigness of Things: New Narrative and Visual Culture*. They are the editor of *Libertines in the Ante-Room of Love: Poets on Punk*.

*Alysia Abbott* is the author of *Fairyland: A Memoir of My Father*, which won the ALA Stonewall Award and the Prix Madame Figaro, and has been translated into French, Spanish, Polish, and Portuguese. Her work has appeared in the *Boston Globe*, *The New York Times Book Review*, *Vogue*, *Psychology Today*, *TriQuarterly*, *Lit Hub*, and elsewhere. She leads the Memoir Incubator at GrubStreet in Boston and lives with her family in Cambridge, MA.

# NIGHTBOAT BOOKS

Nightboat Books, a nonprofit organization, seeks to develop audiences for writers whose work resists convention and transcends boundaries. We publish books rich with poignancy, intelligence, and risk. Please visit nightboat.org to learn about our titles and how you can support our future publications.

Kazim Ali
Anonymous
Jean C. Ballantyne
Photios Giovanis
Amanda Greenberger
Elizabeth Motika
Benjamin Taylor
Peter Waldor
Jerrie Whitfield & Richard Motika

Nightboat Books gratefully acknowledges support from the Topanga Fund, which is dedicated to promoting the arts and literature of California.